Freedomland U.S.A.

The Definitive History

Michael R. Virgintino

Theme Park Press
The Happiest Books on Earth
www.ThemeParkPress.com

Theme Park Press publishes its books in a variety of print and electronic formats. Some content that appears in one format may not appear in another.

Editor: Bob McLain
Layout: Artisanal Text
Cover Photo: 1960 Freedomland U.S.A. Park Guide

All photographs, unless otherwise noted, are from the Michael R. Virgintino Collection. Copyright 2018 Michael R. Virgintino

ISBN 979-8-89609-142-4
Printed in the United States of America

Theme Park Press | www.ThemeParkPress.com
Address queries to ben@themeparkpress.com

To my parents, Raphael F. Virgintino and Jennie Tomao Virgintino, for a wonderful childhood, for raising me in a fabulous neighborhood that also would become the home of Freedomland, for the family trips to the park and for sharing so many other experiences that have influenced and enriched my life. You are always in my thoughts and heart.

To my wife, the love of my life, Barbara Virgintino, who also lived close to the park and has supported everything I have undertaken and accomplished for more than 40 years.

To my son, Nicholas R. Virgintino, who prefers coasters to history but, no doubt, would have shared my enthusiasm and passion for Freedomland and the Bronx if he only experienced both as I did in my youth.

To all the employees (the original Friendly Freedomlanders), to the fans of Freedomland U.S.A., and to all who continue to maintain the history, memories, and stories of this wonderful theme park.

Contents

Introduction

My parents came from the Bronx, the South Bronx to be specific. Raphael F. Virgintino came from 436 East 145th Street. Jennie Tomao was from 335 East 148th Street. They met as teenagers. My father was drafted into the U.S. Navy near the end of World War II. After his service, he and my mother were married during 1947.

My parents moved to Elmhurst, Queens, to start their life as a couple. During 1951, they purchased a new brick row house for about $8,000 in the northeast part of the Bronx on a ridge that overlooked the valley that swept into Eastchester Bay. That part of the borough had been open fields with a scattering of houses that dated to the late 1800s and early 1900s. As the veterans returned home, additional streets were established and each became filled with rows of brick homes along with semi-attached dwellings and the occasional stand-alone house. Most of the yards were the size of a postage stamp.

I came along a handful of years after my parents moved to Mickle Avenue. A few years later, Freedomland U.S.A. rose in the valley. Not realizing it at the time, I was at the right place at the right time.

Thanks to my parents, I experienced a wonderful 1950s and 1960s childhood in a neighborhood filled with kids and places to play ball, even if some of those places were the streets. The sewer plates served as home plate and second base, or the goal lines for touch football. Part of my childhood also included Freedomland.

We all heard about Disneyland, but few, if any, of us traveled to California during summer vacation. Stay-cations mostly were the norm, with an occasional venture to a nearby state.

My summer fun at Freedomland captured my imagination and nurtured my love for American history. With my parents opening doors for me to experience Manhattan's many museums, the Gettysburg battlefield, and the history of the Hudson Valley, my passion for our history continued to grow long after Freedomland closed its gates.

I never forgot about that wonderful place where it all began for me. Over the years, as a writer, journalist, public relations executive, and history buff, I have written about many different topics for newspapers, magazines, newsletters, and online publications while also hosting and participating in radio and television programs. During more recent years, I began to focus more on Freedomland. With the coming age of social media, I started the Freedomland Facebook page (Freedomland U.S.A.—The World's Largest Entertainment Center) and then added Twitter and Instagram accounts to reach more people who shared my interest in American and theme park history, 1960s culture, and, specifically, a great park in the Bronx.

A lot of the research about Freedomland appears in these social media spaces, dovetailing with the articles I have written, media interviews, and presentations. Considerable time is dedicated to correcting other past and current articles and social media posts that contain misinformation about the park. A lot of effort, research, and time also have been poured into this book.

For several reasons, not everything about Freedomland appears between these covers. Some stories never have been documented in notes or archives. Memories have been lost as papers and photos were discarded and when people died as part of the journey of life. Some stories still require additional research. Several new pieces to the overall Freedomland puzzle will be located while you are paging through this book. Finally, I determined that not one more word could be squeezed within the covers.

Thanks to the creation of social media and the digitization of old newspapers, magazines, and other printed material, the research, documentation, and stories related to Freedomland will continue to add to the overall storyline of this magnificent park that could have and should have lasted to this very day. Unfortunately, other factors that were beyond the control of all who loved the park took Freedomland away from us after only five seasons.

Now, if you are ready, let's go back in time. Ask your mom and dad to take your hand and bring you out to Freedomland!

Michael R. Virgintino
Freedomlandusa@yahoo.com
New York, February 2018

The author in a Freedomland snapshot taken by his father.

CHAPTER ONE

The Bronx!

I can't seem to escape
the sins of my smart-alec youth;
Here are my amends.
I wrote those lines, "The Bronx?
No thonx";
I shudder to confess them.
Now I'm an older, wiser man
I cry, "The Bronx?
God bless them!"

—Ogden Nash, 1964

The Bronx is the northernmost of the five boroughs of New York City. Anyone who is from the Bronx (or "The Bronx," as some emphatically capitalize the "t") proudly will remind other city dwellers that their home borough is the only part of the city on the U.S. mainland.

The name originated with Jonas Bronck. He established a settlement in the area as part of the New Netherland colony of the 1600s. The land presently situated within Bronx County originally was the southern portion of Westchester County that sits just north of New York City. In this southern district, the village of West Chester (now the area of Westchester Square) maintained courts, a jail, and county business operations to supplement the county seat at White Plains. Though White Plains was centrally located within the original county, the southern district was established at a time when round-trip travel to White Plains required a multi-day investment.

The consolidation of the southern portion of Westchester County into New York City occurred in two stages. During

1873, the state legislature annexed (effective 1874) certain sections to New York City. The remainder of the territory was annexed to the city during 1895, three years before New York's consolidation with Brooklyn, Queens, and Staten Island. The community of City Island, which is immediately adjacent to the mainland, voted to join the city during 1896. On January 1, 1898, the consolidated City of New York was established with the Bronx as one of the five boroughs.

Historic Location of Freedomland U.S.A.

The location for the Freedomland U.S.A. theme park was natural marshland. The ground experienced rising and falling levels of salt water from the tides of nearby Eastchester Bay to the east, and it contained typical wetlands vegetation. A mill, Reid's Mill (sometimes misspelled "Reed"), operated on the land before the Revolutionary War and until the Civil War. The operation was the first tidal mill to be built along Eastchester Creek and the Hutchinson River. The mill began during 1739 under Thomas Shute. It subsequently was operated by Joseph Stanton and then by John Bartow (Bartow Avenue now enters and passes through Co-op City and the Bay Plaza Shopping Center that occupy the site of Freedomland). John Reid was the miller during 1790 and his son, Robert, continued until the 1850s. After the Civil War, the mill was abandoned and stood forlornly on the salt meadows for decades. It was destroyed during a 1900 storm.

About a half mile north of the area, wetlands today retain an appearance that would have been familiar to people who lived, fished, and hunted in the region from before the 1600s. This area included a settlement that became the home of Anne Hutchinson, whose name now is associated with the nearby river and parkway. Also in the area are remnants of a colonial road (Split Rock Road) along which George Washington's troops under the command of General John Glover fought against British and Hessian soldiers during the American Revolution. These same men from the Marblehead Regiment (14th Continental Regiment) of Massachusetts also saved the army after the Battle of Long Island and ferried troops across the Delaware River to capture Trenton. Another path (Gun Hill Road) in this community received its name from various skirmishes that occurred during the Revolution.

Marshland is visible along both sides of the Hutchinson River Parkway. On the east side of the northbound lanes of the parkway and exactly where the Interstate 95 (New England Thruway) overpass crosses it, the preserved Split Rock stands behind a stone wall. This rock was cut by a retreating glacier and gave its name to the road that passed it.

Freedomland was established about a mile south of the Split Rock Road and a bit farther south from the approximate home site of Anne Hutchinson. It is ironic that a theme park focused on American history would be situated so close to sites of actual events associated with the early stories of the country. But the location of the park actually had less to do with the historic landscape and more to do with the availability of undeveloped land in crowded New York City, access to the location by car and public transportation, and deals by real estate developers and city planners involved with the project.

Billingsly Aviation Field opened on the property on August 5, 1927. It was named for Logan Billlingsly, a real estate developer and builder. The first plane to approach the field was a Curtis biplane piloted by Walter Mitchell. It crashed into a car, a Ford owned by William Critter of 3714 Dyre Avenue. A week earlier, before the official opening, the same plane had crashed and lost both wings when it struck a tree. Just two years later, the newly formed Curtiss Airports Corporation bought the land as one of 18 parcels across the country that the company intended to develop into airports. Soon after, the company suspended development of this specific location and a few weeks later the stock market crashed. A second attempt to build an airport on the site failed as did a post-World War II attempt to build a helicopter field.

Years later, the land housed a cucumber farm and pickle factory, and it once was a good location to grab some clams and blue claw crabs. Then, it became a trash dump.

Though the property was marsh, a late 1950s plan was considered to prepare the land for a potential housing or business complex. To accomplish this, construction plans needed to meet certain conditions that addressed issues related to the soft ground. While the modern development of the land began with a theme park, the overriding objective by developers and politicians was to build Co-op City, the largest cooperative housing development in the world.

CHAPTER TWO

Creation of the Theme Park

Amusement Park: An entertainment facility featuring rides, games, food, and sometimes shows.

Theme Park: An amusement park in which the rides, attractions, shows, and buildings revolve around a central theme or group of themes.

Trolley Park: An amusement park that typically opened in the late 1800s or early 1900s that was built by a streetcar company as a way to generate business during the weekend.

—National Amusement Park Historical Association

Outdoor areas for entertainment or recreation have existed for centuries. Roots can be traced to 16th century Europe. In the U.S., the creation of these outdoor areas relieved the unpleasant living conditions in growing cities, and housed the festivals and fairs of rural communities.

In colonial New York City, which was confined to the lower tip of Manhattan Island, outdoor areas of entertainment began before the Revolutionary War. The pleasure garden concept was exported to America with the opening of Vauxhall Gardens during 1767. By the early 1800s, this venue became the home to one of the first carrousels in the country. (Throughout the book, the word "carrousel" will be written, as necessary, in either the French style with two "r" or the English style with one.)

Vauxhall Gardens included a theater, exhibits, and an outdoor wax museum. As the city grew, so did the number of amusement areas. To compete, owners of these parks always looked for new and unique attractions.

The east side of Manhattan was the home of Jones' Woods. Steeplechase Park arrived in the Coney Island section of Brooklyn. Other parks in New York City were Golden City Park in Brooklyn, Fort George in the Washington Heights section of Manhattan, South Beach and Midland Beach on Staten Island, North Beach (on the site of today's LaGuardia Airport) and Rockaways' Playland in Queens, and Clason Point and Starlight Park in the Bronx.

Some family entertainment centers became known as trolley parks. During the 1800s and 1900s, most employees worked six days a week from Monday through Saturday. Sunday was a day for the family, and companies created entertainment venues to provide enjoyment for the families of employees. Some parks were located near beaches, lakes, and rivers. All relied on access to transportation. Some trolley companies created amusement areas at the end of the lines so that customers would use the trolleys, and deposit fares, even on Sundays. At the beginning of the 20th century, at least half of all amusement areas nationwide were owned by trolley or rail companies.

Palisades Amusement Park was conceived as a trolley park during 1898. It was located in Fort Lee, New Jersey, across the Hudson River from Manhattan. As transportation improved, including use of the automobile, guests arrived from farther distances to enjoy this park.

Two parks in Connecticut hold unique distinctions in amusement park history. Lake Compounce in Bristol opened during 1846 and is considered the oldest continuously operating amusement park in the United States. Quassy Amusement Park in Middlebury opened during 1908 and, according to the National Amusement Park Historical Association (NAPHA), it is one of 11 trolley parks in the nation that operate on original sites.

The other trolley parks as of 2018 are:

- Sea Breeze Park, Rochester, New York, 1879
- Dorney Park, Allentown, Pennsylvania, 1884

- Lakemont Park, Altoona, Pennsylvania, 1894
- Waldameer Park, Erie, Pennsylvania, 1896
- Midway State Park (formerly Midway Amusement Park), Maple Springs, New York, 1898
- Kennywood, West Mifflin, Pennsylvania, 1898
- Canobie Lake Park, Salem, New Hampshire, 1902
- Camden Park, Huntington, West Virginia, 1902
- Oaks Amusement Park, Portland, Oregon, 1905
- Clemonton Amusement Park, Clemonton, New Jersey, 1907

Birth of the Theme Park

Santa Claus Land, which opened in Santa Claus, Indiana, during 1946, is considered by many historians as the first theme park in the United States and a precursor to the modern-day theme park.

Evansville industrialist Louis J. Koch created the park as a retirement project. He was troubled that the tiny hamlet of Santa Claus was visited by children who searched for but could not find Santa. Koch's Santa Claus Land included a toy shop, toy displays, a restaurant, themed children's rides, and, of course, Santa. During the 1980s, the park expanded to include Halloween and Fourth of July sections, and the park's name was changed to Holiday World. Splashin' Safari Water Park was added during 1993 and the Thanksgiving holiday section opened during 2006.

Some theme parks, including Knott's Berry Farm in Buena Park, California, evolved from more traditional entertainment enterprises. During the 1950s, Walt Disney's imagination provided themed family entertainment in Anaheim, California, as an extension of his movies, cartoons, and television programs.

Many people reference Disneyland as the nation's first theme park. Taking into consideration the arguments of providing this designation to Holiday World or Knott's Berry Farm, at least Disneyland can be considered the country's first modern theme park.

Closing the Gates

While a number of parks have survived and flourished for more than a century, many more have vanished after short or long runs. In most instances, the land that outdoor entertainment venues occupied achieved greater value when developed for the public welfare or for private investors. Parks have been razed for airports, highways, housing, and industrial/corporate projects. Freedomland U.S.A. succumbed to the same fate.

CHAPTER THREE

Cornelius Vanderbilt Wood

A pioneer whose leadership was crucial for
bringing Walt Disney's dream to life.

—Van Arsdale France, founder and professor emeritus,
Disney University, author of *Window on Main Street*

C.V. Wood Jr. may be the greatest contributor to America's theme parks, possibly with the exception of Walt Disney. Yet, so many theme park fans have never heard of him.

Cornelius Vanderbilt Wood was born in Waynoka, Oklahoma (Woods County on the border with Kansas), on December 17, 1920. The population at the time was about 1,500. Throughout his early life, he was referred to as Junior and "Woodsy." Later on, friends and business colleagues called him "C.V. Wood" or "C.V." or "Woody."

The family moved to Amarillo, Texas, when Woody's father received a promotion from the Santa Fe Railway. After high school, Woody attended Hardin-Simmons University in Abilene and became a champion trick roper for the school's Cowboy Marching Band. At the school, he has been remembered as "probably the most mischievous student ever to enroll" and also a student "whose brain never enjoyed an idle moment." Woody later transferred to the University of Oklahoma and received a bachelor's degree in petroleum engineering.

Woody's employment background began during 1941 and included nine years at Convair (formed in 1943 by the merger of Consolidated Aircraft and Vultee Aircraft), an American aircraft manufacturing company that later expanded into rockets and spacecraft. He became a Convair chief industrial engineer and he contributed to innovations for the manufacture of planes. His first supervisor was Fred V. Schumacher, who would see Woody again at Disneyland and Freedomland.

Walt Disney met Woody when C. V. was leading the Stanford Research Institute (now SRI International) team that had been hired to crunch the numbers and find the location for the park that would become Disneyland. The organization, located in Menlo Park, California, was a nonprofit research and development organization founded by the trustees of Stanford University. It separated from the university in 1970.

The investigation conducted by the team probably was the most comprehensive study for an entertainment park up to that time. Woody analyzed a variety of criteria, including site location, traffic flow and access, attendance patterns, entertainment trends, weather issues, and economic feasibility of operations. Harrison Alan "Buzz" Price, who contributed significantly to the research for Disneyland and later would work for Disney, was part of the SRI team.

Woody was able to solve problems and he was excited about the Disney concept. When all the preliminaries were completed, Woody joined the Disney company during 1954. At 34 years old, he tapped into Walt's imagination and brother Roy Disney's bottom line to help bring Disneyland to life. He didn't do it alone. He worked closely with the brothers and other employees. He also hired old Texas friends and others he had known in previous businesses. He employed set designers, artists, special effects technicians, and anyone else who could breathe life into the park.

Woody was influential in the purchase of the land on which Disneyland was built and he delivered many additional contributions to the construction and early successes at the park. He was considered Disneyland's first employee, serving as vice president and general manager.

Woody often said that Walt initially treated him as a son. Over time, though, the relationship became strained. While Woody had many great ideas, hired talented people to complete certain tasks, and exhibited unchecked energy to build the park and ensure its success, certain actions along the way concerned the Disney brothers. Walt, specifically, sometimes felt uncomfortable around Woody.

Various stories have been told about the Walt-Woody relationship and the eventual schism. While all the stories probably maintain some percentage of truth, exaggerations and loyalties to either Walt or Woody have tinted facts and opinions. One longtime Disney Imagineer loyal to Walt stated that Wood was a con man. Many others did not share that opinion.

Several stories about Woody mention shady deals or solutions that would not have pleased Walt. The word embezzlement has been uttered, but that could be a theory or an extreme opinion. Conclusive documentation could not be located to indicate that Woody bit the hands that fed him the great opportunity to be involved in the construction of Disneyland.

By successfully winning sponsorships and contracts for the new park that amassed millions of dollars, Woody felt that he deserved a raise in salary. Walt refused and Woody allegedly created an opportunity to increase his income through the small companies that were brought in to lease park shops. Woody was enterprising and maybe more than a few of his actions caused Walt to wince until the only solution was to sever the relationship. The bottom line was that Walt and Roy did not feel comfortable with someone like Woody running the park in this same manner now that it had opened to the public.

Some of the other issues that may have caused office friction between Walt and Woody included:

- Walt was not pleased that Woody received much public credit for the early success of Disneyland. Woody billed himself as the master planner of the park after he left Walt's employ, and this resulted in legal action.

- Woody received more media attention than Walt. When Vice President Richard Nixon visited the park, cameras were snapping as Woody, not Walt, presented the politician with the key to Disneyland.

- Stories claimed Walt learned that Woody planned to create his own company and that Walt did not like the idea of non-Disney parks patterned on his design.

- Woody was a slick, ambitious, and unapologetic business-man. He was driven by sales and developed plans to finish assignments on time. Walt was equally ambitious, but, as seen by Woody, a man who was a dreamer rather than one who worked in the business world of budgets and sales projections. Woody moved fast, too fast for Walt.

- Walt was irked by the mixed media reviews for the special opening day of Disneyland for invited guests while Woody celebrated the creation of the world's first large theme park with his team. Actually, Woody felt the park was not ready to open for at least several months and his quick thinking prevented a public relations meltdown when the following day's public opening was marred by flames from a broken gas line.

- The Disney brothers did not understand or oversee a number of Woody's deals for the park. So, Walt and Roy decided to investigate the process. This made Woody uncomfortable and prompted him to ask Roy to fire the recently hired attorney who was reviewing agreements. One of those agreements, reportedly, involved signing over merchandising rights for a small amount to an unknown company with unknown people. Allegedly, several years after Woody was fired, the Disney brothers determined that Woody and a friend had set up the company to receive all the merchandising money.

- Woody and Walt often would feud, with Woody frequently complaining about Walt's methods for the park. Woody, however, had a version of this story that indicated his important work consisted of keeping the brothers from fighting.

Woody shared Walt's eye for innovation, but long ago he was stricken from the Disney family records. He rarely is mentioned by the company. If records about Woody do exist at the Walt Disney Company, the files seem to reside permanently in an inaccessible vault. His name does not adorn a window on Main Street, U.S.A. along with all the other significant contributors to the creation of the park and the development of the Disney brand.

According to Van Arsdale France, whom Woody brought on board and who later worked at Freedomland before he returned to Disney, C.V. was "a pioneer whose leadership was crucial for bringing Walt Disney's dream to life." But, for more than six decades, definitive answers to Woody's departure have remained elusive. France believed the two men were so fiercely independent that their relationship could not survive. He recalled that during one week Woody was holding his regular meetings with his office packed during every minute of the day. Then, overnight, Woody was out. According to another employee, Walt had Roy fire Woody.

Woody reportedly was offered several weeks' notice before he left the company. The media reported that Woody resigned from Disney, effective February 1, 1956. An unidentified Disneyland representative stated that the resignation was "five months ahead of schedule," explaining that Woody had agreed to stay through the first year of the park that ended on July 16. Some media stories reported that Woody planned to organize a company, Telesearch, Inc., to research and market television productions. Nothing more is known about this company.

A Space-Age Barnum

After departing Disneyland, Woody created Marco Engineering, Inc., which specialized in the design and construction of entertainment attractions. The business also has been referenced as Marco Engineering Company, Marco Company, Marco Development, Marco Engineering & Design, and Marco Design. Woody enticed a number of Disney employees to join him.

A unique talent, Woody was attractive to the executives and investors who wanted to replicate and profit from the Disney success. With former Disney employees and others, along with investors looking to turn a profit, Marco Engineering created Magic Mountain in Golden, Colorado (1957); Pleasure Island in Wakefield, Massachusetts (1959); Freedomland U.S.A. (1960); and Six Flags Over Texas (1961). The first three parks and the early years of Six Flags Over Texas enjoyed many similar attractions, promotions, and events. About 20 parks were anticipated by Marco, but the company did not build another park.

An *Associated Press* story about Woody just as Freedomland opened referred to him as a space-age Barnum who relied on slide-rule and research instead of hunches and stunts to collect the crowds. But, Woody insisted that he was "not a showman. I simply hire people whom I feel can get things done."

Concealed behind the layout of Freedomland's 40 attractions, according to the article, was a design and statistical method adapted from the assembly-line industry. The pedestrian path through the entire park was just a bit more than a mile in length. Woody's investigators found that one mile is exactly the distance a typical family can be expected to stroll.

"People can go through the whole thing in four and one-half hours—that's because," said Woody in the article, "only one group in 10,000 will buy more than one meal. ... If they have to stay longer they will get mad. Of course they won't see everything in that time—we figure on return visits. But it will enable people to travel here, see the park, and get home in an average total time of eight hours. Displays will take between two-and-one-half and 12 minutes—you can't hold people's interest longer than that."

Freedomland promotional information championed Woody's talents: "Wood is the leader in the field of thematic entertainment for the masses. Show business is now in the hands of scientists and Wood's creative achievements mark him as the outstanding creating specialist in the realm of outdoor entertainment."

At the time of Freedomland's opening, Woody had finalized the mathematical details for Six Flags Over Texas and Discoveryland for Miami. The Arlington park opened and has celebrated its golden anniversary. Discoveryland was removed from the drawing board.

Publicity Department Touts Freedomland

The Freedomland publicity department turned out information and photographs leading up to the park's grand opening and then it continued the promotion through the five seasons of operation. The following promotional material featured Woody:

Dynamic Engineer Builds Dream Into Reality

"I wanted to tell everyone the great history and future of our country." Thus does dynamic, 38-year-old C.V. Wood, Jr., explain his response to a "personal challenge" which led him to design and create the world's largest outdoor family entertainment center.

This Texas-born engineer-showman started in the entertainment field by doing a feasibility study for California's Disneyland. He then joined the Disneyland staff in 1954 as general manager and vice-president; there he remained until 1956, when he formed the organization that has carried out the design of Freedomland.

"In building this world's champion outdoor entertainment park," Wood explains, "I told my design staff I wanted to tell the whole American story in one vast area shaped like the nation's map and segmented into regions. We came up with 500 thrilling American themes, discussed and discarded until we had the top 14 major stories now in the park, some of them with four or five separate attractions.

"This is our way of dramatizing the American heritage." Of designing mammoth outdoor "themed" entertainment centers, he says: "I view it as an imaginative combination of big business, show business, design creativity, and mass education through entertainment. What more could a person want?"

Wood often works around the clock at an oversized sofa and coffee table rather than an executive desk. A typical breakfast is hamburger and a bottle of cola.

His only disappointment with Freedomland—a project he says he has been carrying around in his mind for a dozen years—is that limitations made it necessary to leave out his home state, Texas.

"We're planning to add this in 1961, when there will be more time to do full justice to everything the Lone Star State represents. In its place, we combine all the flavor and color of the region in 'Tucson-Santa Fe and the Great

Southwest.' We hope this will satisfy loyal Texans, since they can find their way of life represented here.

"But then," he adds wryly, "you know Texans. I'm really a little worried about making a trip back home. I'm afraid they'll ride me out of town on a rail for being a deserter."

A Disney Lawsuit

After leaving Disney, Woody billed himself as the "Master Planner of Disneyland." Walt felt that his former employee invoked the Disney connection too often and, in so doing, placed most of the emphasis on himself. Lawyers for Disney sued to protect the brand's copyright.

Before Freedomland opened, Disneyland, Inc., and Walt Disney Enterprises requested the Los Angeles Superior Court to permanently enjoin the Marco Engineering Company and C.V. Wood, Jr., from representing themselves as having developed Disneyland. The *Sandusky Register* of May 24, 1960 reported:

> Disneyland, Inc. and the Walt Disney Enterprises has asked a Los Angeles Superior Court to permanently enjoin the Marco Engineering Co., and C. V. Wood, Jr., a firm that did an economic survey last spring for Cedar Point, from representing itself as having "conceived the idea of Disneyland, or designed, engineered or constructed" the west-coast park.
>
> The suit also asked the court to stop the defendants from using the Disneyland trademarks or name in their promotional activities.

The action was accompanied by exhibits to show that Marco Engineering and Wood made the alleged misrepresentations in promoting amusement projects, with specific mention of Circusland in Sanford, Florida; Magic Mountain in Colorado; and Freedomland. Disney contended that Woody's position was as an operations manager and did not involve decisions in creative concepts, design, or construction of the park.

The newspaper article continued:

> George R. Roose, president of G.A. Boeckling and Co., operators of Cedar Point, said Marco had this spring

conducted an economic survey as to potentiality of the area for new rides proposed at the resort.

Roose pointed out that Marco did not lay out the local park nor design it.

"At no time did the concern hold itself out as representing Disneyland," Roose said.

Donn Tatum, Disneyland executive vice president, said that in filing the suit the Disney firms are not asking for monetary relief or damages. Purpose of the action is to set the record straight that Disneyland was designed and built by the Walt Disney organization and no connection exists between it and the Wood projects.

Woody's Post-Freedomland Career

On November 22, 1960, a feature story in *The Daily News-Texan* of Grand Prairie, Texas, indicated that Wood and others from Marco Engineering, including Freedomland designer Randy Duell, were concentrating on designing and building Six Flags Over Texas. Woody and Marco Engineering handled initial work and Randy completed that assignment. At about the same time, the company was hired for the feasibility study that led to the creation of the San Antonio River Walk.

During Freedomland's second season, Marco Engineering merged with the McCulloch Corporation, a Freedomland sponsor. Robert Paxton McCulloch had built companies in engine manufacturing and aviation. He also owned an oil company and produced outboard motors. Robert purchased Lake Havasu and other property in Arizona. He and Woody then collaborated on a plan to attract tourists to this part of the state.

Woody achieved worldwide recognition with the purchase of the original London Bridge. He had it disassembled stone-by-stone, transported across the pond, and reassembled in Arizona. Woody became Lake Havasu's city planner and he created its original garden walks and themed shopping districts. Today, a bronze sculpture of Woody and Robert is located near Arizona's London Bridge.

During 1985, Woody received a credited role as the bar-keeper in the film *Trinity: Good Guys and Bad Guys*. Two years later, he was an assistant to the chairman of Lorimar Telepictures and helped merge that company with Time Warner. He then was retained by Warner Bros. to pioneer its entry into the studio tour attraction business. As the president of the Recreation Enterprises Division, he planned, built, and opened the company's first attraction, Warner Bros. Movie World, on the Gold Coast of Australia.

A lifelong devotee of chili, which he considered America's national dish, Woody twice was a chili cook-off world champion and spent nearly a quarter-century presiding over the annual World Championship Chili Cookoff that he co-founded with race car designer Carroll Shelby. His personal chili recipe included such unusual items as limes and Pepsi-Cola.

At the time of his death on March 14, 1992, Woody had been married for 20 years to actress Joanne Dru. Her brother was actor, singer, and television game show host Peter Marshall whose *Hollywood Squares* television show featured Charley Weaver, an American history buff who once operated a small Civil War museum at Freedomland.

Woody's Revival

Woody's obituaries did recognize his contributions to Disneyland, but Woody never reconciled with Walt. Woody also was recognized by the International Association of Amusement Parks and Attractions (IAAPA). He was inducted posthumously into its hall of fame during 1994.

Only recently has the Disney company become more recep-tive to acknowledging Woody's contributions to the industry and to the creation of Disneyland. During 2011, an official Disney travel magazine offered a bit of trivia about London Bridge, identifying Woody as one of the men responsible for its relocation to Arizona. Also of note, though it might just be a coincidence, is that "Woody" was tabbed the lead character in the 1995 Pixar animated film *Toy Story*.

CHAPTER FOUR

The Building of Freedomland U.S.A.

The imagery of Freedomland centers about a fictional character named "Johnny Freedom." He is representative of the American spirit of hard work and ingenuity coming to the fore whenever the growing nation was in jeopardy.

—Freedomland Promotional Material

Bronx residents had an abundance of family entertainment venues from which to choose during the early 1960s. Anyone seeking a carnival atmosphere enjoyed Brooklyn's Coney Island and Rockaways' Playland in Queens. Some people traveled to Palisades Amusement Park along the Hudson River in New Jersey, or Rye Playland, which continues to operate today in Westchester County. Small neighborhood amusement areas could be found throughout the five boroughs of the city, in Westchester, and along Long Island.

Freedomland U.S.A. was different than the conventional amusement parks. It was a theme park that featured the story of America through attractions that included Fort Cavalry, the Chicago Fire, the Civil War, and the Northwest Fur Trapper ride. It even embraced the present and future of space flight.

The research and design team that created and constructed Freedomland consisted of about 200 leading artists and architects. Many were former Disney employees. Others were veterans of the film industry.

The building of Freedomland begins with the corporate structure that was created to find the land, finance the park, and manage operations. While Walt Disney was cautious about bringing his park concept to the east coast, claiming that the eastern audience was perceived to be more sophisticated than the audience in the west, C.V. Wood absorbed all he had learned and experienced with the construction of Disneyland. He formed his Marco Engineering company and took the show on the road to Colorado, Massachusetts, New York, and Texas.

Woody created family-friendly concepts for the Magic Mountain park in Golden, Colorado, and the Pleasure Island park in Wakefield, Massachusetts. Freedomland was family-oriented, too, but it also was different in concept and design than any other park. As Freedomland opened its gates, Woody already was working on the Six Flags Over Texas project.

The feasibility study for Freedomland was under the direction of Marco's Patricia Kimball, a research economist, and James E. Thompson, who had been a consultant, especially on traffic assessments, for the planning of Disneyland. Their study looked at the potential paying customers within a 50-mile radius of the park. The preliminary plans for the land also included an industrial park, a hotel, and residential housing. The commercial and residential plans were tabled until Freedomland closed. The hotel foundation was placed in the ground and then covered with landfill.

Key Dates In Freedomland History

- Late 1958. C. V. Wood unveiled the Freedomland concept in Manhattan to Webb & Knapp.

- April 14, 1959. Formation of International Recreation Corporation (60 State Street, Boston, Massachusetts).

- April 30, 1959. Freedomland project announced at New York City Hall.

- May 14, 1959. International Recreation Corporation filed a registration statement with the SEC seeking registration of 2,750,000 shares of common stock.

- May 21, 1959. New York City's Planning Commission approved zoning changes for the property.

- May 25, 1959. News conference to introduce the Freedomland project held at the Empire State Building.
- June 1959. William Zeckendorf, Sr., of Webb & Knapp, asked Walt and Roy Disney to become partners in Freedomland. A spring 1960 date for this request also has been cited.
- June 12, 1959. The project received authorization from the New York City Board of Estimate.
- July 20, 1959. 580,000 shares of common stock of the International Recreation Corporation offered at $17.50 per share.
- August 1959. Marco Engineering provided a report to International Recreation Corporation that explained the park design along with cost estimates, attendance potential, and income projections.
- August 26, 1959. Groundbreaking ceremonies. Construction originally was estimated alternately at $15 and $16 million. Combined with the land lease, expenses ballooned to $65 million due to inflated value of the land.
- September 10, 1959. Frederic V. Schumacher is appointed vice president and general manager of Freedomland. He had served as vice chairman of the management and operations committee at Disneyland since that park opened.
- November 1959 / January 1960. Ground is moved, foundations secured, and maintenance buildings constructed.
- March 23, 1960. Fire razes a few small buildings, including one associated, reportedly, with the buccaneer ride. Burned remnants are used to enhance the scenery for the Chicago Fire attraction.
- June 18, 1960. Preliminary opening and charity event.
- June 19, 1960. Opening Day. Singer Pat Boone and family cut the ceremonial ribbon. Television's *The Ed Sullivan Show* features the new park for about 15 minutes.
- June 25, 1960. A stage coach overturns and injures 10 people, two of them seriously.

- August 28, 1960. The Great Freedomland Office Robbery. A portion of the $28,000 cash was found in a fish tank.

- September 1960. Frederic V. Schumacher leaves Freedomland to take a post with the Century 21 Exposition in Seattle. Other changes are made to park management.

- October 1960. Leases for three Webb & Knapp New York City hotels—Commodore, Astor, and Manhattan—are purchased by the International Recreation Corporation. Webb & Knapp, in turn, leases the properties from International Recreation Corporation and provides Freedomland with additional working capital.

- October 5, 1960. Three companies file liens against Webb & Knapp.

- November 11, 1960. Lien filed by Turner Construction Company.

- June 11, 1961. Second season opens with the addition of two entertainment venues: the Moon Bowl in Satellite City and Hollywood Arena in San Francisco.

- May 24, 1961. Freedomland requires $8 million infusion to reduce debt.

- June 10, 1961. International Recreation Corporation gives Webb & Knapp control of Freedomland.

- August 1961. William Zeckendorf, Jr., of Webb & Knapp is named president of Freedomland, Inc.

- March 21, 1962. Arthur K. Moss is named Freedomland's executive vice president and general manager.

- May 26, 1962. New attractions include a circus in the upgraded 5,000-seat Hollywood Arena and a state fair midway with amusement rides.

- June 28, 1962. A "family vacation" evening (6pm) price goes into effect when guests are admitted for $2.50 plus tax. The price provides access to park attractions as well as all shows and exhibits.

- September 5, 1962. Benjamin Moore, the paint company, sues to void its lease and to collect $150,000 in damages, alleging the addition of amusement-type rides removed the historical and education aspect of the park. The suit is dismissed on September 18.

- June 30, 1963. Auction announcement for the Freedomland Inn property.
- June 30, 1964. Webb & Knapp avoids possible bankruptcy by paying $120,000 overdue interest on sinking fund debentures. The company transferred 60 percent interest in International Recreation Corporation and its subsidiary Freedomland, Inc., to National Development Corporation. In a separate transaction, Webb & Knapp transferred 80 percent interest in its consolidated subsidiary National Development Corporation to Hyman Green and his associates. Hyman and the others also own the remaining 20 percent interest in the company.
- September 14, 1964. Freedomland files for bankruptcy. Management indicates that the New York World's Fair contributed to the park's loss of patronage.
- August 30, 1965. Freedomland adjudicated a bankrupt.

Freedomland by the Numbers

- Acres: 205 total acres with 85 acres for attractions and the remaining land for maintenance facilities and parking.
- Attractions: 41 spectacles rolled into one.
- Buildings: 248.
- Building the park: 298 days.
- Cost: $65 million, including $15–16 million to lease the land, equal to 22 star-studded movies, 130 hour-long television spectaculars, 195 Broadway musicals.
- Earth moved: 1.2 million cubic yards.
- Eateries: 18 to as many as 27 restaurants and snack bars, not including certain specialty retail shops, food carts, and picnic grounds.
- Electrical wiring: 150 miles.
- Employees: 2,000–3,000 (some employees were hired by Freedomland while others were hired by the sponsors, or lessees, of park attractions and shops).

- Parking capacity: approximately 7,200 cars for guests and a separate 1,800 spaces for employees. ("Parking Area, as well as most of the park, is built on former swamp and trash dump," according to Freedomland publicity material.)

- Official Freedomland address and phone number: 2800 Baychester Avenue, Bronx 69, New York; TULIP 1-0600.

- Paving: 500,000 yards.

- Plaster: 75 tons.

- Signs: 4,000–5,000.

- Talent: 19 Oscar winners among hundreds of designers and other creative people and actors.

- Telephones: 35 phone booths were scattered throughout the park with the largest concentration in Little Old New York.

- Trees and shrubs: 50,000 total plantings with about 10,000 trees.

- Visitors: original estimates were 32,000 at one time with up to 90,000 during a day. (The population within a 50-mile radius of Freedomland during the early 1960s was estimated at 27 million. This covered Albany to the north, almost to Delaware to the south, past New London, Connecticut, to the east and through New Jersey to Wilkes-Barre, Pennsylvania, to the west.)

- Waterways and lakes: 8 miles of navigation; 15 million gallons of water filled the Great Lakes and other waterways.

Complex Web of Freedomland Oversight

A news service article shortly before Freedomland opened correctly explained the management structure of the enterprise: "Ownership and control of Freedomland is about as complicated as the government of the country it depicts."

The land for Freedomland was controlled by William Zeckendorf, Sr., and his Webb & Knapp, Inc. The other companies involved with the park were National Development Corporation, International Recreation Corporation, and Freedomland, Inc.

Webb & Knapp, the major stockholder of National Development Corporation, was a real estate development firm, founded in 1922 by Robert C. Knapp and W. Seward Webb, along with architect Eliot Cross. Zeckendorf, Sr., joined the firm during 1938 and acquired it during 1949. Webb & Knapp also owned controlling interest in International Recreation Corporation that operated the park under the company Freedomland, Inc. Many of the executives on the board of directors of Pleasure Island, Freedomland's sister park in Massachusetts that opened during 1959, were on the board of International Recreation Corporation. Zeckendorf, Sr., as the chairman of Webb & Knapp, exercised control over these companies and Freedomland.

Through this confusing corporate structure, the land for Freedomland was leased by International Recreation Corporation (parent of Freedomland, Inc.) from National Development Corporation. The lease was for $15–16 million and, reportedly, for 51 years.

The cost estimate has been reported variously as $16 million and $17.5 million to build just the theme park. Unanticipated items inflated the cost to $22 million. The total project cost then was reported at $65 million. According to Woody, this included the inflated value of the land and intangibles such as expensive union labor and New York construction costs.

The original construction estimate was within reason since a handful of years earlier $17 million was invested to build Disneyland. The difference, though, was that Walt Disney purchased and owned his park's land while Freedomland was charged millions for rent.

Zeck, Sr., was the principal stockholder in Freedomland. He also had connections with Woody's other parks—Pleasure Island and Magic Mountain—and he was invested in the Great Southwest Corporation that built, under the oversight of Woody's Marco Engineering, the Great Southwestland park (later named Six Flags Over Texas).

The Principal Players

Woody generated excitement for Freedomland through the work of Marco Engineering. The rest of Freedomland's fate was in the hands of many others. With so much corporate, investor, political, and union involvement with Freedomland, the picture is clear that Woody built a great park, but he did not have control over its management or the land prior to and after it opened, and the park was doomed to fail even before it opened the gates as various plans had been discussed about future development on the same property.

Marco Engineering

- Cornelius Vanderbilt Wood, Jr., president.

Webb & Knapp

- William Zeckendorf, Sr., chairman.
- William Zeckendorf, Jr., president.

International Recreation Corporation

The investors in Pleasure Island partnered with others to form International Recreation Corporation, the parent company of Freedomland, Inc. The principals listed in the Securities and Exchange Commission application of International Recreation Corporation to obtain permission to offer stock were:

- Gerald W. Blakeley, Jr., president of Cabot, Cabot and Forbes, identified as director and promoter. (The company, which continues today as a Boston real estate management firm, was an investor in Woody's Pleasure Island park.)

- Peter DeMet, listed as an industrialist, identified as president, board chairman, and director. (In some media reports, Chicago attorney Milton T. Raynor was listed as president, but this could have been confusion with his role with Freedomland, Inc.)

- Herbert C. Lee, listed as an industrialist (president, A.S. Beck Shoe Company), director, and treasurer.

- Robert C. Linnell, vice president of Cabot, Cabot and Forbes, as director and promoter.
- Thomas B. Slick, as director, from San Antonio and member of a Texas oil family.

Other directors included Salim L. Lewis, Joseph Crosby, Robert Vasselais, David Burstein, William A. Hawkes (president of Pleasure Island), William Zeckendorf, Sr., William Zeckendorf, Jr., and C.V. Wood, Jr., who also was named on the SEC application.

> International Recreation Corporation, 60 State St., Boston, filed a registration statement (File 2-15113) with the SEC on May 14, 1959, seeking registration of 2,750,000 shares of common stock. The company proposed to offer 2,250,000 shares for public sale at $11 per share through an underwriting group headed by Paine, Webber, Jackson & Curtis, which will receive a $1 per share commission. The additional 250,000 shares are under option to Webb & Knapp, Inc. ... The company was organized April 14, 1959, to construct and operate directly or through subsidiaries open-air recreation and entertainment park; and this stock offering is primarily for the purpose of obtaining funds to enable the company through subsidiaries to construct parks in New York City and Miami, Fla. ... It has leased from Webb & Knapp approximately 212 acres of land in the Borough of the Bronx, New York City, which is part of the unimproved land known as Baychester Center, on which it plans to construct a recreational open-air park at a cost estimated at between $14 and $19 million, to be completed by July 1, 1960.
>
> An engineering and management agreement has been entered into with Marco Engineering of the East, Inc., the sole stockholder of which is C.V. Wood, Jr., who is a director and promoter of the issuing company. The latter has also entered into a contract for engineering services with Cabot, Cabot & Forbes Co., and a construction contract with the latter's subsidiary, Aberthaw Construction Co. Gerald W. Blakeley, Jr. and Robert

C. Linnell are the principal shareholders and officers of Cabot and also are directors and promoters of the issuing company.

The prospectus lists Gerald W. Blakely, Jr. and Robert C. Linnell of Boston as holders of 187,500 shares of deferred stock; Peter DeMet of Coral Gables, president, 187,500; Herbert C. Lee, treasurer, of Boston, 187,500; Thomas B. Slick, of San Antonio, a director, 93,750; and C.V. Wood, Jr., a director, 93,750.

> —*News Digest* published by the Securities and Exchange Commission, May 15, 1959.

On July 20, underwriters headed by Bear, Stearns & Co., Reynolds & Co., and the Lee Higginson Corporation offered 580,000 shares of common stock of the International Recreation Corporation at $17.50 per share to fund Freedomland. Webb & Knapp agreed to allocate $7 million for 400,000 additional shares of International Recreation Corporation stock. Besides financing for this park, the company expected to have sufficient funds from the offering to acquire the site for the Miami park.

The Bronx location for the theme park was a 205-acre site at the southern part of about 400 acres of marshland. The park and its attractions would be located on 85 acres, with the remaining 120 acres reserved for maintenance and parking. Part of the grand plan included the $6 million 600-room hotel (Freedomland Inn), also referred to at various times as a 300-, 350-, and 400-room hotel but never constructed at the southern end of the property. At the northern end of the property, the possibility existed for an industrial park and housing. Original blueprints indicated a plan for a movie studio there as well.

Suddenly, one of the prime underwriters, Paine, Weber, Jackson & Curtis, pulled out of the deal. Wall Street sources said the investment firm had become wary of sinking the $47 million it had promised into an untried amusement venture. Zeck, Sr., was determined to keep a promise he had made to New York City Mayor Robert Wagner that the park would open during the summer of 1960.

"We figured that this [the park] would be a good way to enhance our property," said the junior Zeckendorf at a later date, "so we picked up $7 million of stock with the proviso that the rest of the stock issue [a million shares worth about $10,150,000] be sold."

The balance of the stock was sold to various investors, although Webb & Knapp's stock purchase gave it control of Freedomland. For Freedomland's second season, the Zeckendorfs invested $3 million in cash into the park to cover unbudgeted construction and pre-opening costs. Webb & Knapp's cash commitment now totaled about $10 million.

National Development Corporation

This company, controlled by the Zeckendorfs, leased the Baychester marshland to International Recreation Corporation, the parent company of Freedomland, Inc.

At the end of the 1960 season, John C. Mullins of Denver was named president. After several years, Hyman Green became the key player at National Development Corporation, serving as president when the pension fund of the International Teamsters Union assumed Webb & Knapp's interests in the company and in most of the land.

Freedomland, Inc.

- Milton T. Raynor, president.
- Frederic V. Schumacher, vice president, general manager.
- Russell D. Levy, executive vice president, and the executive vice president of International Recreation Company; he also oversaw property management for Webb & Knapp during May 1962.

Additional Freedomland Players

Ed Werner was the opening season advertising and public relations director. Stanley Bailey was the park's director of marketing and John McGarry was the director of group sales.

John Wagerer was an official Freedomland photographer. Sid Ascher, a newspaper columnist and public relations/advertising executive, wrote publicity copy. Writer and publicist

Abel Silver also was involved in the early stages of the park along with photographer Arty Pomerantz. According to Silver family members, the Silver-Pomerantz duo won a contract bid. Both worked at the *New York Post* at the time and their work for Freedomland possibly was handled as a freelance arrangement. During a long newspaper career that included photography of countless celebrities, Arty was nominated for a Pulitzer Prize.

Ellington & Co. served as the park's ad agency during the opening season with Emil Byfield, Jr., as the account executive. The campaign that promoted the park's historical and educational value generated huge crowds. The turnout was so large that management curtailed the advertising campaign. This proved to be an error, according to the agency, as crowd size thinned during the summer months.

Don Drager from Pacific Ocean Park in California was brought in as an executive manager of operations for the 1961 season, with Fran Crews, special services manager, implementing the plans. Stu Ludlom was named vice president of public relations. Cole, Fischer & Rogow, Inc. became the second season advertising agency of record. The campaign sold fun and excitement while de-emphasizing the history and education.

Newspaper advertisements were aimed at adults, convincing parents that for a relatively small amount of money they could bring children to the park for a day. Television was aimed at the children. Radio, through the disc jockey shows, reached teenagers and the evening dating crowd.

The advertising also featured a new ticketing concept that was not used during the previous season: for one admission payment ($2.95), the purchaser could enjoy unlimited access to every ride and attraction in the park.

Profiles of Key Executives

Peter DeMet (sometimes "Demet" or "De Met")

Peter DeMet was a Chicago business executive prominent in the automotive business as the owner of a large Pontiac dealership. His family owned DeMet's Candy Company. Through Peter DeMet Productions, he was involved in filmed sports television shows that included *Championship Bowling, All Star Golf,* and *Pocket Billiard of Champions*. In the SEC filing, he was listed as an industrialist from Florida.

Hyman Green

Hyman Green came to Freedomland during the final phase of the park. Born in Canada, he was involved with real estate and knew the Zeckendorfs. He also was known to the International Teamsters Union, which was involved with the park during the building and operations phases. Later, one of its pension funds would become involved financially with the park and the land.

Hyman was a co-developer of Florida properties that included Tierra Verde, East Bay Country Club, and Coquina Key. He was an officer of Honeymoon Isle Development Corp. near Dunedin. During 1961, according to newspaper reports, a counterfeit bond scandal investigated by U.S. Attorney General Robert F. Kennedy traced $1,000 Ohio state turnpike and Shell Union Oil coupon bonds to a late confidant of labor union leader James R. Hoffa. The bonds had been deposited in the Guarantee Trust Co. in the Bahamas. Hyman, as a reported official of the bank, allegedly escorted an associate of the confidant to Nassau to deposit the bonds. Hyman and nine others were indicted by a federal grand jury.

Milton T. Raynor

A native of Chicago, Milton T. (Ted) Raynor graduated from Northwestern University, where he played varsity basketball and baseball. He turned down opportunities from the Philadelphia Athletics and the Chicago Cubs to pursue a law degree from Northwestern Law School. Upon graduation and during the establishment of Freedomland, Ted operated a Chicago law firm that became known as Raynor and Mitchell. It focused on trade association business.

Already associated with Peter DeMet, Ted broadened his activities to include collaboration with successful television sports programming such as *Championship Bowling* and programs connected with major league baseball and professional football. After Freedomland, Ted moved to California and became involved with producing the films *Viva Max, Julius Caesar,* and *The Magic Christian.*

Herbert C. Lee

From Newark, New Jersey, Herbert C. Lee began his career in merchandising at the local Bamberger's Department Store and then moved to Kobacher's in Columbus, Ohio, where he met his future wife, Mildred "Micki" Schiff. After World War II, Herbert joined his wife's family business, Shoe Corporation of America, where he served as vice president of manufacturing. He also was named to the board of directors. He served, in succession, at A.S. Beck, Shoe Corporation of Canada, Clark Shoe Company, and shoe importer MDA, Inc.

Frederick V. Schumacher

From San Diego, Frederick V. Schumacher was an industrial engineer and also involved in public relations. Associated with the 1939–1940 New York World's Fair, he was Woody's first supervisor at Convair, the aircraft manufacturing company. Woody invited Fred to work for Walt Disney as they prepared to open Disneyland, where Fred served as vice chairman of the management and operations committee.

Fred was vice president and general manager of Freedomland, Inc., on the opening day of the park. At the close of the first season, during September 1960, he decided to leave Freedomland for the Century 21 Exposition in Seattle. At about this time, Freedomland president Ted Raynor vacated his position. Rumors within the industry indicated that the interests of Zeck, Sr., were overseeing policy decisions and creating differences in operating philosophy.

Russell B. Levy, a colleague of the Zeckendorfs, became the acting boss at Freedomland. He persuaded two of Fred's top executives, Earl Shelton and Fran Crews, to remain with the company. Both also had worked with Disney. Bob Smith, who had operated a Kiddieland at a shopping center (possibly the Zeckendorfs' Roosevelt Field) on Long Island, joined Freedomland as executive vice president to assist Russell.

The Zeckendorfs

William Zeckendorf, Sr., was an employee of Webb & Knapp, one of the largest real estate investment and development firms of the 1930s through the early 1960s. He eventually owned the company and developed a significant portion of the New York City urban landscape. William Zeckendorf, Jr., maintained a lower public profile and became known for large-scale projects that transformed neighborhoods.

One day in 1958, in Webb & Knapp's executive suite in Manhattan, Woody met with both Zeckendorfs. He unveiled a scale model of Freedomland and the two real estate tycoons agreed to lease their land for $800,000 a year (this eventually rose to many millions on a 51-year lease). The park would operate, according to Woody, from May 15 until October 15, and it would draw five million people annually.

"Wood is one of the real great salesmen of our time," recalled the younger Zeckendorf during 1965. "He can sell anything, and he sold us on Freedomland."

During 1961, the son was elected president of Freedomland, Inc., while maintaining his position as executive vice president of Webb & Knapp.

Others

With so many artists, set designers, and others who had worked in Hollywood and on stage productions, Freedomland was similar to a movie studio backlot. The creators used studio techniques that manipulated the visual perception of buildings. A structure would appear larger, taller, or farther away by adjusting the scale of surrounding objects in relation to the viewer. This increases or decreases the perception of depth. Many of these techniques remain popular in the entertainment field.

Maurice Ayers

Maurice Ayers was the park's special effects superintendent. He came from the film industry, where he was involved with pre-Freedomland *The Pride and the Passion, Cleopatra,* and *The Ten*

Commandments, and post-Freedomland *Paint Your Wagon* and *The Blue Max*. He received the 1949 Scientific and Engineering Academy Award for an invention that aided set construction.

At about the time of Freedomland, Maurice started to concentrate on amusement park design that included dark rides. Along with his wife, Dorathea, he designed attractions at such venues as Pacific Ocean Park (Santa Monica, California), Six Flags Over Texas (Arlington), Kennywood (West Mifflin, Pennsylvania), and Astroworld (Houston, Texas). Maurice was instrumental in the design of the Chicago Fire attraction and known at Freedomland as the man who "burned Chicago down every 30 minutes."

Randall Duell

A former art director at MGM Studios, Randall Duell received three Academy Award nominations. His movie credits included *Singin' in the Rain* and *Blackboard Jungle*. He also worked on a number of pictures without film credit, including *The Wizard of Oz*.

After departing MGM in 1959, Randall briefly worked with Woody and Marco Engineering as co-art director. He collaborated with Woody and art director Wade B. Rubottom on Pleasure Island in Massachusetts and then Freedomland. He designed many of the structures at Freedomland and specified the color scheme for the railroad and other areas of the park.

Randall also designed other themed parks and structures under his own company, R. Duell and Associates. His work included Six Flags Over Texas, the Universal Studios Tour in California, and the Texas Pavilion at the 1964 New York World's Fair. He developed the Duell Loop concept for amusement parks that provided a connected pathway through a park to link attractions and themed areas. Many of today's parks have abandoned this concept.

Freedomland, according to its promotional material, had been in the blueprint stage for two years in Hollywood under the supervision of Wade B. Rubottom and Randall Duell, "graduates of MGM and Disneyland."

Joseph Linesch and Arnold Dutton

Joseph Linesch had worked with pioneering landscape designer Morgan "Bill" Evans to create the landscape at Disneyland. Joseph then landscaped Freedomland with Arnold Dutton, representing the company Evans, Linesch and Dutton.

Joseph created designs for many other world-renowned parks, including the Magic Kingdom and EPCOT Center at Walt Disney World, Disneyland in Tokyo, Universal Studios in Florida, Busch Gardens in Houston and Van Nuys, Astroworld in Houston, Hershey Park in Pennsylvania, and the Shinen-kan Pavilion Garden and East Sculpture Garden at the Los Angeles County Museum of Art. He also devised landscape plans for multiple-acre regional parks in various locations throughout the United States, the pool at the Fontainebleau Hotel in Miami, the Beverly Hilton Hotel, and the Los Angeles Sports Arena.

Around 200 gardeners were digging around Freedomland's Great Lakes, building the Rocky Mountains, creating the Great Plains, and planting scale-size forests on the property. Arnold was the landscape architect in charge of the project. He said that the work, when completed, would dwarf the landscape of Disneyland.

"Our aim is to give visitors a look into regions of America they would not ordinarily be familiar with at first hand," said Arnold at the time. "A city-bred youngster from the East Coast might never have seen a real live cornfield, one of the symbols of American agriculture. So in Freedomland we're going to have a full-size cornfield complete to ears of corn on the stalks."

Arthur K. Moss

Not much is known about Arthur K. Moss. He had been a movie camera operator and director, a night club entrepreneur, a talent scout, and an advertising and promotion expert.

For the 1962 season, Art was named executive vice president and general manager. He was tasked with brightening the park's profit picture. Art immediately shaved the park's $150,000 weekly payroll by 20 percent and banned overtime. He also invested heavily in celebrity musical entertainment for performances at the Moon Bowl and Hollywood Arena, two venues that had been added for the 1961 season. Art appears with prominent entertainers in a number of Freedomland publicity photos.

Art replaced George A. Hamid, who stepped away to concentrate on rebuilding the Steel Pier in Atlantic City that had been damaged by a storm. George had built a portfolio of piers and eight boardwalk theaters in Atlantic City and was known as "King of the Boardwalk." He remained a consultant in the development of Freedomland's entertainment policy.

As Art assumed greater responsibilities, he realized that the park faced a poor public relations image. Everyone was knocking it, especially taxi drivers. Art got the cabbies on his side by paying for advertisements in their trade publications to announce that drivers and their families would be admitted at no cost to the park.

Under Art's oversight of the Moon Bowl venue, Freedomland attempted to attract more teenagers, a move that ultimately transformed the park into a conglomeration of rides, skill games, and midway attractions.

"We learned that you just can't drag teenagers to a park to be educated," Art said at the time, "so we tried to put on a face of fun and excitement."

Tex McCrary

John Reagan "Tex" McCrary was a journalist and public relations specialist who popularized the talk show genre for television and radio along with second wife, model/actress Jinx Falkenburg. They hosted the first radio talk show, *Meet Tex and Jinx*, along with the radio show *Hi Jinx* and the television talk shows *At Home* and *The Swift Home Service Club*. Fully engaged with the candidacy of Dwight D. Eisenhower for president, Tex was a friend and public relations consultant of Zeck, Sr. He was called upon to employ his expertise to help promote Freedomland.

Wade B. Rubottom

A Hollywood art director, Wade B. Rubottom worked on numerous films, including the *The Wizard of Oz*, *The Philadelphia Story*, and *The Shop Around the Corner*. He worked for Walt Disney's private design firm, WED Enterprises, during 1954–1955 as an art director responsible for the small town theme and overall look of Disneyland's Main Street, U.S.A. Wade later worked for Marco Engineering with the title of executive vice president and he contributed to the designs of Magic Mountain, Pleasure Island, and Freedomland. Through his MGM experience, Wade already knew Marco Engineering art director Randall Duell.

Cliff Walker

Cliff Walker was the foreman for the construction of Disneyland's Jungle Cruise attraction. At Freedomland, he was the director of operations for the first four seasons.

Sylvester Weaver and Douglas Leigh

Sylvester Barnabee "Pat" Weaver, Jr., chairman of the board of McCann Erickson, a powerful advertising agency, was named a Freedomland consultant during the formation of the park. So was Doug Leigh, president of Douglas Leigh, Inc. Pat directed radio and television activities for Freedomland and Douglas directed outdoor displays and spectaculars.

Pat was a radio advertising executive who became president of NBC during the mid-1950s. He was involved with a number of huge television ideas such as *Your Show of Shows* and *Today*. During 1958, he accepted the position with McCann Erickson. He was involved with Freedomland until his 1963 departure from the company. One of his daughters, Susan Alexandra, is the actress Sigourney Weaver.

Douglas was an advertising executive and lighting designer. He was a pioneer in signage and outdoor advertising, and he made New York City's Times Square the site of some of the most famous billboards, like A&P's Eight O'Clock Coffee that emitted clouds of steam from a large cup and Camel's advertisement that blew smoke rings. His design of a large illuminated snowflake has decorated the intersection of New York City's Fifth Avenue and 57th Street for many holiday seasons.

Park Design Team

Many people who joined Woody's Marco Engineering team worked on either Magic Mountain or Pleasure Island, or both, before starting the work at Freedomland. The Marco Engineering team for Freedomland, besides lead designers Wade B. Rubottom and Randal Duell, included John Welker (architect), Paul Groesse and Bob Stahler (art directors), Bob Minkus, Ted Rich, and Bob Brown (assistant art directors), William Minker (color consultant in charge of props and dressing), and Richmond "Dick" Kelsey (art director in charge of rides).

Richmond had been an animation art director with the Disney company and he assisted with the design of Disneyland. He was hired by Woody to work with Wade on the development of Magic Mountain and Freedomland. He later returned to Disney.

Other departments consisted of sign shop artists, staff shop, mill crew, construction advisors, ride and special effects, and scenic shops. According to Freedomland promotional material, 19 Oscar winners were among 133 scenic artists who designed the 457 sets. The sets dwarfed a dozen circuses, motion picture spectacles, and a season of Broadway musicals and extravaganzas, covering more space than six Hollywood studios.

What's in a Name

Freedomland was referenced in a number of different ways in print, advertising, and promotion by park employees and the media, with slight differences in style. Pleasure Island, a little older than Freedomland, first was tagged with the description as "The Disneyland of the East." Soon after, Freedomland also would receive this same description.

- Park Name: Freedomland, USA / Freedomland U.S.A. / FREEDOMLAND.

- Taglines: The World's Newest and Largest Outdoor Entertainment Center / The World's Largest Entertainment Center / The World's Largest Family Entertainment Center / The World's Largest Outdoor Entertainment Center.

A lesser known generic tagline, "A World of Fun for Everyone," later was introduced by marketers. One that did not make the cut: "Freedomland is fifty states of happiness!"

The park also was identified by its original promotional jingle: "Mommy and Daddy take my hand, take me out to Freedomland." Subsequent up-tempo quickie songs for broadcast commercials were sung by entertainer Paul Anka.

Construction Management and Costs

Construction plans were announced at New York City Hall on April 30, 1959, by Zeck, Sr. He said the project would be built and operated by a syndicate to which his company would lease the southern portion of its 400-acre tract of vacant land. Tentative plans included the construction of middle-income housing and a "motor hotel" on other portions of the property.

A few weeks later, on May 25, a news conference was held at Manhattan's Empire State Building to officially unveil the world's largest outdoor entertainment center, Freedomland U.S.A. The engineering firm of Andrews & Clark of Manhattan estimated the cost of planning, surveying, land fill, and leveling at $1.5 million. Tentative plans at the time indicated the possibility of a celebratory fireworks gala at the property on the evening of July 4, 1959. Documentation has not been located to support the occurrence of the fireworks show.

General contractors for Freedomland were Turner Construction Co. of New York and Aberthaw Construction Co. of Boston. Ambrose Burton was the president of Aberthaw and this company completed the construction of Pleasure Island. Ed O'Brien was the project manager for Turner-Aberthaw. Engineering was the responsibility of Cabot, Cabot and Forbes Associates, Inc.

Woody requested a construction budget of $15.5 million. By ribbon-cutting time on June 19, 1960, the park was about 85 percent complete and construction had already cost approximately $22 million. Before Freedomland's first cash customer passed through the turnstile, the park was facing mounting debt.

Groundbreaking

The official publication of the Bronx Board of Trade featured the arrival of Freedomland as its cover story. Several of the park's preliminary promotional points were altered by opening day:

> On Wednesday, August 26, the ground breaking ceremonies of the new Freedomland, U.S.A., The Bronx took place. Many city and borough officials, along with representatives of The Bronx Board of Trade were present.
>
> This new enterprise will occupy 205 acres in the northeast section of The Bronx at a cost of $65,000,000 and will be the largest outdoor entertainment center in the world. It is scheduled to open on July 1, 1960.
>
> It will be the American story brought alive. ... It will be a telescope back through time. ... It will be a rollicking fun trip through our nation's past and future.
>
> Freedomland will be a "historyland," with 41 elaborately detailed installations where visitors will live through the actual and fictional events that played a significant role in the romantic growth of the United States. Families at the park will see our history!—and become a part of it!
>
> They will leave this century when they enter the grounds through "Little Old New York" as it was in the 1750–1850 period. They will see bright and gay Chicago as it was in its early days, San Francisco at the time of the Barbary Coast and they will live through its earthquake. They will re-live the era of the hearty whalers of the fishing coasts of New England.
>
> They will ride in a stage coach, buckboard and covered wagons, a sternwheeler across the Mississippi River, in antique autos and on an old-time steam-engine railroad. They will journey into exciting Creole fiestas and alligators will attack their swamp "buggy" as they ride through the Florida bayous. They will travel in a war correspondent's wagon at the time of the Civil War and get caught in a cross-fire between the Blue and the Gray. They will span a century or two as they visit Cape Canaveral and learn the role of the U.S. in space travel.

They will actually fly in the "space ship" of the future. The ship will circle the "earth" in a six-minute voyage as they see many of the globe's most famous landmarks through the ship's twelve viewing ports.

Appropriately, Freedomland, U.S.A. will be built in the contour of the United States on its Bronx site bounded by the Hutchinson River, Hutchinson River parkway, the New England Thruway and near the Pelham Bay Park (Lexington Avenue-Local) and Baychester Avenue (Seventh Avenue-Express) IRT subway stations.

Its builder is Marco Engineering Co., headed by C.V. Wood, Jr., who participated in the design, construction and management of Disneyland. It will have a 12,000-car parking lot and is designed to entertain a peak daily attendance of 90,000 persons. Exhibitors using its space are expected to invest $14,000,000 on their projects which will depict their particular contributions to our American traditions and progress. There will be many restaurants serving foods popular in their related locales, and also snack bars from one "coast" to the other.

The coming of Freedomland, U.S.A. early next summer has elicited warm response from New York City officials and educational leaders. Mayor Robert Wagner has expressed himself as "delighted" because New York has been selected as the site for the center. The city's Board of Education president, Charles Silver, has said: "The Freedomland project will serve the vital purpose of refreshing the memories of all of us in a visual and dramatic way. ... I have a feeling that history teachers all over the country will be grateful."

Perhaps Mayor Wagner sums up its purpose with this statement: "I know that Freedomland, U.S.A. will help refire the imagination—as well as entertain—all those who visit it!"

The Bronx Board of trade, always vitally interested in bringing new industry into our borough, welcomes Freedomland, U.S.A.

—Bronxboro, Fall 1959

Groundbreaking ceremony attendees included:

- William Zeckendorf, Sr., chairman, Webb & Knapp.
- C.V. Wood, president, Marco Engineering.
- Ambrose Burton, president, Aberthaw Construction.
- Abe Stark, president of the New York City Council whose business advertising gimmick ("Hit Sign, Win Suit. Abe Stark. 1514 Pitkin Ave. Brooklyn's Leading Clothier.") once adorned the scoreboard of Ebbets Field, the home of the Brooklyn Dodgers.
- James Lyons, Bronx borough president who, a few months earlier, was quoted as stating that the city's board of estimate had "done everything necessary" to prepare the way to develop the park. He also said that he was agreeable to changing the name of the Baychester section of the Bronx to Freedomland, "as long as it's 'Freedomland in the Bronx.'"
- Charles Van Doren, the emcee, who later would be linked to the television quiz show scandals.

The day after the shovels turned over the ground *The New York Times* reported: "Out of a cloud of dust and thundering hoofbeats in the Bronx yesterday rode two cowboys, four showgirls, a bulldozer ballet and a posse of press agents—all hired to publicize what they called the 'greatest outdoor entertainment center in the history of man.'"

The reporter was then a little known journalist by the name of Gay Talese. The exact location of the ceremonies that began at 10am has not been determined, but the events likely occurred close to the main access road to the property, approximately where Bartow Avenue currently emerges after passing under the New England Thruway.

Local troops of Girl Scouts and Boy Scouts participated during the flag ceremony. Costumed actors represented the various historic eras to be featured at Freedomland. The 60-piece New York City Sanitation Department band entertained the crowd.

Large tents were erected for the event. One was a catering tent for the guests while another tent was reserved for VIPs and guest speakers. A helicopter was hired to allow news photographers to snap aerial pictures of the property. The chopper landed shortly after the start of the ceremony, disturbing a lot of dirt and spreading it into the tents.

The host for the festivities, Charles Van Doren, was a teacher at Columbia University. He was the son of Pulitzer Prize-winning poet and literary critic/teacher Mark Van Doren and novelist and writer Dorothy Van Doren. Less than three months later, Charles appeared before Congress during its investigation of the television quiz programs scandal. On November 2, Charles said to the House Committee on Legislative Oversight that "I was involved, deeply involved, in a deception. The fact that I too was very much deceived cannot keep me from being the principal victim of that deception, because I was its principal symbol."

Freedomland Suppliers

As with any large entertainment venue, contract vendors provided the goods and services required for the construction and daily operation at Freedomland. Vendors of various sizes and from around the country included amusement attraction developers, food management companies, electrical contractors, and suppliers of furnishings.

Arrow Development

Founded during 1946 as Arrow Development Company by Karl Bacon, Ed Morgan, Bill Hardiman, and Angus Anderson, the company originated as a machine shop at 243 Moffett Boulevard just north of downtown Mountain View, California. The company initially sold used shop equipment and performed general machine work, design, and fabrication for a handful of local companies. By 1949, Arrow had begun building playground equipment, merry-go-rounds and horses, and kiddie rides for amusement parks. Arrow's owners responded to an inquiry from Walt Disney about its stern-wheeled paddle boat during 1953, but Walt hired the company to help design and build the ride systems for several of Disneyland's other early attractions. These included Mad Tea Party, King Arthur

Carrousel, Mr. Toad's Wild Ride, Casey Jr. Circus Train, Snow White's Scary Adventures, Dumbo the Flying Elephant, Autopia, and Alice in Wonderland. Disney also invested financially in Arrow, purchasing one-third of the company in 1961.

As Disneyland's general manager, Woody worked closely with the company and later, as he was designing his parks, he again would work with Arrow. For Freedomland, Arrow built several attractions—Spin-A-Top and the freeway cars for the Satellite City Turnpike—that had been adapted from rides created for Disneyland. For Freedomland, Arrow designed and built about one half million dollars of attractions, including antique cars for the Horseless Carriage, two Danny the Dragon electronically guided trackless trains, horse-drawn streetcars, and four dark rides: Buccaneer, Earthquake, Mine Caverns, and Tornado. In some publications, Tornado is identified, erroneously, as one of just three Arrow-designed attractions at Freedomland.

Arrow's 1961 price list included gas-powered antique cars for $1,750–2,350 each and individual gas powered freeway cars for $1,750, a trackless train (Danny the Dragon) for $15,000–25,000, and dark theme rides for $16,000–30,000.

Throughout the 1960s and 1970s, Arrow continued to create ride systems for Disney and other parks. Significant advancements in flume rides and coasters are credited to Arrow. During the early 1970s, the founders sold the company. After a series of financial setbacks, the company's remaining assets were purchased by Sansei.

Edaville Railroad

This heritage railroad in South Carver, Massachusetts, opened during 1947. The 2-foot narrow gauge line was built by the late Ellis D. Atwood (initials E.D.A. for Edaville) on his cranberry property. He died during 1950. The family sold the operations during 1957 to F. Nelson Blount, who leased the steam engines and the cars to Pleasure Island and Freedomland.

Enco National Corp.

The Enco National Corp. in New York City, also identified as Enco Inc., provided souvenirs to Freedomland's shops.

Located at 242 Fourth Avenue, Enco maintained a trading post outlet that sold western goods and souvenirs at the park's Fort Cavalry.

The Brass Rail

This food-services company operated or managed most of the park's food concessions. The "stockyards restaurant" in Freedomland's Old Chicago became known as the Brass Rail Steak House.

When Freedomland opened, the Brass Rail already had a long New York history. It had managed food services for more than 30 years at Jones Beach State Park and it operated five restaurants at the 1939–1940 New York World's Fair. The Brass Rail restaurants and coffee shops in New York City were located on Park Avenue at 40th Street, Fifth Avenue at 43rd Street, Seventh Avenue at 49th Street, Eighth Avenue at 36th Street, and on Nevins Street in Brooklyn. The company also operated at New York International Airport (often referenced as Idlewild Airport and later renamed John F. Kennedy International Airport) and managed domestic and foreign airline dining services, company executive and employee contract food services, special events, and group catering.

Todd Shipyards

The Freedomland sternwheelers were built by the Hoboken (New Jersey) Division of Todd Shipyards Corporation. The facility actually was located in Weehawken Cove with the Hoboken-Weehawken city line passing through the site. The company used a Hoboken address in all its literature and the division closed soon after Freedomland, on September 1, 1965.

This company maintains a link to the Civil War. For the historic battle of the ironclads, Cornelius DeLameter's company, DeLameter Iron Works, built components of the USS *Monitor*. This company is the earliest ancestral connection to Todd Shipyards, the corporate entity that, after several name and ownership changes, became the William H. Todd Corporation.

Stephens-Adamson Manufacturing Company

The Speedwalk Division of Stephens-Adamson Mfg. Co. of Aurora, Illinois, provided the passenger conveyer system (moving sidewalk) for Satellite City. A full-page trade advertisement for the technology in the March 1961 issue of *Progressive Architecture News Report* included a photo of Freedomland's "speedwalk passenger conveyer system":

> Modern superhighways and other convenient time-saving methods of transportation have given greater access to parks and amusement centers across the nation. Increasing multitudes of people flock to these areas for enjoyment and relaxation during their leisure hours. Now our parks and amusement centers are faced with growing pedestrian traffic problems.

The following is a partial list of additional suppliers for construction or daily operation.

- Bethlehem Steel Company (Bethlehem, Pennsylvania) for sky ride cable.

- Bliss Display Company (Long Island City, New York) for animated display units.

- Camera Equipment Corporation (location undetermined) for the Braniff Space Rover auditorium installation.

- Chrysler Airtemp (Dayton, Ohio) provided more than 150 units to supply the "perfect indoor climate" in park shops, restaurants, and other buildings. The company also maintained an exhibit about the story of air conditioning in Satellite City.

- Crown Paper Company (Yonkers, New York) remains in business today. The company manufactures corrugated boxes and sheets, die-cut mailers and shipping room supplies, and a range of floor maintenance products. Crown was a supplier during the inaugural season and possibly other seasons.

- Fischback and Moore (New York City and elsewhere) electrical contractors helped wire the park.

- Gignac Coach Company (Chicago, Illinois) for the western stage coaches.

- Lawrence Labriola Nurseries (Scarsdale and Armonk, New York) provided more than 50,000 trees and shrubs.

- Macglashen Guns (Stanton, California) for shooting gallery equipment. However, a few months later, P.E.P Corporation, also of Stanton, was identified for air-gun equipment.

- Minneford Yacht Yard (City Island, New York) for New York Harbor's tugboats and the nine bullboats of the Northwest Fur Trapper attraction. Minneford was established during 1926 and turned out palatial yachts for millionaires. It also built many of the America's Cup racers, including *Constellation*, *Intrepid*, *Courageous*, *Freedom*, and *Enterprise*. During World War II, the yard built torpedo boats, landing craft, mine sweepers, and seagoing tugs. By 1962, it was one of the largest shipyards on the island. The yard closed during 1982 and the current marina on the site opened during 1985.

- Naclerio Pelham Contractors (Bronx, New York) laid more than 50 miles of pipe and wire under Freedomland. Along with George W. Rogers Construction Company, Naclerio delivered a quarter million yards of fill from about 25 different sources in the metropolitan area to raise the ground level.

- National Amusement Devices (Dayton, Ohio) was consulted about providing kiddie rides. Documentation has not been located to determine if the company entered into a contractual agreement with Freedomland.

- Paddock Pool Company (location undetermined) for the reflection pool in Satellite City that later was removed for the Moon Bowl dance floor.

- Percy Turnstile and Globe Tickets (location undetermined) for admission systems.

- Raisler Corp. (possibly Raisler Sprinkler Inc. on Amsterdam Avenue in New York City) maintained fire protection day and night.

- Samuel Lakow & Sons (New York City) provided office furnishings.
- Sound Systems, Inc. (Long Island City, New York) for sound work throughout the park.
- Taylor Lumber Co., Inc. (New York City) delivered lumber and paneling for park construction.
- Von Roll (Berne, Switzerland) for the Tucson Mining Company ore bucket attraction.
- Western Costume Company (Hollywood, California) supplied the film industry since the early 1900s and also supplied Freedomland and other Marco Engineering parks.
- Williamsbridge Parkway Willys-Jeeps Inc. (Bronx, New York) provided vehicles and service for the park.

Additional suppliers included A. Belanger & Sons for waterproofing, A.S. Beck Shoe Company (associated with Herbert C. Lee, who was president of the company and treasurer of International Recreation Corporation), C. H. Cronin for plumbing, Consolidated Laundries, Fulton Roofing Corp., J.I. Haas Company for painting, Slattery Contracting Company for site grading, National Vending Service, and White Plains Iron Works for structural steel and iron work.

The Freedomland Inn

The Freedomland Inn was designed but never built. Only the foundation was placed into the ground in the area currently occupied by an indoor mall and its parking garage. William B. Tabler, Sr., who was raised in a small farming community south of Chicago, was hired to design the facility. He had studied architecture at Harvard University and designed more than 400 hotels in 20 countries.

A newspaper advertisement in 1960 claimed the facility, part of the Zeckendorf hotel group, would open during the summer of 1961 as America's most modern hotel:

> Your visit to Freedomland U.S.A. becomes a truly unforgettable experience when you stay at "Freedomland

Inn." With a direct entrance to Freedomland, you're just steps away from all the fun and adventure provided by the world's largest entertainment center. After a day of excitement touring through our country's past, return to the relaxed atmosphere of America's most modern motor inn...the latest addition to the friendly group of Zeckendorf Hotels.

At "Freedomland Inn" you'll enjoy the ultimate in fine appointments...gracious dining in a unique restaurant and a convenient coffee shop. 400 rooms with air-conditioning. TV and radio. There's an Olympic-size swimming pool for your pleasure, and a separate wading pool and play area to delight the children. Tree-lined promenades, feathery fountains, central gardens—all enhance your visit to "Freedomland Inn."

For inquiries and reservations write or phone: Freedomland Inn, Bronx 69, New York, N.Y. Telephone Tulip 2-1400.

When, during 1963, Webb & Knapp advertised its auction of the property, one of the ads specifically identified the condition of the land: "Completed ground floor slab, grade beams, and pile foundations. All under-slab and in-slab plumbing, drains, and risers are in place." The property was featured as suitable for motel-hotel, shopping center, or corporate use.

The slab was discovered during 2012 as the ground was prepared for construction of the indoor mall. It had been buried under about five to eight feet of landfill for five decades. This footprint was outside the boundary of the park. After much of Freedomland was removed, remnants of the park were bulldozed to this corner property. For more than 40 years, the field contained park bricks, pipes, concrete blocks, one of the wood pilings possibly from the Northwest Fur Trapper attraction, and some of the west's boulders.

A motel not affiliated with Freedomland or the Zeckendorfs was built north of the park's parking lot. Many celebrity entertainers and park visitors from out of town relaxed at the heated pool or enjoyed a drink at the Town and Country Motor Lodge. The three-story building, constructed in 1960, was located at 2244 Tillotson Avenue between Rombouts and De Lavalle avenues. The facility contained 70 rooms, a restaurant, and cocktail lounge. The building still stands, but the pool was removed years ago. During recent years, the location has served as a health facility and a homeless shelter.

CHAPTER FIVE

The World's Largest Entertainment Center

Mommy & Daddy, take my hand
Take me out to Freedomland.
$2.95 is all you pay
At Freedomland today!

You'll see the great Chicago Fire
Look out the flames are getting higher.
Battlefields and shady parks
You're right there on the spot.

—Freedomland Jingle

Freedomland's grand opening had been scheduled for June 1, 1960. It then was rescheduled for a month later to ensure that the park would be ready for the anticipated crowds. Due to the growing excitement generated by aggressive advertising, marketing, and the on-air promotion by the city's popular music radio stations, the official opening date again changed to June, specifically to Father's Day on Sunday, June 19.

With official proclamations, public greetings from politicians, remarks by the president of Freedomland, and a welcome from a famous actress, the park opened to extensive media attention and to a local and national audience.

Preview Day

Saturday, June 18, was preview day at Freedomland. The park was dedicated by New York City Mayor Robert F. Wagner, and

Freedomland's senior management that included William Zeckendorf, Sr., and park president Milton T. Raynor. About 25,000 people attended the preview, which also served as a benefit for several youth charities. One nonprofit was the Children's Village Interfaith Chapel Fund; another was Boys Harbor (now Boys & Girls Harbor), which sold 1,500 tickets at $10 each for the preview event.

The contractors involved in the construction of Freedomland were invited with their families to enjoy the day's festivities along with a barbeque and free admission to all the attractions.

New York City Proclamation

For the opening of Freedomland, the City of New York issued this official proclamation:

> WHEREAS: There has now been established within our boundaries, on a 205 acre site in the Baychester section of the Bronx, the world's largest outdoor, family entertainment center —called Freedomland—whose purpose it is to restage 200 years of the American heritage, from pioneering days to the wonders of the space age.
>
> NOW, THEREFORE, I, Robert F. Wagner, Mayor of the City of New York, do herby proclaim Sunday, June 19, as
>
> FREEDOMLAND DAY
>
> In New York City, and do highly commend the people whose worthy labors have been rewarded in the creation of this unique project, and I do further recommend Freedomland to our citizens and visitors and advise them to take advantage of the opportunity to participate in a living portrayal of all the beauty, art, culture, drama and heroism that added luster to the imperishable history of the United States of America.
>
> —Excerpt From the Official Proclamation, Office of the Mayor, City of New York

Newspaper Supplement Herald's Freedomland

On the morning of opening day, a 20-page advertising supplement ("Our Whole, Wide, Wonderful Freedomland Comes to Life in New York City—World's Largest Entertainment Center") in *The New York Times* heralded the debut of Freedomland. Sponsored by the Bronx Chamber of Commerce and Freedomland's parent company, International Recreation Corporation, the insert provided the public with a preview of the world's largest and newest family entertainment center. The insert was filled with articles, artist concept drawings of the park, and several actual photos of attractions.

The supplement also contained greetings from New York State Governor Nelson A. Rockefeller, the city's mayor, Freedomland's president, and actress Mary Martin.

> Freedomland is the ultimate expression of the effort to dramatize our history and to bring it home vividly to everyone who sees it—an effort which, incidentally, originated on a far smaller scale in the Lake George area of upstate New York, with the reconstruction of Fort Ticonderoga and Lake George Village.
>
> We welcome Freedomland for itself, and as an entertainment center which will attract visitors from all over the world.
>
> —Nelson A. Rockefeller, Governor

> Our heartiest congratulations to Freedomland on its auspicious opening. ... As the world's largest outdoor entertainment attraction, it fits quite naturally into the world's greatest tourist and business metropolis. ... We wish Freedomland good luck in achieving its high-level aims and trust it will help spread the message of Americanism as well as the spirit of New York throughout the nation and the world.
>
> —Robert F. Wagner, Mayor

For us, that big day is here! The final dab of paint, the final geranium is in place and the final rehearsal of our costumed cast of 3,000 is over. The curtain is up today and our show is on!

All of us—designers, architects, craftsmen, artists and all the others who have worked so diligently to create Freedomland—are waiting to greet you. It is our hope to make your visit a rewarding experience.

As you enter Freedomland, you will be embarking on a journey through time—past, present and future—during which you will "live" through the inspiring stories of America and its people.

Because we are dedicated to your comfort and pleasure, we have designed every aspect of Freedomland not only to provide the maximum in fun for every member of the family, but also the utmost in convenience and service.

We feel sure you will enjoy your visit as much as we have enjoyed creating it for your pleasure. Here's hoping we will be seeing you and your family soon.

—Milton R. Raynor, President, Freedomland

Mary Martin Sings Freedomland Praises

It is my pleasure to extend a triple salute to Freedomland today on the occasion of its official opening.

First, as hostess of New York City's "Summer Festival," I am proud that the exciting activities of this gigantic attraction have been added to a program of events which is unmatchable in any other city in the world. Headed by Freedomland, New York is truly "the city with everything."

Next, as one who has spent her life in the entertainment world, I am happy to see the curtain go up on another good show. This "new kind of show business," as it has been called, will provide an entertainment and education for all the world to enjoy.

And, lastly, as a parent, I welcome such a wholesome significant project. Freedomland offers a program of pleasure for children and adults alike. It will also renew in all of us the pride and understanding of America which is so important for each of us to appreciate to the fullest at this time.

Every best wish for a successful run.

Sincerely yours, Mary Martin

Opening Day

On June 19, 1960, New Yorkers were introduced to a unique theme park. Unlike those that came before it and certainly never duplicated since, Freedomland U.S.A. incorporated American history into family entertainment. More than 60,000 people passed through the park gates. They experienced cowboy shootouts, train robberies, and the burning of Chicago. All of this history, education, and entertainment was situated on 85 acres carved into the shape of a map of the continental United States.

As guests entered the park property, they were greeted by 11 tall flagpoles, each flying the U.S. flag. Each pole also contained one large letter to spell the park name. Cars drove past these poles to enter the parking lot, located north of the current Bartow Avenue that travels through today's Co-op City complex. The distinct smell of asphalt was in the air that first day as workers only days earlier had paved the lot.

The park was scheduled to open at 10am, but guests began to arrive as early as 7:30. At 8:30, singer Pat Boone, who lived in New Jersey at the time, cut the opening day ribbon along with his wife, Shirley, and their four daughters—Cherry, Lindy, Debby, and Laury. Soon after, the singer and his family led the opening day parade.

"In the early heat of my career as a recording artist and becoming a movie actor as well," recalled Pat, "I was delighted to be invited to come to the newly created Freedomland U.S.A. and was given the honor of cutting the ribbon officially opening the place! My young wife and our four very young daughters all came, dressed alike—as their mom always saw to it in public—and had the time of their lives! They'd never been to the other highly publicized theme parks yet, and this was a wonderland, and they always wanted to come back.

"Unfortunately, we moved to California after that, rather quickly, so I could do all my entertainment stuff from one place—and never got back to Freedomland U.S.A. Our loss. I saw it as a national treasure and am delighted to have had the honor of cutting the ribbon. It's a treasured memory for me."

Though the entire Boone family never again visited Freedomland, Pat actually did return during 1962. He appears in park publicity photos with bandleader Harry James and contestants in the Miss World contest.

The fanfare for the opening day festivities included New York City children's television program hosts Officer Joe Bolton, Bozo the Clown (New York City version portrayed by Bill Britten) Tom Gregory, Chuck McCann, Captain Jack McCarthy, and cartoon characters Yogi Bear, Huckleberry Hound, and Quick-Draw McGraw. The nighttime entertainment was provided by jazz musician Lionel Hampton.

Missing Boy and Miss Freedomland. This staged publicity photo comforted the public by assuring everyone that children who lost their parents at Freedomland would be reunited with them. The boy was from Long Island. The Lakewood, Ohio, woman was Miss Freedom of June 1961.

That first day was beautiful and sunny. By about noon, radio announcers were advising people not to go to the park since the car lot could not take one more vehicle. But, visitors kept coming. With the car lot filled to capacity, the surrounding residential community became clogged with traffic. Hundreds of cars (maybe more than a thousand) parked on the main streets of Gun Hill Road, Eastchester Road, and Allerton Avenue, and along the side streets. Some people walked more than a mile to reach the main gate that day. C.V. Wood said park planning had estimated that 23 percent of guests would arrive by subways and the remainder by vehicles.

By 3pm, Freedomland closed the gates. Three of the 10 admission counters were reported to have malfunctioned after more than 50,000 people were recorded.

"It was a very hot day," recalled one Freedomland executive. "The water fountains weren't working and none of the concessions were in shape to serve food. If you wanted to go to the bathroom, it was like going to a privy—if you could find one. There were a lot of unpainted and unfinished exhibits. They shouldn't have opened like that, but it was an attempt to keep the opening date."

Satellite City was not accessible due to electrical issues. It opened a few weeks later. The Chicago Fire also experienced early operation difficulties that were corrected within a few weeks. Despite these glitches, the opening was no different than the debut of Disneyland five years earlier. The California park had experienced a rush at the gates, mechanical issues with some attractions, a short supply of food and beverages, and a plumbers' strike that limited the number of working water fountains.

Freedomland was scheduled to close that first day at midnight. But, due to the large crowd and safety concerns, management closed the park at 9pm.

Freedomland's Historically Themed Attractions

Freedomland was arranged into seven themed periods throughout American history: New York City from the late

1800s, Old Chicago at the time of the great fire, the plains country of farms and forts, San Francisco at the time of the great earthquake, the untamed southwest, the Mardis Gras celebration in New Orleans, and the present and future of space flight at Cape Canaveral. From the concept stage to opening day, a variety of rides and attractions were proposed, some were discarded, and the names of others were changed.

Among the names altered by opening day were Merry Mule (possibly Mule-Go-Round), Dragon Parade (probably Danny the Dragon), Magnetic House (Casa Loca), Future Autos (Satellite City Turnpike), Earth Satellite (probably Braniff Space Rover), and Northwest Passage (Northwest Fur Trapper).

Several additional areas of the park were planned but never constructed. These included a re-creation of Bunker Hill, a Gloucester fishing village, and Plymouth Rock for the New England portion of Little Old New York, a movie lot that presumably was a re-creation of a Hollywood set to be located below San Francisco, a re-creation of the Florida Peninsula

Suffrage Rally. A rally to promote a woman's right to vote frequently was held in the streets of Little Old New York. A Freedomland politician is in the middle of this demonstration in front of the Kodak store.

that was to be situated below Satellite City, a Daniel Boone compound, and a Mexican village.

Freedomland's Complete Official Guide with Maps

Freedomland published two park guides that were souvenir booklets of about 16 pages. The first welcomed the grand opening of the park and was sold through the 1961 season. Surplus copies again were sold during the park's final season. Published before the park officially opened, this guide featured the original color artist renditions of park attractions. The cover displayed a family of four gazing upon a map of the United States and all the attractions to be seen at Freedomland.

For the 1962 season, Freedomland published a second park guide with multiple photographs for each area of the park. This guide included one of the Freedomland cartoon kids on the cover. Others appeared throughout the guide. The cartoon kids became part of the park scene after the first season.

GREETINGS:

No trip to New York City is complete unless it includes a tour of the exciting panorama of America provided by FREEDOMLAND. It is family entertainment at its best, as each guest relives the many action-filled era of American history, which are re-created in the wonderful world of FREEDOMLAND.

We in the Borough of the Bronx take pride in the fact that this show place of fun and laughter chose the Bronx as the home for its authentic replicas of the American Scene. We thank you for visiting us and we hope you will tell your neighbors of the unique entertainment which is provided for young and old alike at FREEDOMLAND. May you return soon.

Sincerely,

JOSEPH F. PERICONI
Borough President

—1962 Official Guide Complete with Maps

During five seasons of operation, additional park publications included the *Freedomland Eagle,* the *Freedomland Enterprise,* and *Brass Tacks* (published by the Brass Rail restauranteur). These publications heralded daily news, information and events schedules.

Freedomland After Dark

One of the most vivid memories of Freedomland is the variety of color and glow emitted at night. Freedomland installed colored spotlights rather than neon lights to showcase the park's attractions.

At the Civil War ride and the Northwest Fur Trappers ride, the figures and animals were bathed by bright gold and pink hues. With the fireflies providing that extra touch of nature along with the night songs of crickets and other insects, guests actually experienced a battlefield or a boat ride on a river. They certainly forgot for a while that they were in the Bronx.

Bright spotlights illuminated the prominent buildings of Old Chicago and Little Old New York, and the stockade of Fort Cavalry. Similar to the angles and backlighting of a movie set, Freedomland provided guests with the authentic appearance of buildings and scenes.

Vintage Building Advertisements

On many building exteriors, Freedomland incorporated vintage-type painted advertising and messages. Some signs paid tribute to park executives.

One building advertisement for drums in Little Old New York honored Woody. Another sign was located in the southwest area on a mercantile and dry goods store. This was a tribute to the father of Zeck, Sr., who operated such a store in Arizona during the 1800s.

Getting to Freedomland

Two main highways straddled the park. The New England Thruway (Interstate 95) delivered people from the north and a spur traveled over the recently completed Throgs Neck Bridge to connect with people in Queens and on Long Island. The Hutchinson River Parkway connected to Queens over the Whitestone Bridge. Directions were provided from Manhattan, Brooklyn, Queens, Long Island, Westchester County, southern New England, and New Jersey. Cars parked for 50 cents. Two trackless trams roamed the parking areas to shuttle visitors to and from the main gate.

The directions by train advised guests that shuttle buses to Freedomland were available at the Pelham Bay Park (#6) and Gun Hill Road (#5) subway stations. Longer bus rides included city lines plus the Gray Line from Capitol Greyhound Bus Terminal at West 50th Street (between Broadway and Eighth Avenue). Many people rode to Freedomland on sightseeing buses.

From the northern suburbs, a train would travel to Grand Central Terminal or, possibly, the stop at 125th Street. From there, guests would take a subway and/or bus to Freedomland.

"Jet-setters" arrived by plane. Flotair Seaplane took just five minutes to arrive at Freedomland from Manhattan. Helicopters landed at the park near the parking lot, and some carried celebrity entertainers.

Park guests also had the opportunity to enjoy a bird's eye view of the park in a chopper. Each person who took the fly-over received a Freedomland Helicopter Citation for out-standing ability as a passenger on board the Freedomland Helicopter. The certificate documented the round-trip flight between New York and California and named the passenger a Commander of the Freedomland Helicopter Wing. The certif-icate was signed by the pilot, Captain Henry B. Grudberg, and the officer of the Freedomland Flying Corp., park executive "Colonel" Art K. Moss.

An unidentified newspaper columnist wrote during 1962:

> Hank Grudberg loaded me into the Freedomland thrasher yesterday. You sit in a thing which looks to the unpractical eye like the kind of a plastic bubble the kids blow with those pipes and goo they get in the five and dime. The bubble I was in cost some $10,000.

CHAPTER SIX

Corporate Sponsors and Food Vendors

This comes to you from Freedomland
where we're having a wonderful time!
Look at the map inside
to see the places we've visited.
Wish you were here, too!

—Freedomland greeting card by Hallmark Cards

During the 1950s, C.V. Wood unveiled a new concept to engage potential sponsors. He first employed the strategy at Disneyland.

Corporate sponsors became lessees. Leases for space were sold for a fixed price ($20–$25) per square foot. The park provided structures and storefronts while sponsors were responsible for designing the leased space along with any related construction costs, insurance, and other fees.

While all of today's entertainment venues develop multiple options for sponsored branding opportunities, corporate marketing at entertainment venues had been more reserved until the 1950s and 1960s. In New York, the World War II generation that brought its children to Freedomland initially experienced venue sponsorship during the 1939–1940 New York World's Fair. They would see it, along with their children, on a grander scale at Freedomland and at the 1964–1965 New York World's Fair.

Freedomland opened with a long list of corporate backers that supported the various attractions, shows, and eateries. Rather than associating sponsors with the entire park,

Freedomland management showcased the various sponsors within the seven themed areas. Most sponsors were matched with specific attractions. Sometimes the attractions were created to match the interests of sponsors and to ensure maximum return of invested marketing dollars. Some sponsors displayed goods or services in institutional messaging and others conducted direct sales.

The park encouraged guests to patronize all the advertisers and sponsors, except for the "green stamp undertaker."

Sponsors at Freedomland

Some Freedomland sponsors remain nationally recognized names today. Others are out of business, or have been absorbed by other companies, or were local New York businesses at the time that valued the advertising opportunities provided by the park. While some of the sponsors remained with the park for its five-year duration, many companies were featured at Freedomland for one or just several seasons. Park sponsors included:

Little Old New York

- American Oil Company (Amoco) fueled the Horseless Carriage ride through the New England countryside.
- The Bank of New York was the official bank for Freedomland, Inc.
- The Borden Company managed the 1890s ice cream parlor.
- Eastman Kodak focused on the photography store.
- Nestle's operated the New York Coffee House.
- The Lipton Tea Company, or Thomas J. Lipton, Inc., opened an eatery.
- The Welch Grape Juice Company sponsored the vineyards and juice bar near the Horseless Carriage ride.
- Trunz meat company advertised in this area of the park.
- Shuntz's Delicatessen served New York-style pastrami and corned beef sandwiches along with cheesecake.
- Schering Corporation operated the old apothecary shop and a pharmaceutical exhibit.

- R.H. Macy re-created its original New York City store.
- An insurance exhibit was sponsored by Continental Casualty Company.
- Scripto wrote the agreement for its pen shop.
- The F & M Schaefer Brewing Company sponsored a replica brewery. For the park's last season, John's Bargain Stores sponsored a haunted house in the same building.
- Pato's Bakery from the borough's Pelham Parkway area sold baked goods near the main gate.

Old Chicago

- Hallmark Cards supported the communications center and a card shop.
- The authentic steam-powered railroad was sponsored by the Atchison, Topeka and Santa Fe Railway Company.

The Great Plains

- American Express sponsored the Overland Tour stage coach through the Rocky Mountains.
- The Borden Company, in addition to its New York sponsorship, operated a farm (Elsie's Boudoir, the fully furnished apartment for Elsie the cow) and a milk bar.

Old Chicago, July 1960. The train station and the fire house in Freedomland's Old Chicago. The Brass Rail restaurant was steps away.

- The Tandy Corporation leather supply operation from Texas had a retail shop. Soon after, the company acquired a number of other retail companies, including RadioShack.

San Francisco

- Chun King operated a Chinese restaurant.
- A&W Root Beer featured a restaurant and soda exhibit that opened for the 1962 season.

The Old Southwest

- The Frito Lay Company operated a Mexican restaurant.
- The New York area Pepsi-Cola operation (the Pepsi Cola Metropolitan Bottling Company) sponsored the saloon and music hall that included silent movies and stage shows. It also featured a Pepsi-Cola bar.

New Orleans

- The L.D. Harris Pop Corn Corp. sold its kernels at a popcorn store and wagon.
- J.D. Jewell, the chicken company, operated a plantation restaurant that many guests considered the best eatery in the park.

Satellite City

- American Oil Company (Amoco) maintained a petroleum exhibit in this themed section and supported the cloverleaf Satellite City Turnpike attraction.
- Braniff International Airways sponsored the Space Rover that simulated space flight.
- Chrysler Corp. handled an exhibit about heating and refrigeration.
- Coca-Cola featured a hospitality area.
- The McCulloch Corp. had an outboard boating and chain saws attraction.
- Benjamin Moore & Co., the paint manufacturer, sponsored the Science of Color exhibit.

And throughout the park, the Hamilton Watch Company kept the clocks ticking.

Freedomland's Corporate Sponsors Today

Attempts have been made to contact the remaining companies, or corporate successors of Freedomland sponsors, to determine if any information could be learned about each company's involvement with the park. Corporate archives, with the exception of Coca-Cola, revealed little additional information.

Coca-Cola was a prominent sponsor in Satellite City and a three-plus-page article filled with photos from Freedomland was featured in a 1960 issue of *The Coca-Cola Bottler*, the official publication of the Coca-Cola Bottlers' Association.

> Coca-Cola first on Mars? The year 1990 may see some of us pausing to refresh in the familiar manner on a nearby planet after blasting off from Satellite City!

> In an imaginative way, this is what is happening at the Coca-Cola Company's new Spaceport Refreshment Center at Freedomland, U.S.A. Satellite City is a section of Freedomland, a 205 acre park in the Bronx, New York City.

The article explained the other features of Freedomland before returning to the Coca-Cola presence at the park:

> Transition from past to future begins with the company's large pavilion named the "Spaceport Refreshment Center." Working together, Metropolitan Travel Display Inc., New York and Ted Duffield of the Coca-Cola Company Advertising Department evolved "A Concept For the Future."

Illuminated and animated space travel posters decorated the walls and a moon scale allowed earthlings to calibrate their weight on the satellite. A bar in the pavilion was designed as a "33-foot gracefully curving unit with an unusual top treatment. The only red in the room is seen in the dispensers, with the color echoed in a red mosaic circle under the revolving parabola."

While sipping their Cokes, visitors could "gaze through the pavilion's glass walls, across a champagne-colored lagoon [before the Moon Bowl and dance floor were added], to the huge Braniff space ship launched on its launching pad. At night, the machine fires off eerie purple and blue lights reflected against its silver skin."

The article ended with commentary about Coke's future as science advancement continued:

> It is not inconceivable that in the future something like Satellite City will really exist. When it does, it is reasonably certain that the Coca-Cola Company and the Coca-Cola Export Corporation will have made provision to permit the pause that refreshes...with ice-cold Coke somewhere out there!

A follow-up article in the October 1961 issue of the same publication profiled the "gaily colored, ingeniously designed Pre-Mix carts" that helped the Coca-Cola Bottling Company of New York provide Coke to park crowds. Six carts operated at Freedomland with each manned by an operator in "Gay 90" attire. The wagons had red and green colored stripes on the sides. Each unit served a drink below 40 degrees and maintained a compartment for hot frankfurters and rolls.

For the Freedomland rails, the successor to the railroad company that sponsored the park's steam trains located the executive who wrote the annual sponsorship check. During 2009, Bill Burk, the retired vice president of public relations for the Santa Fe Railroad, provided a few details about the sponsorship: "I can confirm that Santa Fe did sponsor it and I was in it from the beginning till the end. I have forgotten the details, and I have a hazy recollection it was only for about three years. I remember I signed the voucher each year for $50,000."

On the farm, a young public relations executive at Borden Inc. was surprised to learn about Freedomland and did not know that Elsie the cow once had a popular boudoir in the Bronx.

Freedomland Restaurants

The Freedomland Enterprise ran this piece about food in the park:

> **Food, Glorious Food!**
>
> There's a fantastic array of festive fare to please every palate at fabulous new Freedomland. The aroma of

epicurean achievements from all parts of the world emanates from every restaurant and food mart in the park. The hungry traveler will find treasures precisely to his taste in one or another of Freedomland's eating emporia.

Do you fancy a satisfying plantation-style dinner of fried chicken with all the fixin's? Then try the Plantation Restaurant in the New Orleans area, and dine with the airs of a Dixieland band accompanying a magnificent meal.

Or does your taste turn to thick steaks, done precisely to your order? Then Chicago's Steak House is your dish, with its wide range of hearty fare served with elegance and zest.

Or do you favor something from foreign lands—an oriental delicacy, or the savory specialties of expert Italian chefs? San Francisco can offer you both: a touch of the East in Chinatown; and a host of Italian inspirations at the Barbary Coast and the Fisherman's Wharf, including all your fish-fry favorites.

No trip to the Great Plains would be complete without a visit to the famous Chuck Wagon, frequented by cow-pokes and dudes alike. Here you will find, among other mountainous morsels, a veritable behemoth of a bean-pot, the world's largest. Visitors are invited to have their plates heaped from this colossal cauldron.

If the lilting melodies of meandering "mariachi" attract you, you will always find them near the Mexican restaurant in the Southwest area. Enjoy their songs while dining on chili, tortillas, frijoles, and other specialties from South of the Border.

At Freedomland, you're never far from refreshment. In New York, there's an old-fashioned ice cream parlor, and a grape juice bar; in the Great Plains, Borden's Milk Bar; and well-stocked snack stands at almost every turn."

—The Freedomland Enterprise, Vol. 1 No. 1 (eight-
page newspaper published for the 1961 season)

At the time, park management did not consider food as a significant source of revenue. Food was viewed as a service for guests before they continued their journey to the next attraction. At Freedomland, food and beverage locations came and went during each season. For the 1960–1962 seasons, Freedomland operated more than 20 locations where guests could grab a bite or drink, including the mobile carts. The number of culinary locations does not include some of the specialty shops, such as the Candy Kitchen and Trunz Quality Meats in Little Old New York and New Orleans' Pop Corn Store and Pop Corn Wagon by L.D. Harris Pop Corn Corp.

- **Little Old New York**: Welch's Juice Bar was in the New England section of the area. The old-fashioned ice cream parlor was sponsored by Borden. The New York Coffee House was sponsored for at least some of the time by Nestle. The Lipton Tea Company operated a tea house and eatery.

- **Old Chicago**: Besides a snack bar, the area featured the Chicago Steak House at Freedomland that also was known as the Brass Rail Steak House. It was considered the largest restaurant in the park, seating more than 300 people. A beer garden also was located in this area.

- **The Great Plains**: The popular Chuck Wagon barbecue/snack bar was located in Fort Cavalry. It simulated the Conestoga-covered wagons of a wagon train. Borden's Milk Bar was near Elsie's Boudoir.

- **San Francisco**: This area of the park featured the Chun King Shangri-La Restaurant, a Fisherman's Wharf Snack Bar, and an Italian restaurant known as the Little Pizza Shop. A&W Root Beer's exhibit and restaurant opened for the 1962 season.

- **The Old Southwest**: The Opera House and Saloon (also known as the Music Hall, the Wild West Show Palace, and the Red Garter Saloon) included the Pepsi-Cola bar. (Pepsi-Cola featured sponsorships of theme park music halls in its marketing strategy. The company was the original sponsor of the Golden Horseshoe Revue at Disneyland from July 17, 1955, until September 30,

1982, and the sponsor of Pleasure Island's Diamond Lil Saloon.) The Frito Company maintained Libby's Frito House Mexican restaurant, or Libby's Hacienda, that premiered this company's version of sloppy joe on a bun. A snack bar also was located in this area.

- **New Orleans**: The Creole Café served waffles and pancakes. The Jesse Jewell Plantation House Restaurant was known for its chicken dinners supplied by J.D. Jewell, Inc., a popular southern chicken company of the time. This area of the park also featured the Jolly Roger Galley.

- **Satellite City**: The area included a snack bar and a separate soft drink bar featuring Coca-Cola hospitality.

Freedomland also operated a cafeteria. Carts throughout the park hawked Coca-Cola, ice cream, pretzels, and Fritos. Many menu items were similar at the various park eateries, but themed areas also provided a few unique food and drink choices.

- At Welch's Juice Bar in New England, grape-ade was sold for either 15 cents or 25 cents.

- At the Lipton Inn, or Lipton's Tea House, in New York, hot tea was sold for 15 cents, iced tea for 25 cents, soup with crackers for 35 cents, and a tossed green salad with Wishbone dressing for 35 cents.

- At Borden's Old Fashioned Ice Cream Parlor in New York, a double-dip cone sold for 25 cents, ice cream cone for 15 cents, Walk A Way sundae for 45 cents, ice cream sundae for 55 cents, and a Freedomland sundae for 75 cents. The ingredients of a Freedomland sundae remain a mystery. An ice cream soda was 45 cents (the menu noted that 43 cents was for the soda and two cents for tax). A milk shake was 40 cents and cake (pound, raisin, or marble) was 20 cents. The cakes were offered at several venues throughout the park.

Sandwiches also were available at various locations. Several of the eateries served the popular cream cheese and nut on whole wheat raisin bread for 35 cents but only on Fridays. At this time, the Catholic Church required meatless Fridays and this sandwich likely was on the menu for that reason.

- At the Brass Rail Steak House in Chicago, originally open daily from noon until 10pm during the early years of Freedomland, char-broiled steaks, golden-fried fantail shrimp, and open sandwiches were featured. A complete filet mignon dinner was just $4.50. The restaurant served Coca Cola and Pepsi Cola, both of which sponsored attractions in the park, and a children's menu was available.

- At the Chuck Wagon in Fort Cavalry, a frankfurter on a bun sold for 25 cents, a hamburger on a bun for 35 cents, French-fried potatoes for 25 cents, a chili dog for 40 cents, barbecued beef on a bun for 50 cents, and a bowl of chili and beans for 60 cents. Fritos, Cheetos, potato chips, hard pretzels, and cookies each were 15 cents.

- At Borden's Milk Bar in the Great Plains, ice cream, milk, and chocolate milk, along with a malted milk and frosted milk shake, each sold for 40 cents.

- At the A&W outlet in San Francisco, root beer floats cost about 50 cents.

- At Fisherman's Wharf in San Francisco, golden-fried filet of flounder with French fries and tartar sauce went for 65 cents, and fish sticks with French fries for 40 cents.

- At the pizzeria in San Francisco, individual pizza sold for 40 cents; spumoni and tortoni deserts were 25 cents each.

- At the Frito House restaurant in the Old Southwest, the menu included much of the same fare as many other eateries in the park with a few added "specials." A bowl of chili and beans with Fritos cost 60 cents, a Mexican platter (two cocktail tamales, chili with beans, frijoles Fritos, and Fritos corn chips) was 99 cents, Frijoles Fritos was 25 cents, and two cocktail tamales cost 30 cents. The restaurant also displayed a collection of cattle brands that were a "fascinating reminder of the cattleman's long struggle for law and order." The Frito Company of Dallas, Texas, was selected for exclusive distribution of Fritos Corn Chips and other products throughout the park.

The southern-fried chicken at the Jesse Jewell Plantation House Restaurant in New Orleans still conjures up tasty memories. A 2012 online comment about the restaurant recalled: "It was where I had southern chicken for the [first time], till today I think it was the best ever!! Older brother thinks so also."

Elegant Eating At Old Plantation

New Orleans—"You'd have to travel mighty far south to find fried chicken like the Old Plantations!" one more-than-satisfied guest exclaimed.

"We haven't tasted real honest-to-goodness homemade pies like the Plantation's since we raided the berry patches on Grandma Logan's farm!" said another.

The exclamations vary, but the subject's always the same. There's royal fare at the Old Plantation—and the guest is king. Freedomland's penchant for delightful dining has truly triumphed in this culinary palace of pleasure.

And there's no more pleasant setting for enjoying the fruits of the chef's labor than the Old Plantation with its lovely antebellum veranda, and its tranquil, mirror-like lagoon. A Dixieland combo is always nearby to help meet your mood as only New Orleans music can.

—The Freedomland Enterprise, Vol. 1 No. 1(eight-page newspaper published for the 1961 season)

Jesse Jewell (1902–1975) is credited with making Gainesville, Georgia, the "poultry capital of the world." For the state's poultry industry, he pioneered vertical integration—the combining of all phases of the business, such as raw materials, processing, and distribution, within a single company. Jewell was a national leader of the industry. His enterprising and genial personality made him a popular figure throughout north Georgia. He is not known nationally today because he sold his company to a group of investors during the first half of the 1960s. The company eventually filed for bankruptcy in 1972.

CHAPTER SEVEN

Little Old New York: 1850–1900

*New York was the "golden door" for millions who
came to America seeking—freedom.*

—Freedomland's 1960 Complete Official Guide with Maps

Freedomland's Little Old New York replicated the big city
during the second half of the 19th century, providing park
guests with a nostalgic look at the lives experienced by their
ancestors. The miniature re-creation was authentic to the last
detail with shops, horse-drawn trolleys and tracks in the
streets, the cop on the beat, and replica signs on buildings and
windows from the days of grandpa and grandma.

Visitors boarded tugboats that departed regularly from the
harbor dock. F&M Schaefer re-created one of the many popular
breweries that once populated Manhattan. Shops included an
apothecary, photo studio, a functioning bank, candy store,
bakery, and ice cream parlor. Merchants changed from season
to season. Just north of the city, guests could enjoy a horseless
carriage drive through the scenic New England countryside.

Main Attractions

Park guests walked through the main entrance and past
a Dutch style building that resembled a churn and captured
the image of New Amsterdam. The location provided park
information and guidebooks. Stroller rentals and lockers were
available in this area.

- The Bank of New York featured a financial exhibit (the building also served as an actual office believed to be one of the first bank branches in an entertainment park).

- F&M Schaefer Brewery was converted into a haunted house for the 1964 season and sponsored by John's Bargain Stores.

- Harbor Tug Boats provided a pleasant trip in the New York waters.

- The Horseless Carriage through the New England countryside became known to many as the Antique Car ride.

Little Old New York. The friendly police officer on the beat in Little Old New York comforts a young child.

- Horse-drawn streetcars and horse-drawn surreys traveled from New York to Chicago.
- Kandy King Candy Shop (Candy Kitchen), Borden's Ice Cream parlor, and the Nestle Coffee Shop / Lipton Tea Shoppe were popular stores.
- Political and women's suffrage rallies, bank robberies, German oompah band.
- Vineyard and Welch's Grape Juice Bar.

The streets (Broadway, Cortlandt, Greenwich, Hudson, and Liberty along with 14th, 19th, and Mineta Alley) of Little Old New York contained numerous shops and offices. While a handful of buildings were false fronts to create the illusion of businesses—a sign in the barbershop window indicated that the owner was fishing for the day—many of the shops offered food, souvenirs, and other features that coaxed guests to enter.

The stores were separate retail units similar to actual street shops. Guests could not walk inside one shop and then meander from store to store. Rather than creating a straight Main Street, Freedomland's streets weaved with numerous curves that provided additional charm to the park.

The Old Apothecary Shop

Located on Hudson Street and down the block from the main entrance, the Old Apothecary Shop was sponsored by the Schering Corporation (now part of Merck & Co.). The company promotion provided guests with free samples of the decongestant Coricidin. The samples were placed in paper packets that showcased the Freedomland logo on the front and medication information on the reverse side. Freedomland publicity information indicated that "nurses' caps for little girls, health badges for the boys, and Coricidin in a smart Freedomland package will be given out."

R.H. Macy

The three-story structure on Freedomland's 14th Street replicated Macy's original New York City store. The outlet sold an assortment of toys, pennants, park guidebooks, and hats (cowboy, Civil War from both sides, boat skipper, and others) that were representative of the park's themed areas.

The Glass Blower Shop

Owned by Martin Finkel, this popular shop provided demonstrations of traditional glassblowing. The store fascinated many park guests, and it continues to conjure fond memories. Decorative blown-glass items were available for purchase.

William Cahn was one of the glassblowers. According to his son, Jeff, Cahn started glassblowing after World War II and continued in the profession for about 10 years before he moved into another career. He only returned to glass blowing on a temporary basis when Martin, his former boss, opened the Freedomland glassblowing shop.

"My dad worked there every Saturday during the 1960 through the 1962 seasons," said Jeff. "My father took me to work with him in Freedomland almost every Saturday he worked there."

Not much is known about Martin. His last residence of record was cited as Massapequa, New York, on Long Island. His work was part of Broadway shows and he appeared at the New York World's Fair.

Morgan Press

This company from Westchester County maintained a print shop that was a few steps from the brewery and post office. The company handled a considerable amount of printing for Freedomland, including maps, the *Freedomland Eagle* newspaper, broadsides for the park, and posters that guests could purchase for a few quarters.

Brothers Douglas and Lloyd Morgan established Morgan Press, Inc. Printers and Typographers in 1958 in Hastings-on-Hudson, New York. From 1973 until it closed more than a decade ago, the business was located in the converted Anchor Brewery near the Hudson River in Dobbs Ferry. Douglas pursued graduate work in printing management. Lloyd maintained a passion for forestry.

During its existence, Morgan Press published many books that showcased photographers, including a monograph series of eminent photographers such as William H. Jackson, Andreas Feininger, and Ansel Adams. The company also published instructional photography books.

The men's mother, Barbara, was a photographer whose subjects included popular modern dancers and choreographers. She was a co-founder of the photography magazine *Aperture*. Their father, Willard, was the first picture editor for *Life* magazine, the first director of the department of photography at the Museum of Modern Art in New York, and the founder of photographic literature publisher Morgan & Morgan.

Douglas maintained an extensive collection of rare 19th century wood-type letterforms that helped start a graphic design revival. The Morgan Press Type Collection was the largest of its kind in the United States. These woodblock letters and fonts were used during the previous century for advertisements, posters, and handbills. Darker and larger than more delicate metal typefaces, the woodblocks are the bold lettering on vintage western wanted posters. Many variations of classic wood type were intricately ornamental to grab the attention of passersby in an increasingly cluttered advertising environment. The Morgan collection today is housed at the Smithsonian National Museum of American History, in the Hall of Printing and Graphic Arts.

Other Shops

Continental Casualty was located on 14th Street. Information about a variety of insurance policies was provided to guests. For just a quarter, a $10,000 accidental death policy was available for purchase. With this policy, children received fire hats.

Kandy King Candy Shop, also known as Candy Kitchen, was located on Hudson Street.

A.S. Beck shoes was located on Hudson Street. The store carried a line of shoes with some special "flats" for women to ensure they enjoyed a comfortable visit to Freedomland.

Borden's Ice Cream parlor also was located on Hudson Street. Pato's Bakeries, found on Cortlandt Street, was a Bronx business located on the borough's Lydig Avenue. It operated for several seasons at the park. The Scripto shop on Broadway featured an exhibit of historic pens that were used to sign historical papers and, according to Freedomland promotional material, "reaffirm our Freedoms."

The Eastman Kodak store on Cortlandt Street sold cameras and equipment. The store also rented still and movie cameras. According to Freedomland promotional material: "Kodak will set up 150 picture-taking posts throughout the park to encourage visitors to shoot all exhibits to show the folks back home."

The area also featured a store by park sponsor Consolidated Laundry along with shops for flowers, records, antiques, and magic items. An artist studio and a tobacconist operated during the opening season.

Horseless Carriage

This attraction harks back to a time when men with googles invited ladies with veils for a spin in a gas-powered buggy. The

Chuck Schmidt driving the Horseless Carriage. A 1960 photo of New York journalist and author Chuck Schmidt enjoying his drive in the New England countryside on the Horseless Carriage. Photo courtesy Chuck Schmidt.

Freedomland cars were scale models of a 1909 Cadillac. Ride attendants dressed with bow ties and straw hats.

The attraction was duplicated in many other theme parks around the country for many years and some parks still maintain a version usually called Antique Cars. Today's attraction, though, has at least one significant difference from Freedomland's Horseless Carriage. While the driver still can steer the cars and use the pedal to start and stop, each car today is positioned over a metal guide rail. The cars will not drift too far to the left or to the right. Freedomland's Horseless Carriage did not have this guide rail. But it did have a "governor," a device that regulated fuel supply to ensure cars operated at a safe and comfortable speed.

The Horseless Carriage simulated a country drive through New England. Actual vineyards were nearby and the Welch Grape Juice Bar provided refreshments. The attraction particularly was a hit with the children. If they were taller than four feet, they could get behind the wheel of a car to steer and they could place their feet on the pedals. While some park literature boasted that the fleet included 40 cars (at a cost of about $100,000), other sources indicated that 30 replicas of the 1909 Cadillac Jennys were ordered from Arrow Development Company for $75,000.

Old style billboards appeared on the roadway landscape. A car prop was placed nearby to snap a family picture with an American Oil Company (Amoco) replica billboard as the backdrop and an American logo on the side of the vehicle. As the sponsor, Amoco also featured a talking gas pump that mesmerized children. The voice came from a nearby building where an Amoco employee could see park guests, especially children, and engage them in conversation.

F&M Schaefer Brewery

A brick building was constructed to replicate a working Manhattan brewery of the late 1800s. The New York landscape was dotted with breweries in those days. The attraction was sponsored by the F&M Schaefer Brewing Company. Today, the title to the company is held by the Pabst beer company and the Schaefer brothers rest in a family plot in the historic Woodlawn Cemetery only several miles from the Freedomland site.

In the heart of Old New York...you'll walk through the door into another century—see the vaulted chambers where Schaefer's famous lager was first brewed and mellowed...relax in the hand-hewn hominess of the old Schaefer office. Through another door, and you'll be in the world of Schaefer today...airy and bright and modern as tomorrow. Gone are the brewery horses and the oaken casks and the beamed ceilings. But still very much in evidence are the pride and skills and traditions of the old-time brewers. Please stop in. You'll enjoy a historic welcome...and a most entertaining exhibit.

—Freedomland newspaper advertising supplement, *The New York Times*, June 19, 1960

The workers in the attraction could be classified as gnomes. Kevin Butler, a children's television historian, indicated the characters could have been the work of famed television puppeteer Paul Ashley. Kevin recalled that Ashley once told him that he had worked with a group of artists to create rides and attractions for Freedomland.

The building did not serve as Schaefer's sponsored attraction for the entire five years of Freedomland. When Schaefer turned its attention to its exhibit at the New York World's Fair, the Freedomland brewery building was converted into a haunted house sponsored by John's Bargain Stores, a local business with locations throughout New York City, in Yonkers, and on Long Island.

The Bank of New York

The Bank of New York, the city's first bank established during 1784, was Freedomland's business bank of record and it maintained a branch in the park. Employees could cash their Freedomland checks there. Its location on Greenwich Street is believed to be one of the first functional bank branches in a theme park. Besides processing money transactions, the bank also offered an exhibit about the history of America's currency.

The branch office was designed to replicate the atmosphere of the Bank of New York from the mid-1800s. Employees wore the appropriate apparel of the time. The exhibit included the first warrant, or promissory note, signed by Secretary of the Treasury Alexander Hamilton. The branch offered keepsake facsimiles of the warrant along with Freedomland money orders in $1, $5, and $10 denominations that could be used anywhere, redeemed in full at any time, or retained as a souvenir. The images on the money orders depicted scenes from American history that were re-created in the park.

Horse-Drawn Trolley

The two horse-drawn trolleys, or streetcars, in Little Old New York that transported guests to and from Old Chicago were built for $24,600, according to the park guide. Some reports indicated that additional trolleys may have operated during Freedomland's five seasons.

Harbor Tug Boats

The New York Harbor Tug Boats *Totsie* and *Pert* (reportedly named for the wives of two park executives) were built by the nearby City Island Minneford Yacht Yard at a reported cost of $38,000. These boats were flat-bottomed, 36-foot imitations of the side-wheel tugs used in New York harbor during the mid-1800s.

Designer Henry Devereux patterned the boats for 50 standing passengers from an old photograph of a 100-foot tug. The side paddles were designed as props, spinning realistically but not contributing to propulsion. The boats did not operate on a track. The power was generated by Mercedes Benz 74-horsepower diesel engines. Triple rudders were installed for sharp turns in the winding Freedomland waterway.

CHAPTER EIGHT

Chicago: 1871

*Mrs. O'Leary's cow really started something when she
kicked over a barn lantern one night in 1871.*

—Freedomland's 1960 Complete Official Guide with Maps

This sentence may not be historically accurate, but it did create the narrative for one of the most popular attractions at Freedomland. An event that destroyed much of the city of Chicago became spectacular entertainment in the Bronx.

Freedomland's Old Chicago re-created a number of that city's streets: Dearborn, Michigan, Stewart, La Salle, De Koven, Forest, and State. Guests heard the call "All Aboard!" for a ride on the two authentic steam trains that included clanging bells and the hiss of steam. Musically pitched whistles floated through the air from the two sternwheelers at the city's docks. Then, the yell of "Fire! Fire!" spread through the streets.

Main Attractions

- Chippewa War Canoes on the Great Lakes (1960 and 1961).
- The Fire House featured the antique water pumper used to fight the Chicago flames.
- Great Lakes Cruise (sternwheelers *The American* and *The Canadian*).
- Hallmark Cards Shop and park communications center.
- Harbor Tug Boats (another dock was added for 1962 season; two boats were added to the fleet that resembled the Northwest Fur Trapper attraction bull boats).

- State Fair Midway (added for the 1962 season and included children's rides).

- Santa Fe Railroad (Chicago Station) took passengers around Freedomland on the Iron Horse, stopped at San Francisco, and returned.

- The Chicago Fire (times of the inferno changed with the seasons, beginning at about every 20 minutes, then hourly, and then several hours apart).

- The Relic House souvenir shop located near the fire attraction.

- The "stockyards restaurant" that became known as the Brass Rail Steak House.

Chicago Fire

Every day in Old Chicago guests would greet Mrs. O'Leary and her cow. The term "Mrs." is referenced loosely as "she" mostly was portrayed by one of the park's male actors. Mrs.

The suspected cause for the Chicago Fire. It was the cow and not Mrs. O'Leary or the family visiting from Revere, Massachusetts.

O'Leary and the cow quietly disappeared just before Chicago burst into flames.

> In 1871, the great Chicago fire was a disaster; today it's spectacular entertainment. Chicago burns every twenty minutes at FREEDOMLAND. It's the greatest deliberate conflagration since Nero burned Rome. But these flames are scientifically controlled—there is no danger at any time. At the cry of "Fire!" the old Chicago fire department springs into action. Quickly, the hand-drawn, hand-pump engine is wheeled out through the fire house doors. The call goes out for volunteers: volunteers to help pull the engine through the streets, volunteers to help man the see-saw pump. This means you, for all volunteers come from the audience. It won't be easy—the flames are stubborn, but gradually the fire-fighters bring them under control with a 200-foot jet of water. The fire is over—there's nothing left now but acres of smoking ruins—until Chicago bursts into flame again.
>
> —Freedomland's 1960 Complete
> Official Guide with Maps

The Chicago Fire remains one of the best recalled attractions at Freedomland. During the five seasons of park operation, the fire erupted at various scheduled intervals from about 20 minutes to several hours. Firemen would rush the antique water pumper to the scene and park guests, often children, would handle the pump to douse the flames.

Manually operated gas burners were located in each of the windows of the building located on Forest Street. The gas cost more than $30,000 each season, depending on the frequency of fires. Flames would rise about seven feet and even higher with the wind.

The Chicago Fire likely was the most photographed attraction at Freedomland. Not only was a burning building a great Kodak moment (Kodak was a park sponsor), but the thrill of firemen rushing to the scene with the old-fashioned hand-pump and then getting kids involved to pump water to fight the flames became perfect images to capture on cameras and 8mm movie cameras. Even when all was quiet between flare-ups, the scorched building served as the perfect backdrop for family photos, group photos that included scout troops, and publicity pictures of visiting celebrities that included Timmy (actor Jon Provost) and Lassie.

Chicago Fire Department

From a Freedomland postcard:

> CHICAGO FIRE—Flames sweep through the charred ruins of a Chicago business district as Freedomland re-creates the Great Fire of 1871, bringing to life a dramatic page of American history.
>
> —Description with the Freedomland
> Chicago Fire postcard

Once they heard the screams, the brave men of Chicago Engine Company 8 grabbed their hand-pumper and raced through the streets. All other activity stopped as park guests watched them rush to the scene of the disaster. Their heroic efforts, however, could not beat back the flames. The firefighters needed assistance from the citizenry to manage the pump and douse the inferno.

A lot of kids often ran alongside the firemen. If they were tall enough, boys and girls were allowed to pump the water to assist Chicago's bravest. Youngsters considered themselves very lucky if they were chosen for the fire brigade. Many shorter and younger children were moved away from the pumper (described as a see-saw pump in the first park guide) for safety reasons— imagine your feet leaving the ground as your side of the pump handrail rose into the air. The circa 1840s pumper was from Tennessee. Its post-Freedomland history remains a mystery.

Children who helped extinguish the fire received a certificate that was signed by Fire Chief Sidney Wohlfeld:

> The
> Chicago Fire Department
> Little Giant Engine Company
> Freedomland, U.S.A.
> certifies that
>
> [guest name]

has been sworn in as Honorary Fire Chief for
Meritorious service in fighting the Chicago Fire.
FREEDOMLAND
Sidney Wohlfeld, Chief of Fire Dept.

Sidney was a real person and not a Freedomland character actor. He had served as captain (1949–1953) of a Fire Department of New York company (Engine 71) located in the Melrose section of the Bronx. One of the park's first-aid stations, staffed by a doctor and a registered nurse, was located, appropriately, near the Chicago Fire attraction.

The Great Lakes

Though the park was built on marshland, the 10-acre Freedomland Great Lakes was a man-made waterway. About 10 million gallons of water filled the lakes to a depth of about six feet. A submerged guide rail provided direction for the sternwheelers.

A leak-proof fabric lining created by Cincinnati's Philip Carey Manufacturing Company served as the base for the lakes, along with the small lake for the Horseless Carriage attraction in Little Old New York and the bay in San Francisco. The company used panels of asphalt plasticizes and inert materials. Many people initially thought the lakes contained a concrete base.

The same body of water served the sternwheelers, the New York harbor tugboats and, for the first few seasons, the Chippewa Indian canoes. An island in the waterway known as Bird Island was created as a habitat for turkeys and other fowl. These animals would be scooped up at the end of the season and brought back to the island during the following spring.

Turbulence caused by the sternwheelers' paddles created regular maintenance issues as water leaked from the lakes. The water was drained completely when the park closed each year and the lakes were refilled the following spring.

The Sternwheelers

Freedomland touted its sternwheelers:

From Chicago, the queen city of the Great Lakes, the Great Lakes Cruise takes you round FREEDOMLAND's man-made waterways. You sail through all five of the lakes, on one of two 110-foot, 400-passenger stern-wheelers. The last sternwheel steamers to be built in the United States, they were specially constructed for FREEDOMLAND by Todd Shipyards. There'll be music and singing as you sail; each boat carries a band featuring a calliope, and you can join in the community singing with words and music that one of America's top composers has written for FREEDOMLAND.

—Freedomland's 1960 Complete
Official Guide with Maps

The American and *The Canadian* sternwheelers were designed by Gene Angel (boat) and Earl Hart (ornamentation). These men had designed and built the sternwheeler used in the MGM musical *Showboat* and other films.

The sternwheelers were identical and each was crafted to carry 400 passengers. Confusion still reigns about the

Sternwheeler and Tugboat. One of the sternwheelers shares
the Great Lakes with a New York Harbor Tug Boat.

propulsion of these boats. Some stories indicated that the boats did not have engines (accurate) and were considered floating barges with paddle wheels that provided the propulsion. Other stories indicated that each boat had a Mercedes motor. The long-reported story that both boats operated on a track located under the water actually is a reference to a guide rail in the lake bottom that directed the boats and supported docking.

The Todd Shipyards Corporation's Hoboken Division in New Jersey delivered the two 110-foot hulls to the park, where final ornamentation was added to the boats. The sternwheelers were moved to the Great Lakes by Nicholas Brothers Building Movers. Five years earlier, Todd Shipyards' San Pedro, California, operation delivered Disneyland's *Mark Twain* riverboat hull.

The total budget for the design, manufacture, transportation, and installation of both sternwheelers was about $400,000.

Of the two Freedomland sternwheelers, *The American* survived until recently and it never traveled far from the park. During the 1960s, when it was renamed the *Mark Twain*, it was docked at the Showboat Hotel (later the Greenwich Harbor Inn) in Greenwich, Connecticut. A number of years ago, it became a waterfront party boat on the Byrum River in the Westchester County community of Port Chester. During 2018, it was sold for $1,020 at auction and destined for Korea to serve as a restaurant. Severely damaged during transfer to a ship, the boat was relegated to the scrapyard.

Due to false information that was repeated in newspaper articles after Freedomland closed, many people believed and continued to convey the story that *The Canadian* became the *Mark Twain*. Actually, *The Canadian* traveled farther into Connecticut (Johnsonville Village in East Haddam) before it was destroyed.

Raymond Schmitt was a local business owner who owned the Johnsonville Village land that once had been a thriving mill community. Raymond and his wife planned to convert the property into a tourist attraction. They purchased and moved vintage buildings from throughout New England to Johnsonville. The structures included a Victorian stable and chapel. They also purchased and moved *The Canadian* to the mill pond.

A Connecticut newspaper during the mid-1960s reported that the Schmitts bought *The American*, and this may have been the original source of the error that led to the misidentification of the two Freedomland sternwheelers. Additional information in the article was accurate—specifically, the boat was towed up the Connecticut River and then carried by truck to the community of Moodus, a village in East Haddam, and placed in the Johnsonville mill pond. The boat was situated near the shore for about 30 years.

Another article about Johnsonville Village in the December 30, 1982, issue of the *Hartford Courant* featured photographs of the boat with the "Canadian" name between the smoke-stacks as it had appeared at Freedomland. This article, though, did contain some misinformation about the boat—that it was built during 1954 (actually 1959) and that it was purchased during the early 1970s (actually 1966). Due to the lack of maintenance, the boat, according to the article, continued to deteriorate at Johnsonville Village. Another article from the *Hartford Courant* on September 8, 1983, featured a different photograph of *The Canadian*. The name of the boat still could be seen between the smokestacks.

Then, it was gone. During February 2005, the boat, reportedly, was moved across the pond to the side with access to the road, then carted away after it was sawed or chopped into pieces.

While gone, *The Canadian* is remembered on Riverboat Dave's Paddlewheel Site. Among the listing of boats is the picture of a model of *The Canadian*. Accompanying information identifies the boat and mentions that it was located at Freedomland. The listing identifies the owner of the model as Ray Harrington. He references the boat as the *Eugene*, providing more confusion and mystery about the life of the old Freedomland sternwheeler.

Ray wrote:

> I purchased the *Eugene* at an auction in Connecticut at a place called Johnsonville. The owner, Ray Schmit[t], died of cancer a couple of years ago and then the whole place went up for auction. Schmit[t] had a lot of money and his goal was to rebuild an old village on his property.

And he did. Everything from original houses and buildings that he moved, carriages, furniture, sleds, etc. Everything you could think that would be in a town back in the late 1800s. He also purchased a sternwheeler from what use[d] to be Freedomland, an amusement park in New York back in the 60s. He had the vessel floated up from New York, up the Connecticut River, and then moved over about 4 miles of land.

The listing on this riverboat website is the only known reference that *The Canadian* may have been renamed *Eugene*. No evidence has been located that a new name had been assigned to the boat. With efforts unsuccessful to locate Ray Harrington, mystery continues to surround the removal and fate of *The Canadian*.

Santa Fe Railroad

The two Freedomland trains—steam engines, coaches, and open cars—were the property of the Edaville Railroad in South Carver, Massachusetts. Edaville is a heritage railroad that operates excursion trains for tourists.

The trains were leased to the park. The engines and cars were transported to Freedomland during April and the equipment returned to the railroad company at the end of each season. Numerous roundtrips occurred on a specially designed flatbed truck that carried a couple of cars. The truck traveled along the Connecticut Turnpike and then to the New York State Thruway before arriving at the Gun Hill Road exit for entrance to the park. These trains were not needed by Edaville to meet its summer activities, but were used for the popular excursions during its Christmas festival.

The coal-fired engines were known as Monson No. 3 (built 1914) and Monson No. 4 (built 1918). An Edaville employee served as an advisor at the park each season to ensure proper maintenance for the engines. Due to New York City union rules, Edaville personnel could not operate the trains.

The trains were 2-foot narrow gauge that included the vintage passenger coaches and the more modern open cars. Monson No. 3, along with cars, originally was leased to the

Pleasure Island park for its 1959 debut season. Monson No. 4 started its working life hauling quarried slate six miles in Maine from Monson to Monson Junction, where it met the Bangor and Aroostook line. It was sold for scrap to a Rochester, New York, railyard during 1943. Following World War II, this locomotive was rescued by the Edaville Railroad.

Both steam engines featured at Freedomland now are in Maine. Monson No. 3 is at Boothbay Railway Village in Boothbay. Monson No. 4 is at Maine's Narrow Gauge Railroad and Museum in Portland. The engines have been in machine shops during recent years for repairs or major overhaul.

The Freedomland train stops were in Chicago and San Francisco. The trains traveled an approximate one-mile loop around the park and crossed several trestles. While mostly a pleasant ride, passengers often would be confronted by masked robbers when the train traveled through the Wild West.

During the park's early seasons, a train passenger received a pocket-size fold-out brochure that promoted the Santa Fe rail system. Contemporary pictures on one side included the diesels that powered the freight and passenger trains, the high-level *El Capitan* with seats on the scenic top level of each car and the Turquoise Room private dining room on the *Super Chief*. The reverse side featured engines of the past, including the "Last of the steam giants, No. 2921, built in the 40's was retired when Santa Fe became a completely dieselized railroad."

The last panel of the brochure provided a space for a person's name to certify that he or she "is an honorary engineer on the Santa Fe Railway at Freedomland U.S.A." The brochures eventually were eliminated and replaced with a card to certify honorary engineers.

Chippewa War Canoes

The Chippewa War Canoes were featured only during the first two seasons of the park. Each of the five canoes accommodated 19 people and two employee guides. The 34-foot canoes were built in Maine for $4,700. The guides, reportedly, were actual members of the Mohawk tribe who most likely lived in Brooklyn. They or their parents had moved to the borough years earlier to work on the city's steel structures for bridges and buildings.

Every youngster on a canoe received a 6x8-inch certificate that included several Indian images. The certificate for a boy proclaimed:

Freedomland
Indian Tribal Council
New York City, U.S.A. Council of Tribes
Penobscot, Cherokee, Mohawk, Sioux, Ojibwa, Chippewa
have accepted

[guest name]

As an Honorary Brave and he is now a member of the
Freedomland Indian Council
Black Hawk, Chief

The Hallmark Store: Freedomland's Communications Center

A television film adaptation of William Shakespeare's *Macbeth* was presented as the November 20, 1960, episode of the anthology series *Hallmark Hall of Fame*. An exhibit of scenes from the program was featured in the Hallmark exhibit at Freedomland during the 1961 season.

The Hallmark store served as the park's communications center. The main telephone switchboard for park operations, however, was located in another part of Chicago, on the floor above the first-aid station that was a few steps from the Chicago Fire. The Hallmark store sold cards with specific Freedomland artwork and messages, picture postcards, and the collective series of postcards with park concept artwork.

The State Fair Midway

During the 1962 and 1963 seasons, Freedomland added several new attractions, including a state fair midway that was an acceptable addition to the historical backdrop of the park. However, several typical amusement park rides also were introduced and this distanced the park from its historic theme. The decision angered some sponsors.

The rides, some located in the Chicago midway area and others in New Orleans, included a Meteor Monorail Roller Coaster, Astro Ride, Bumper Scooter, Drive a Go-Kart to Pike's

Peak or Bust, and Wiggle Worm. A kiddie land (Kiddie Kountry Fair sponsored by King Korn stamps) was established and included a Junior Santa Fe train along with several other child attractions (karousel, boats, helicopter, whip, fire engines, buggie, jeep, and coaster).

The Meteor Monorail Roller Coaster was classified as an Italian monorail coaster and described as a steel roller-coaster sit-down thrill ride of three cars per train. Riders were arranged inline in two rows for a total of six riders per train. Manufactured by Mack Rides GmbH & Company of Germany, it arrived for the 1963 season. Research leans to the ride's relationship with Sportland Pier in Wildwood, New Jersey, possibly before and also after its time at Freedomland.

The Astro Ride operated from 1962 to 1964. Manufactured by the Allan Herschell Company, the model was described as a wild mouse or mad mouse. The single-car trains arranged riders inline in two rows with a total of two riders per car.

Some park fans recall a Ferris wheel in the park during latter seasons. An August 1964 newspaper gossip columnist article confirmed its presence: "Lionel Hampton, doing a concert at Freedomland, led his band—still tootling—off the bandstand, onto a Ferris wheel and up into the air."

CHAPTER NINE

Friendly Freedomlanders: The Park Employees

It was the best seven weeks I have ever spent in a lifetime.

—Tony Sozio, Tug Boat Sea Captain

Van Arsdale France received a phone call from C.V. Wood during August 1954. Van and Woody had been old acquaintances from their days at Convair, the aircraft manufacturer, where Van had supervised that company's training program. Woody told Van that he had left the Stanford Research Institute and was involved in, as Van phrased it, "something called Disneyland."

Just six months before Disneyland's opening day, Woody suggested to Walt Disney that Van should join the team. Woody then hired Van as a consultant to design training programs for Disney's cast members that stressed the best opportunities to "create happiness" within the park. According to Van, Woody advised him that "Walt is a wonderful guy and this studio is nothing like any place you or I have ever worked. It's like a family and Walt treats me like a son." Woody then added that "Roy [Disney] hired me as a vice president and general manager, and when I told Walt, he said, 'That doesn't leave much room for advancement.'"

Soon after Woody left Disneyland, Van also departed for a short time to develop the employee training program ("It's Been My Pleasure") for Woody's Pleasure Island park. Then,

Van created another program ("Be a Friendly Freedomlander") for Freedomland. The Freedomland employee handbook, which included an image of a friendly American Indian on the cover, offered tips to assist workers as they engaged the visiting public. A photo of Van at Freedomland has not been located, but he did share interesting stories about Woody and the park.

In his book, *Window on Main Street* (published by Theme Park Press), Van recalled that Woody may have been a bit unconventional for the times, but he was able to sell his ideas:

> In the back of my mind, I remembered that Woody had been involved in some crazy ideas, and he was a masterful salesman. He could easily compete with the legendary P.T. Barnum. ... Woody was only about 32 years old at that time, one of those born leaders, and had been ever since he was a kid."

Van also documented a number of insights about Woody from their Freedomland days.

When Van walked into Woody's Manhattan hotel room, Woody pointed to a table and a check for $13 million to begin Freedomland. Unfortunately, the land had not been as carefully selected as had the Disneyland site.

Van wrote in his book:

> One way the project had been sold was by using some low-cost land fill in the Bronx area of New York. When piledrivers would pound down great poles for foundations, the poles would simply disappear. Wood commented, "This is the last time I'll ever build a park on a thousand gin bottles."

As at Disneyland, the asphalt for the parking lot and the striping for the spaces occurred just a few days before the grand opening:

> But at Freedomland, underneath the black top were mattresses and mattress springs and other assorted trash. These springs popped up through the black top, and myself and many guests tripped over the hazards.

Van also was assigned the responsibility of creating direction signs and coordinating traffic to the park. He worked with the city's traffic and police departments to direct the flow through the boroughs on opening day.

Van eventually returned to Disney and created additional training programs for Walt Disney World and Tokyo Disneyland. His window was unveiled on Disneyland's Main Street, U.S.A. in 1994.

Recollections by Cheri France and Susan Webb Fields

Cheri France is Van's daughter. Susan Webb Fields refers to herself as a surrogate daughter. Their memories of Van touch on both his career and his personal life.

Cheri was about 15 years old at the time of Freedomland, but she never saw the park. She also didn't visit Pleasure Island.

"I remember we spent a summer in New York and stayed at the Paris Hotel," said Cheri. "I remember more about the Paris Hotel and all the places Mom and I visited while Dad was at work. The only thing I remember is a story that Dad told us, and I don't know if it was about Freedomland or Pleasure Island, but it must have been a very hot day and the asphalt had not really settled yet. A family got one of those big tacks in the tire and Dad tried pulling it out and succeeded, and then tried putting it back in as the tire was going flat."

Cheri added that her father "always was busy and put 24/7 into his work. When we lived in San Diego and he worked in Los Angeles, we only saw him one weekend a month and that was back in the mid-1950s. When we moved to Newport Beach in mid-1955, he was home every night mostly, but way after my bed time."

Cheri's parents divorced after France returned to work at Disney. Susan and Jonathan Webb, the children of Estelle (Stel) O. Webb, then entered Van's life. Even though Stel and Van never married, Susan said the small unit was a family. Van rarely talked much about his work, according to Susan, who could not locate any details about Freedomland in her personal papers.

"We spent holidays together and my mom and Van often traveled," said Susan. "They visited Walt Disney's hometown on one trip. Van loved Disneyland. He knew everyone and they knew him. He often worked the graveyard shift so that he knew the gardeners and maintenance crew. One of the Clydesdale horses that pulled the street car down Main Street was named after him.

"After Freedomland was completed, Van, C.V. Wood, and, I imagine, other people went to the 21 Club in Manhattan. They were celebrating and C.V. had a tower of champagne glasses set up and was pouring a huge bottle of the best champagne. Van just happened to cross his legs and knocked the whole thing over. After it was cleaned and C.V. asked for more glasses and champagne, he looked at Van and said, 'Van, take your chair and back away from the table.'

"Van was always spilling coffee, burning holes in his clothes with his cigarettes, or just spilling food on beautiful new suits and shirts. He liked to drink out of crystal glasses, which he constantly broke and had to replace. None of these things bothered him at all."

Susan said her two children adored Van and he loved them as well.

"He always treated them like little adults and I think they really liked that," recalled Susan. "They never questioned why Grandpa and Grandma didn't live together, but my daughter was only 10 and my son 13 when Van died. One of my favorite stories about my kids is the day Van decided that, at the ages of five and eight, they should learn to play poker. They sat down at the table and my kids listened seriously as Van explained the rules of the game. After the explanation and dealing the cards, Van turned to my son and said, 'Ryan, I'm going to wax your ass.' Ryan laughed so hard he fell off his chair to the floor. And so did my mother and me."

Van and Susan's daughter, Stacey, had an especially close bond. They enjoyed walks and talked non-stop. Susan's mother rented a beach house in San Diego for about eight years. Van and Stacey took long walks on the beach to look for shells and discuss life.

"When we would visit my mother in Costa Mesa, Van always came over for dinner. When we knew Van would be walking over from his apartment, I would stand with my daughter in front of the house and as soon as we saw him round the corner on our street I let Stacey run to meet him. He would open his arms and she would run in for a hug and he would ask her, 'How's my princess?' She loved being called a princess."

Susan maintains a charming essay that Van wrote about taking her mother and Stacey to Disneyland. Since he always was thinking, as he had done for years for the Disney company and then with Woody at Pleasure Island and Freedomland, Van identified an opportunity to prepare a "guide" for the senior set, especially if they were enjoying Disneyland with the grandkids.

Van called it the "Guide for Two Old Crocks with a Kid on a Hot, Crowded Day at Disneyland." He even developed sections that included planning for the fatigue factor (for the grandparents and the kids), enjoying It's A Small World, and traveling around the park by train. A wise tip in the guide: "Never mention some attraction if you aren't going to follow through. 3-year-olds remember…and hold you to it."

The essay ended with a sweet sentiment that reflects the thoughts of many grandfathers about their grandchildren: "It was a memorable day, though it left us with a touch of sadness. Stacey is going to grow up, and won't be 3 forever."

Susan added that Van always gave her sound business advice and even dating advice (never date a man who wears a pinky ring and always carry mad money in case you want to leave and need to call a cab).

"We were lucky to have Van in our lives," added Susan. "He helped me secure my first job at Disneyland and he was very funny."

Friendly Freedomlanders

Freedomland's employees were slotted within 54 categories, some of which were not listed by big city employment agencies at the time. Many employees were required to possess unique skills, including buffalo wrangler, carrousel horse jeweler, totem pole carver, and stage coach harness-maker.

Other odd occupations at the park included pretzel bending, seal keeping, doughnut rolling, can-can dancing, glassblowing, and space tracking. The park also employed a skin diver who regularly inspected the Great Lakes for purity and maintenance.

Every park employee—from phone operator to office worker to lovable undertaker Digger O'Toole—was a Friendly Freedomlander.

Boat Operators

John Provenzano was a sternwheeler operator. He lived nearby on Crosby Avenue in the Pelham Bay section of the Bronx. His daughter, Andrea Provenzano-Nation, does not recall which of the sternwheelers her father operated, but it is possible that he piloted both *The American* and *The Canadian*. John was an insurance agent by trade.

"I recall Freedomland and visiting my father on the boat," said Andrea. "The park was so different than anything we had in the Bronx. It was a magical place."

Tony Sozio, who now resides in Florida, piloted a tugboat.

"I worked there for only seven weeks [during 1962], because of a union strike at the company I worked for, which was Lockheed Aircraft at [New York International Airport/ Idlewild Airport]. I was part of administration, so I was non-union. I could not cross the picket line. So, the company gave me the time off.

"Lucky me! I was lucky to get the job of the tugboat sea captain. Of course, I had to pass their test requirements. It was the best seven weeks I have ever spent in a lifetime. My first daughter was only seven years old when I took her on the *Totsie* on my day off. As amazing as it may seem, she remembers the ride and said she could never forget it."

Another unnamed tugboat operator was a college student who possessed some boating experience. The boats had about eight operators and all were required to join the Teamster's Union and become trainees for an operating engineer's license. One day, after heavy rain raised the water level in the Great Lakes, several tugboat operators were needed to tow one of the sternwheelers back into position. To aid docking, the sternwheelers followed a guide rail in the lake bottom. This one had been lifted away from the guide rail by the rising water.

Food Service

Connie Capobianco started working at Freedomland before the park officially opened. She had just graduated from Cathedral High School in Manhattan, and she planned to attend nursing school in the fall. Connie traveled by subway each Freedomland work day from her apartment building near the Hub, the neighborhood of the South Bronx at the crossroads of 149th Street and Third Avenue.

(While speaking with Connie, the author learned that his mother and grandparents had lived in the same building—335 East 148th Street. Connie's grandparents owned the building.)

At Freedomland, Connie was employed in food service, and she met another young lady who would become a long-time friend. Connie and Carole (Avondoglio) Fantel were the maids of honor for each other's weddings and godmothers to each other's children. Back then, though, they were just teenagers who enjoyed their work to get Freedomland ready for its debut.

"I was helping set up the pizza shop located in the San Francisco area," said Connie. "Part of my job was to put up the curtains and the signs. I also helped clean the tables after they were removed from the delivery truck."

That's where Connie first met Carole, who had attended Blessed Sacrament High School in Manhattan.

"I was living in Astoria [2029 28th Street, an apartment complex near the Grand Central Parkway as it travels into the Triborough Bridge] and my neighbor was Thomas Gardner who worked for the Brass Rail restaurants," recalled Carole. "He lived one flight upstairs and I was friendly with the entire family. He told me about Freedomland, that his company was managing the food locations and suggested that I come in for an interview. My mother advised me to dress to the nines for the interview and I was hired immediately."

Carole started that same day. She found herself, in dress and heels, standing on a table to help prepare San Francisco's Italian restaurant for opening day. Once the park opened, Connie and Carole worked in the pancake restaurant, the Creole Café, in New Orleans. The shop also served waffles.

"We wore a white dress with puffy sleeves and had the Aunt Jemima type of aprons," remembered Connie. "Occasionally, I also worked at the Jesse Jewell Plantation House. Early on, at the pancake restaurant, we ate pancakes every day during our meal breaks and I always covered them with boysenberry syrup. Food Services finally allowed us and all the other restaurant workers to take meals at the other food locations."

Carole added that restaurant management had noticed that many of its employees were not eating enough protein. She said staffs then were allowed to sample hamburgers and other food options during their breaks. Pancakes, though, remained a popular item. Before the park opened each day, Connie, Carole, and others served pancakes for their fellow park workers.

"We didn't charge them for it," said Connie, "and one day Bob Silverstein, one of the young managers of the Brass Rail food service company, noticed that I wasn't taking any money, but he never said anything about it."

Carole remembered that everyone had a good time that summer and that working at Freedomland was a great adventure.

"One day, I went to serve ice tea to a customer, but I forgot the ice and the very hot tea melted the plastic cup," said Carole. "Another time, Bob was making dough and just doing it all wrong. All the flour got on him. Then, on another day, somehow detergent got into the mixer and the batter turned green."

Connie fondly remembered the various themed sections of the park and enjoyed walking through each one when she arrived before the gates were opened to the public.

"When you walked through those streets, you actually felt you were in the actual locations. The music was created especially for each themed area and as you listened to the music you imagined that you were in San Francisco or old-time New York. I can still hear the music."

Connie also enjoyed the park's attractions when she had free time.

"I liked the carrousel, because I liked the music," recalled Connie. "It was near the pancake house and not too far from the Chicago Fire, which I found interesting along with the re-enactment of the stage coach robbery."

Carole also enjoyed the carrousel and often went with Connie to Elsie's Boudoir to see Connie's late brother. Faust Capobianco took care of the barn along with Elsie and her twins, Larabee and Lobelia, at Borden's sponsored attraction.

"When we were young, we spent summers at a farm in Pennsylvania and my brother really enjoyed it," said Connie. "He graduated from Farmingdale [the State University of New York at Farmingdale, Long Island] and studied agriculture. He later continued his studies at the University of Georgia. He was the manager at the barn for the 1960 and 1961 seasons and maybe also for the 1962 season. He cleaned the stalls, walked Elsie into and out of the barn, and he milked her every day."

Connie remembered Elsie living in "a fancy brass rail enclosure with red velvet drapes and chairs. There was even carpeting. The furthest thing from a stall that a cow would ever see. My brother also cared for the two little calves on either side that were in their brass and red velvet cribs."

Faust greeted visitors and answered bovine-related questions. According to Connie, Faust's friend (she recalled his name as Tony Restivo) from SUNY Farmingdale worked there, too.

During the park's second year, Connie also worked part time at Freedomland and even helped her brother at the barn. While she couldn't regularly enjoy the pancakes and the boysenberry syrup, she was just steps away from the ice cream and milk shakes at Borden's Milk Bar.

Guest Relations

During Freedomland's debut season, a number of college students from around the country served as hosts for the many celebrities and other special guests who visited the park. Diana Karasik Levin of Chicago was one of the young ladies assigned to the hospitality department.

Diana, who was almost 21 at the time, learned about Freedomland from a family friend. Sam Greller was in the Chicago trophy business. The plan was to let his wife run the business for a couple of months during the summer while he went to New York as a consultant for Freedomland. He had been invited to New York by his nephew, Ted Raynor—the same Milton T. Raynor who was president of Freedomland and also a friend of the Karasik family. Sam's work at Freedomland was related to special events. He had handled special events for the 1933–1934 Chicago World's Fair.

Sam planned to rent a two-bedroom apartment in New York. He was taking his secretary along to help with the Freedomland assignment and he offered Diana the opportunity to join them and explore the city. Diana was offered a position to host the park's VIPs, and Sam said that she and his secretary could share one bedroom while he would take the other bedroom in the apartment.

Within a couple of days of settling on these New York City plans, a phone call from a relative in Washington, D.C., provided Diana with another summer job opportunity. The position was as an assistant to David Brinkley, then the co-anchor of *The Huntley-Brinkley Report* on NBC.

"I had a choice," said Diana, "and you just knew I was going to go to New York City and work at a theme park."

Sam's wife and Diana's mother found the trio their New York apartment on 66th Street between Second and Third avenues, "and to our surprise," recalled Diana, "they were waiting for us when we arrived."

About 10 or 12 college students, according to Diana, worked in Freedomland's guest relations department that first season.

"We were trained extremely well," said Diana, who recalled escorting singer Pat Boone and his family on opening day after Pat had cut the ceremonial ribbon to officially open the park. "One of the good things about such a job was that you also got to go at the head of the lines for all the attractions. I recall Pat, his wife, and daughters going on the carrousel in New Orleans and asking me to come along, but carrousels make me dizzy so I just watched them have a great time."

Another park VIP that Diana escorted that season was actress Sandra Dee, who already had appeared in several popular films and opposite some big screen stars. Later that year, Sandra married singer and Freedomland entertainer Bobby Darin.

Diana also recalled working a day or two with Barbara Walters to help her prepare for a television broadcast. At the time, Dave Garroway was the host of the NBC morning program *Today* and one show was broadcast from the park that first season. Barbara previously had been a publicist with Tex McCrary's public relations agency that had its connection to Freedomland through William Zeckendorf, Sr., and then she was a writer at *Redbook*. She became associated with *Today* in a behind-the-scenes role as a researcher, and it was during this time that Diana was assigned to work with her.

One of Diana's biggest thrills at the park occurred on her birthday. She was born on July 4 and Freedomland that first season offered many activities throughout the park to celebrate Independence Day.

"Freedomland always had these parades in Little Old New York," recalled Diana. "On my birthday, they placed me in a carriage with my name on a sign and I was part of that day's parade. I still can recall all the festivities through the streets with bandleader Paul Lavalle and the Freedomland band leading the way."

Diana met one of her long-time friends during Freedomland's debut season. Alice Faye Harris of Arizona also was assigned to the guest relations department. She is a daughter of actress and singer Alice Faye and comedian, musician, and bandleader Phil Harris. In a show business newspaper column from 1960, Alice's mother stated that "my oldest girl, Alice, is now 18, and working...at Freedomland in New York. She recently showed Rudy Vallee and his wife around Freedomland."

After Freedomland's first season ended, Diana remained in New York and shared a Manhattan apartment with three other young ladies that included Alice and a stage actress (Lois Greenfield) who appeared in *Gypsy*. Diana eventually returned to Chicago for a real job and, much later with her husband, owned a private school.

"Freedomland was a great place to work for college grads and out-of-work actors," said Diana. "To this day, my daughter, Laura Levin Jordan, who knows of my Freedomland training and how I always organized family trips to amusement parks, tells friends that if they plan to visit any theme park that they should make sure they take me with them."

Maintenance Crew

John Brennan was the foreman of the painting crew at Freedomland. He worked there until the park closed. His daughter, Barbara Brennan Burke, recalled that her father brought her with him a few times during the spring before the park opened for the season. They got to walk around the park and through the attractions.

"We went to Freedomland each year and my dad would explain how the rides worked," said Barbara. "It was a really great place. ... I still remember vividly the Chicago Fire, San Francisco Earthquake, the Civil War ride, and the walk-through Casa Loca where everything was tilted."

Park Security / Fire Brigade

Freedomland's security corps employed a security manager, captain, four lieutenants, five sergeants, and approximately 90 security officers. Many had experience in the New York City Police Department, industrial security, and military security. Among the corps were Mauro Contristano as supervisor of the security team, Captain Vito Taglienti, Maury Altes, and Thomas Dolan. German Shepard guard dogs were used to patrol the grounds.

A fire lieutenant and approximately one dozen firemen also were part of the park's security staff. All were former New York Fire Department employees. They were supervised by Fire Chief Sidney Wohlfeld, a former New York Fire Department battalion chief who was the park's director of fire and safety.

The chief surveyed the property prior to construction. He stressed the importance of water mains, hydrants, building sprinklers, roads, lights, and radio communications. The brigade provided around-the-clock protection with the most trusted fire prevention methods available at the time. A close liaison was maintained with the city's fire department, according to Gary Urbanowicz, a Fire Department of New York historian. The firefighters inspected Freedomland daily for safety issues and compliance with fire prevention ordinances. Park employees and others employed by sponsors received extensive training.

A 24-year-old 750-gallon-per-minute Seagrave pumper (the company is the oldest fire apparatus manufacturer in the country) was purchased from the Smithtown Fire Department on Long Island. The park also purchased a 300-gallon booster tank. More than 300 water, dry chemical, and carbon dioxide portable fire extinguishers, along with mobile hose reels, were distributed throughout the park. The park installed 19 manual fire alarm boxes. The chief ensured that the 29 hydrants were installed on a 10-inch water main loop system to access the millions of gallons of water in the park's artificial lakes.

A pump house was installed at the edge of the Hutchinson River. Sprinklers were installed in all buildings. The fire pumper, ambulance, and fire-fighting jeeps were equipped with two-way radios. Walkie-talkie radios were carried by all members of the brigade as they exited the fire station. The fire-fighters also maintained the five first-aid treatment stations in the park and they assisted with emergencies that occurred during storms.

Parking Attendant

Eugene Edelstein was a parking lot attendant during the inaugural season. He lived on Ogden Avenue in the west Bronx at the time and the 1960 season followed completion of his senior year of college at CCNY.

"In order to work there, I had to join the Teamsters Union," said Gene. I'm afraid I don't still have my union card! It was the first and only time I joined a union.

The first day, we were instructed *not* to park cars in a certain area, because the lot had sunk [due to the construction on marshland]. We weren't really given any instruction as to how to do our job, just to wave cars in. There were a few experienced parking guys who led us. You would either be on a line of attendants waving cars along, or standing in front of the parking spot, "pulling" them in, motioning to your left to get the driver to turn the wheel in that direction [his right], and vice versa. There was one guy who would just give a signal like he was grasping and turning a wheel back and forth, and no one could tell in which direction the driver should turn. When asked, he insisted they just had to see which way he turned the wheel first.

"When it rained all day, and the park didn't open, we didn't get paid," added Gene. "My mother said I should never take an outside job again. There was an area where the employees, including the parking lot attendants, changed into their uniforms. I don't remember much about the uniform, but I do remember that we got safari-type hats to wear, good for both sun and rain, and we had yellow slickers for rainy weather.

"Once, a guy returning to his car found he had a flat tire. He asked us if there was some service to change the tire. One of our guys said he would call the park mechanic. I had changed a tire on my father's car before and, sensing a possible gratuity, said we could do it ourselves. We got out his jack, jacked up the car, but, because the surface of the lot was so uneven, the car fell off the jack. The guy said he probably had a broken axle now, and we did call the mechanic, who brought a much more substantial jack and changed his tire. The strange thing was, he gave us (I think there were two of us) a tip anyway, even before he found out that he did *not* have any damage to his axle.

"I had a friend who had gotten a job there as a security officer. He had a badge and a uniform. He did tell me that if anything happened, he would run in the other direction.

"We had breaks, and a lunch break. I remember that I quickly figured out where the closest air-conditioned areas were to cool off. I remember being on break, standing under an awning during the rain, watching the Chicago Fire. A security guy came up to me and said, 'You got a good post.' We were both wearing the yellow slickers and safari hats. His was only slightly different, and he thought I was another security guy assigned to a spot where I could stay out of the rain. I did explain that I was a parking lot attendant on break.

"I know we got reduced, maybe it was even free, admission to the park, so I went with my then-girlfriend (now my wife) a number of times. Definitely fond memories!"

Sponsor Employee

Neil Borrell worked in Freedomland during the summer of 1962 before his senior year in high school. He was employed directly by American Oil Company (Amoco), working at the travel exhibit in the Little Old New York area near the main entrance.

"I was 17 and it was a magic summer," recalled Neil. "My brother-in-law, Ed Alcamo, had a job as an 'exhibit attendant' and lined me up a job as 'exhibit attendant casual,' which really only meant balloon blower. I was to only blow up the balloons in the back of the travel exhibit that were given away at the counter in the front along with road maps and 'wet naps,' which became scrip in our hands. A box of American Oil 'wet naps' once bought me a sight-seeing helicopter ride over the park. They also were good for more basic things such as lunch at a restaurant."

Neil loved that summer and the park so much that he wrangled himself into other opportunities. He became the person who went out on the street to give away the balloons and then he started marching at the end of the twice-daily parades handing out balloons to little kids.

Neil lived on Marion Avenue and 197th Street in the Bronx and took a bus to the park.

"I could have gotten off at the main entrance and been right there," said Neil, "but I loved arriving early, as long as possible before the park opened, and entering through the employee gate at the other end of the park. That meant walking through the whole 'backstage' area and then through the empty Wild West and Chicago areas, past the Great Lakes and into Old New York. By the time I arrived, music already was playing through the sound system even though the areas were quite empty. I loved that special feeling of being the only one there. From my perspective, it was a really friendly place to work and within a few weeks I was able to hop on a trolley at any point in its route and then hop off at the dock and jump on one of the little tugboats for a sail around the Great Lakes. I loved the place so much that I would go there on my days off just to walk around."

The American Oil travel exhibit included the talking gas pump Amoco Sam, voiced by one or two of the exhibit attendants.

"I would blow up a ton of balloons in the back of the exhibit and then go across the street and up the stairs of one of the two-story office buildings into the tiny room with a window overlooking the exhibit," recalled Neil. "I would suggest to whomever was the voice of Amoco Sam that I could give them a nice long break if they wanted. I ended up being the talking gas pump quite a lot."

A sheet of acceptable answers to questions was taped to the wall. The only one, other than the obvious "What's your name... etc.," that Neil recalls was the last one. If you were asked, "Who pumped Ethyl?" the voice had to provide a well-thought-out ambiguous answer.

"I made a sign for Amoco Sam," added Neil, "for the unusual time when I was unavailable and the operator had to leave for some reason. The sign read 'Amoco Sam is Sleeping.'"

Neil also became adept at balloon blowing but his hands received cuts when he tried to break the string to tie the inflated balloons.

"We were next door to Pato's Bakery," said Neil. "They used a knife to cut the string tied around a box of baked goods, but that wouldn't work for me standing in front of a tank of helium. There was a concession at the front gate that sold tacky souvenirs and inflated balloons that you had to purchase. They used a little ring with a curled knife edge attached to cut through the balloon string and I offered to buy one from them. The gangster-voiced concession guy stood very close to me and said, 'How many balloons do youse give away in a day?' I answered about 900. He pulled a cutter out of his pocket, handed it to me and said, in his cheap gangster movie voice, 'Make it 500!' I guess he thought our free balloons were cutting into his balloons-for-profit business. I thanked him, went back in, and proceeded to blow up and give away 1,500 balloons."

Neil always felt bad for the kids whose balloons would pop, so he started placing one balloon inside another and blowing both up. If the outer balloon popped, a child still would have the inner balloon.

"We all loved the aromas coming from Pato's Bakery when their products were cooking and it became a gathering point for coffee breaks," recalled Neil. "I loved seeing the actors from the stage coach robbery. One of them told me that they had pulled a few train robberies, too, just for fun, but had stopped after the park tried to make train robberies part of the act."

Working for Freedomland was a different experience than working for a park sponsor.

"I have no idea how good or bad Freedomland was as an employer," added Neil, "but I know that American Oil pretty much left us alone to do our jobs and have a good time. It was the third season, but it was obvious that there were problems. American Oil had a gas station at the other end of the parking lot and our manager got a call one day late in the summer instructing him to make it clear to the gas station that they were no longer to extend any credit to Freedomland.

"I was probably lucky that the park was closed during the winter, because I think I would have wanted to stay. I was devastated when American Oil, along with a lot of other corporate sponsors, didn't return for the next season. I applied for, and was offered, a job working for Freedomland, but I would have had to start before school ended and it was my senior year so I ended up working in a discount store on Fordham Road the next summer."

The Freedomland experience that Neil totally embraced did pay career dividends.

"I'm certain that the 'show business' summer I spent at Freedomland set me up for the rest of my life. I ended up as a television director."

Wranglers

Tony Aiello lived at Swinton and Barkley avenues in the Throgs Neck section of the Bronx at the time of Freedomland. He worked at many jobs as a young man before becoming a correctional officer in central Florida.

Tony was hired just before the park opened. Since he had experience with horses, he became a wrangler and worked with the livestock. He said the wranglers had to break and train many horses and mules. Tony didn't recall how long he worked at the park, but he did remember that he left just before the chariot races were held in the Hollywood Arena. That show was featured during the second season (1961) of the park.

Musicians

All kinds of music played throughout Freedomland. The official Freedomland brass band, with its trombones gleaming and drums booming, set the tempo with its toe-tapping marches through the streets of the east coast-themed areas. The band was under the direction of Paul Lavalle, a conductor, composer, arranger, and performer on clarinet and saxophone.

Born Joseph Usifer on September 6, 1908, in Beacon, New York, Paul's parents were Italian immigrants. He studied music at the Juilliard School and performed in many 1930s bands. He became an arranger and clarinetist with the NBC house orchestra.

Paul worked on numerous radio programs, including *The Dinah Shore Show* (1939–1940), *The Chamber Music Society of Lower Basin Street* (1940–1944), and *Plays for Americans* (1942). He collaborated with Victor Borge, Mario Lanza, and Robert Merrill. His 1944 jazz composition "Always" climbed to number 29 on the top 40 charts. During 1940, *The New York Times* described Paul as "NBC's ubiquitous music maker" and added that he was "of small size, dynamic, dark haired..." Paul told the reporter that "music is my life, and I am happy that it is so."

Paul was selected over several applicants to become the conductor of the Band of America in 1948. The band performed on a weekly radio show (almost 400 programs) on NBC Radio for eight years. Each program began with the introduction: "Forty-eight states...48 stars...48 men marching down the main street of everybody's hometown! Here comes the Cities Service Band of America, conducted by Paul Lavalle!"

During 1964, the Band of America toured extensively and also became the official band of the 1964–1965 New York World's Fair.

Paul conducted the ABC Symphony, CBS Symphony, NBC Symphony Orchestra, New York Philharmonic, and Rochester Philharmonic Orchestra. During 1966, he became the conductor for the Radio City Music Hall Symphony Orchestra, and he returned two years later to serve as director of music and principal conductor until 1975. During 1967, he was instrumental in forming the 100-member All-American High School Band (by 1968 known as McDonald's All-American High School Band).

Besides the Freedomland brass band, music of all kinds played regularly in each of the themed areas of the park. The band's musicians often separated and changed costumes to perform as the German oompah band in Little Old New York and the clown band in New Orleans. Banjo players performed on the sternwheelers. A Dixieland combo played in New Orleans. The park also had a band on wheels that could appear anywhere at any time.

Versatile Employees

Many Freedomland employees were assigned to a variety of jobs during their time at the park. In an online comment a number of years ago, a Freedomland employee wrote:

> I was on the Fur Trapper ride, full-time, in all of '61. In '62, I was the conductor on the horse-drawn street cars on weekends as I was also working at a full-time job. In '63, I split my time between the Earthquake and the Tugboat rides, full-time. ... I remember the Chariot race [in the Hollywood Arena] where the black team of horses unexpectedly won over the white-team. The wandering clowns "Buttons and Bows." Going to the moon-bowl [sic] after my shift to see some of the acts, especially Bobby Darin. We either brought our lunch or looked for something special, e.g., the egg rolls at the Chinese place.

CHAPTER TEN

The Great Plains: 1803–1900

*FREEDOMLAND commemorates the proud strug-
gle of the pioneers in its Great Plains area.*

—Freedomland's 1960 Complete Official Guide with Maps

The Great Plains themed section of Freedomland featured the western growth of America from 1803 (the Louisiana Purchase) through 1900. This section of the park included Fort Cavalry, "a log-by-log replica of an army stockade of Indian-fighting days," according to the Freedomland park guide. The fort featured a frontier trading post and chuck wagons for grub. A nearby working farm, sponsored by Borden,was home to Elsie the cow. Animals were found all around the farm and buffalo grazed the surrounding prairies.

The Wells Fargo stage coach line rumbled guests through Rocky Mountain passes. Danger from gangs of desperadoes lurked behind each bend along the route of the Lewis and Clark expedition. To quickly send your message of good or bad news out of town, a Pony Express rider regularly left the fort in a heap of dust to get the mail of every guest to the park's Old Southwest area.

Main Attractions

- Borden's Farm (Elsie's Boudoir) that included animals, corn, and hay.
- Borden's Milk Bar with dairy delights.

- Buffalo Stockade and other animals, too.
- Cavalry Rifles shooting gallery for marksmen of all ages.
- Chuck Wagons around the fort to grab a bite.
- Fort Cavalry was the scene of gunfights at high noon, cowboy and cowgirl demonstrations, and square dancing. A photo studio offered pictures with the cowhands.
- Fort Cavalry Stage Line with a coach ride by Overland Tour on the Lewis and Clark trail.
- Frontier Trading Post for souvenirs.
- Indian Village for a pow-wow.
- Mule-Go-Round was an old-time single mule-drawn merry-go-round.
- Old MacDonald's country-style hay ride.
- Pony Express station with mail service to the Old Southwest.
- Stage coach hold-ups, farmhands, blacksmith shop; trout fishing (for 50 cents) added later.

Fort Cavalry

The frontier stockade fort had gained renewed popularity at the time from movies and the many western shows on television. Various activities occurred within its protective gates, including lessons in square dancing, lasso and gun demonstrations, street fights and shoot-outs by cowboys, arrests by the marshal, a threatened hanging, and the funeral planning for the bad guys by Freedomland undertaker Digger O'Toole.

The Borden Farm: Elsie's Boudoir

The Borden Farm was popularly known as Elsie's Boudoir. Elsie and her twin calves lived in the barn. Guests could enter and visit with the bovine family. Each animal stood in a simulated bed made from hay.

> Time for a stroll down on the farm—Borden's complete, country-style farm in FREEDOMLAND. It's a showplace of our agricultural past, a treat for the millions of city youngsters who've never seen a real farm before. And

everything on Borden's Farm is real—animals, crops, farm buildings and implements—just as you'd see them in an old Midwestern farmyard. Whether you're a dyed-in-the-wool city slicker or an old hand at the plough, you and your whole family will enjoy a visit to Borden's Farm.

You'll see dairy cows in a real cow pasture, and horses grazing in the corral. In the barn, Elsie the cow is in residence, with a corps of attendants. You'll see a working windmill and a big barn silo, a corncrib and a haystack. Watch the ducks navigating in the pond, the hens and chicks gossiping in the poultry house. There are live sheep in the sheepfold, pigs in the pigpen. You'll see a whole field of growing corn, and a country blacksmith shop. There's a Milk Bar, too, at Borden's Farm.

—Freedomland's 1960 Complete
Official Guide with Maps

Elsie was the most popular animal at the park. Her home was designed by the company of William Pahlmann, a prominent New York-based interior designer who popularized the eclectic style of design to accommodate customers' personal taste preferences and stressed the importance of comfort, functionality, and adaptability.

Elsie always was well-coiffed for Freedomland parades. During the opening showcase for the 1962 season, Elsie was fitted with a wig created by Mr. Anthos, a well-known New York City hairdresser. A Freedomland publicity picture of the hairdresser applying the finishing touches appeared in newspapers across the country.

Elsie was in residence only through the 1963 season, moving to the New York World's Fair for 1964. This change of scenery was announced with typical New York fanfare: her appearance (a large depiction of Elsie on a swing held up by a balloon) in the 1963 Macy's Thanksgiving Day Parade.

When Freedomland opened for the 1964 season, a sign at Elsie's Boudoir indicated that she planned to return to the Bronx when the fair closed. Unfortunately, Freedomland closed before the fair. The Freedomland Elsie, though, never actually made it to the fair. Yes, Elsie was at the fair, but it wasn't the

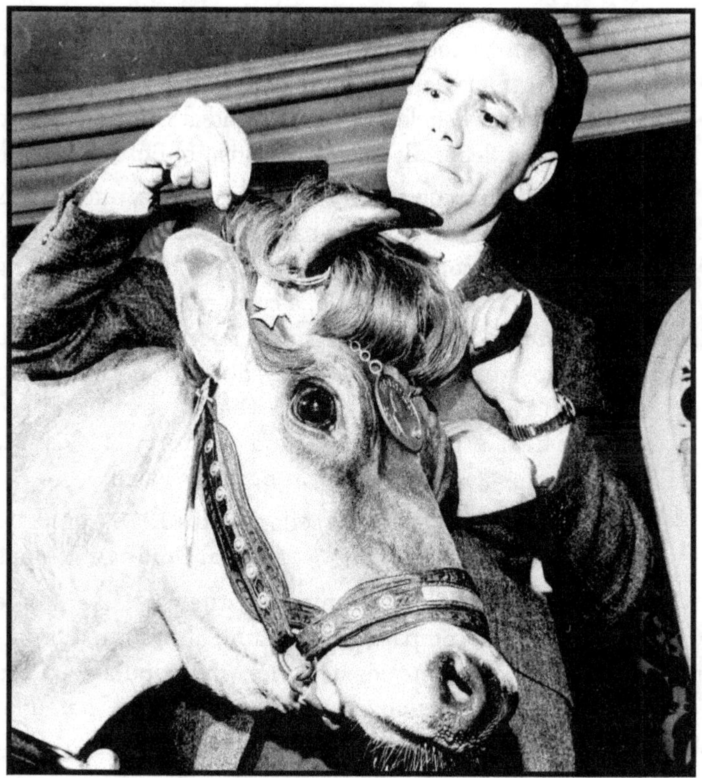

Elsie and her hairdresser. Elsie always looked her best whether at home in her boudoir or during parades and personal appearances.

same cow. At the fair, a Borden executive at the company exhibit explained that "the old Elsie, if you mean the predecessor to this current Elsie, is living a life of luxurious ease on a peaceful farm in upstate New York. She has been retired to green pasture reserved for the senior citizens of cow land."

Stage Coach

The stage coach brought travelers through the west and the Rocky Mountains. Sponsored by American Express, the four coaches of the American Express Overland Tour were created by the Gignac Wagon and Coach Company of Chicago. Some reports indicate that the park actually maintained seven or eight coaches.

American Express Stage Coach. The stage coach makes a splash for these riders as it rumbles through hostile mountain passes. Courtesy Billy Collins.

A driver and a team of four horses drove each of the coaches through mountain passes while encountering buffalo, danger, and the probability of attack by outlaws or Indians. Two horses pulled the coaches after one coach overturned during the first month of the park's operation.

George Oldham was hired when the accident injured the driver. Several passengers suffered serious injuries from the spill. George worked during the 1960 and 1961 seasons. Linda Heikkila, his fiancée, often rode shotgun. She didn't work for Freedomland, but she was allowed to ride along once in a while. They married during the fall of 1961.

Indian Village

An Indian village of teepees and totem poles originally was located in the Chicago area. It was moved to the Great Plains after a couple of seasons. Other Indian experiences at Freedomland included the short-lived Chippewa War Canoes attraction in Chicago and the village that was part of the Northwest Fur Trapper attraction in San Francisco.

CHAPTER ELEVEN

Freedomland's Character Actors

*It's the best thing that's happened to me
in ten summers in New York.*

—John Fortna as Digger O'Toole

Approximately 5,000 original costumes of several hundred styles were designed for Freedomland. The park's promotional information indicated that more than 9,000 different pieces of apparel were used during the 1960 season.

Gordon Weiss was wardrobe director. He provided the same services for Disneyland and then for the 1964–1965 New York World's Fair. With a staff of more than 50 people, the wardrobe unit researched more than 1,000 photos and museum pieces to capture the authentic look for each of the park's themed areas.

Freedomland operated wardrobe buildings for character actors and the many other cast members that included performers for shows at the saloon and Hollywood Arena, clowns, and musicians. Non-actors also required specific Freedomland attire and these employees included security officers, attraction and parking attendants, ticket sellers, restaurant employees, and maintenance workers.

Billy Collins (Billy the Kid)

Some boys who grew up during the 1950s and 1960s wanted to be astronauts. Others wanted to be cowboys, or play for their hometown baseball team. Billy Collins wanted to be a cowboy, and also an Indian chief and a fireman. He succeeded at two of the three—a cowboy at Freedomland and later a firefighter in California.

Billy came from Malverne on Long Island. John Wagerer, the son of Billy's godmother and a cousin through marriage, was an official Freedomland photographer. That's how a kid who was just 15 or 16 at the time was able to don a cowboy hat and holster to earn money at the park. Billy got to the park for the opening 1960 season through his family connection.

"John's office was in the second story of one of the buildings in Little Old New York," recalled Billy. "Sid Ascher [the newspaper and public relations man] was there, too, and wrote much of the park's publicity copy."

Though he was too young to work at the park, Billy used phony identification and his connection to John.

"John was given the photo studio in Fort Cavalry for the 1961 and 1962 seasons, and I worked there along with a couple of young girls," said Billy. "I got dressed up as a cowboy and took

Gunfight at Fort Cavalry. The marshal is the last man standing. John Conant (foreground), Bob Oran (upper left), Mike Hill (lower right), Billy Collins (upper right). Courtesy Billy Collins.

pictures with the park guests. Maybe it cost them a buck to take a picture with a Freedomland cowboy. Cast members also were often asked to be in photos and would do so on breaks between performances. I must have been in hundreds of shots, all of them black and white Polaroids. We stood in front of western scenery that had been created by the park's scenery painters."

Billy also became one of the cowboys in the demonstrations and gun fights. His stage name was Billy Cane and he had to join the AFTRA (American Federation of Television and Radio Artists) actors union. One of the older cowboy actors, Bob Oran, tagged him with the nickname Billy the Kid, an obvious decision considering Billy's name and age.

"Bob was one of the originals and quite a character. He was my best friend among the cowboys at the park," recalled Billy. "In 1961, the song "Barbara Ann" became a hit. We changed the lyrics a bit whenever Bob showed up to the dressing room to get into character. Instead of Ba-ba-ba ba Barbara Ann, we would sing Bob-Bob-Bob-Bob-Bob Oran. He didn't like it!

"All the cowboys took turns as the good guys and bad guys. I often stayed overnight in one of the dressing rooms that was located in the second story of one of the San Francisco buildings. The Northwest Fur Trapper ride was nearby and the sound effects ran all night and you would hear the animals and other sounds at all hours."

When he wasn't sleeping at the park, Billy stayed at the apartment building of one of his girlfriends. He would sleep on the roof, which residents of the Bronx popularly called "tar beach" during the summer. Billy's girl during 1962 was Janice Hall, a Bronx girl who worked at a jewelry shop next to Casa Loca.

Besides the guys, a few cowgirls were part of the Wild West scene at Freedomland. Actress and singer Alice Scott briefly portrayed Jane Freedom and Annie Oakley. Another performer, Margie Walker, also portrayed Annie for a short time.

"Margie didn't appear often," said Billy. "She was a Broadway actress and singer. Her act was to shoot and hit cans off one of the railings. The cans were blown away by air jets."

During his off time, Billy would wander through the park. But, he would always be in costume, which was not appreciated by the park managers. Imagine a dusty cowboy in Satellite City!

"I was reported several times for being in other locations instead of confined to the fort area or the other western locations," said Billy. "But I couldn't be fired, because of my relationship with Freedomland's photographer."

Billy often watched shows at the Hollywood Arena. One act involved an older man with trained dogs. He also remembered Ann Williams, the young and attractive elephant trainer, and he watched her lay on the ground as the elephant sat on her. He also remembered a guy they called Billy the Elephant Boy who was from the south and cleaned up after the elephants.

"The park issued us actual guns and holsters," said Billy. "Bob Oran, though, brought his own two nickel-plated pistols. We gave one of the Freedomland guns to Billy the Elephant Boy and something happened. It blew up in his hand and almost took off his thumb."

Another mishap that Billy recalled was an evening when one of the cables on the Tucson Mining Company ore bucket ride snapped and all the gondolas attached to that cable fell to the ground. No one was in them at the time as the ride had already closed for the evening.

Billy remembered a couple of other Freedomland cowboys—Mike Hill ("he was really nice") and Teddy Burrell (spelling of surname questionable; "I think he was of Lebanese background")—but didn't know much more about them or what they did after leaving Freedomland. He also recalled a fellow named Sam [probably Sam Stewart], who also was the union shop steward.

"He was an ever-present, great guy," said Billy. "We called him 'Whispering Sam.' He got this title because Bob Oran accidentally punched him in the throat and he lost his voice for months."

Billy said the park had many character actors who kept coming and going as they worked at other venues that included the Broadway stage. Billy does remember John Fortna (Digger O'Toole) very well and said he looked much different when not in costume ("he was a tall, handsome guy who was very nice to everyone"). Billy also recalled William Zeckendorf, Sr., coming into the park in his car with "Z" for the license plate and seeing many of the celebrity performers at the Moon Bowl.

"I have a picture of myself in regular clothes and surrounded by girls as I hand out my autograph. Paul Anka was performing and he had to stop giving out his autograph at the side door to get backstage to prepare for his show. The girls were told that I was his brother and they were just happy to have an autograph from an Anka. There is a security officer in the photo that was taken by my cousin, the Freedomland photographer. They were all in on the prank."

During and after his Freedomland days, Billy attended art schools (Pan American and Art Students League) in Manhattan. He also was part of the short-lived "The Gunfighters" that were booked for all kinds of shows, from fairs to corporate events. The group consisted of Billy, Bob Oran, John Conant (the singing sheriff during the first few seasons of Freedomland; stage name Johnny Steele), and Margie Walker. Eventually, Billy moved to California. He didn't star in any westerns, but he was a Hollywood advertising art director and graphic designer prior to becoming a firefighter for both the Orange County and Los Angeles County fire departments. He continues to love the old days and is in the process of remodeling a home built during the Wild West days of 1887.

Donald Crabtree (Johnny Freedom)

Donald Crabtree spent several years as a featured performer at Freedomland. He portrayed Johnny Freedom, the prominent fictional character of the park. According to the publicity material associated with Freedomland and the song "Johnny Freedom" recorded by Johnny Horton, "Johnny Freedom is the image of the American spirit. He was reared in America's past, he lives in America's present and his future will be fulfilled in America's dreams and aspirations. Johnny Freedom is the embodiment of Freedomland U.S.A. where all of America comes to life."

From Borger, Texas, Donald was raised in Oklahoma. A proud member of the Choctaw Nation of Oklahoma, he attended East Central University in Ada, where he held a 30-year track record. He then worked in the Colorado oil fields and, due to his horse-riding skills, with local rodeos. After a two-year stint in the U.S. Army, he moved his family to New York to allow him to pursue a career in music and entertainment.

Donald's long Broadway career included *Destry Rides Again, The Happiest Girl in the World, A Family Affair, The Unsinkable Molly Brown, Sophie, 110 in the Shade, Golden Boy, Pousse-Café, The Best Little Whore House in Texas*, and *42nd Street*. On the big screen, he appeared in *Texas, The Edge of Night, A Man Called Adam*, and *The Hustler*. On television, he was seen on *The Ed Sullivan Show, The Bell Telephone Hour, The Red Skelton Show, Dark Shadows, The Edge of Night*, and many commercials.

John Fortna (Digger O'Toole)

The most beloved personality at Freedomland—undertaker Digger O'Toole in the Wild West—was portrayed by John Fortna. Digger was friendly with children, provided them and adults with his business card, raised a shovel at an outlaw ready to be hanged (and predicted that the outlaw would meet his maker sooner if he could just swing the heavy shovel), and measured the deceased outlaws for the pine box. While John became Digger O'Toole at Freedomland, his acting skills provided unique opportunities before and after his work at the park.

During 1951, the musical comedy *Where's Charley?* appeared at the Broadway Theatre for 48 performances (January 29 through March 10) with Ray Bolger, who reprised his roll from the 748 performance run at the St. James Theatre that started near the end of 1948. John appears in the show credits for the 1951 show. He was one of the cast singers and also the understudy for the role of Sir Francis Chesney, a clueless single father in financial difficulty. John was about 26 years old at the time.

As part of the Freedomland publicity machine, a 1960 national article about John and other Freedomland actors was distributed to newspapers across the country by the Newspaper Enterprise Association:

> The undertaker is a picture of professional sorrow as he measures the dead gunman for a coffin. But, underneath, he's perfectly delighted with his lot. In fact John

Billy and Digger. Billy Collins (Billy the Kid) is just another customer for John Fortna (Digger O'Toole). Courtesy Billy Collins.

Fortna couldn't be happier. He does his undertaking at Freedomland. About once an hour, a gunfight erupts in the "Western" town's streets and Fortna prepares for action. Regular as clockwork, two quick-draws shoot it out; one goes down; the other is captured by the sheriff. And then Fortna swoops down on the scene with his tape measure and sorrowful clucks.

John said that he faced a summer of unemployment compensation before he scored the Freedomland role. When asked about the number of actors who were employed at the park, he could not provide specifics, because not all actors were in acting jobs. John and his fellow western characters were covered by a regular American Guild of Variety Artists (AGVA) contract that did not represent actors who secured summer incomes as railroad workers, Pony Express riders, and concession staffers.

John was 35 years old when Freedomland opened. During previous summers, he had worked in summer stock, sung with a quartet, and was a stage manager for industrial shows. For 1960, he had three stage managing jobs lined up before each one fizzled and he faced a summer as bleak as an undertaker's face. That was until Freedomland opened.

"It's the best thing that's happened to me in 10 summers in New York," said John in the article. "I make a darned good salary—about what a character actor would average if he worked all summer, which he could never do."

The role of Digger O'Toole was strictly improvisation. John thought this was "wonderful." He did not have any lines to memorize. He did not need to listen to a director and he did not need to stand on any chalk lines. John and his fellow cast members, according to the article, "play it differently each time, exercise their histrionic muscles and, they feel, gain in acting prowess by this constant experimentation."

John first looked at the job as a way of eating well during the summer. Then, he thought the Digger O'Toole character could advance his career. Television programs at the park and the ongoing publicity cast the spotlight on him. Since he portrayed a friendly undertaker who always carried a shovel with a ribbon tied into a bow, he felt that he would be the most photographed actor at the park. He also was the only character actor with a business card. The back of the card changed slightly from season to season. That change depended on the sponsor of the season and sponsors included Green Stamps and King Korn Stamps.

In the years following the closing of Freedomland, just a trace can be found about John. It seems he just disappeared from acting work, or credits could not be located for his appearances. The only post-Freedomland "sighting" that has surfaced was a mention in a Florida newspaper column.

John Fortna Offers Course To Church Leaders

John Fortna, longtime New York actor and speech specialist, has just returned to Sarasota from a stay with Mr. and Mrs. Ralph Evinrude of Jensen Beach. Mrs. Evinrude, better known as musical comedy and screen star Frances Langford, reviewed plans with Fortna for his scheduled free vocal dynamics seminar entitled Making "The Word" Heard for area church leaders and teachers. The two-hour course in speech improvement will be offered Aug. 29 from 7:30 to 9:30 p.m. at the Presbyterian Chapel on Siesta Key. The workshop is free to all those involved in speaking to small or large groups as part of church-related activities.

—*Sarasota Herald Tribune*, August 14, 1983

Albert A. Hecker, Jr. ("Colossus" Horseman)

For the 1961 season, "Colossus" was a Freedomland-created extravaganza that featured horsemanship and other spectacles from history. Among the participants was the late Albert Arnold Heckler, Jr. His daughter, Victoria Heckler, shared her father's story.

Al was born in Brooklyn during 1935. When he was about four or five years old, he ran away from home and was found at Coney Island.

"So, he always had a fondness for amusement parks," said Victoria. "A neighbor boy in Brooklyn had a horse that he wasn't riding much, so his father asked my father if he would like to ride it. That's how he learned to ride."

The family relocated to Bethel, Connecticut, during 1950. Al attended Henry Abbott Technical School and, at 15, he left school when he received his journeyman license in electronics. At about this same time, Al started to work for Bud Chase, a rodeo stock contractor from Kent, Connecticut.

"It was like you see in the old westerns, where the farm hands lived in bunkhouses and all ate meals together," added Victoria. "My dad traveled the local rodeo circuit with the

Chase family and, at times, competed as a bull and bronco rider. By his own admission, he 'wasn't very good.' He also worked as a rodeo clown. During the 1950s and 1960s, dude ranches were very popular in New York State and in parts of Connecticut. They would put on rodeo shows at various ranches such as Cimarron Ranch in Putnam Valley, New York, or at state and county fairs."

Al enlisted in the U.S. Army in 1955 and he was assigned to boot camp and basic training at Fort Dix, New Jersey. He remained in the U.S. Army Reserves until he was honorably discharged at the end of 1962.

"He worked at Freedomland while he was in the reserves," said Victoria. "My aunt told a story of how she once brought a family friend, a young boy, to Freedomland to see my father in the show and to this day that friend still

A "Colossus" star. Al Heckler appeared as a cowboy, a Russian Cossack, and an Arabian horseman. Courtesy Victoria Heckler.

counts that visit as one of the best days of his life. Clearly, Freedomland was something special."

After "Colossus," Al worked at various dude ranches in upstate New York, ending up at Arrowhead Ranch in Parksville as a barn foreman and one of the ranch managers. Victoria's mother and her mother's sisters often were weekend guests at the ranch, taking a bus from New York City on Friday nights and returning home on Sunday evenings.

"That's how my folks met," recalled Victoria. "They were married during the early 1970s and eventually settled down in Danbury, where my father owned a television repair company.

Al died in 2010 from emphysema. The last time Victoria saw him on a horse was when she worked at a horse farm in Westchester County during the mid-1990s.

"He came by one evening and we put his old saddle on this big black quarter horse we used for lessons. He took the horse around the arena a couple times, putting him through his paces, and for a few minutes it seemed as if he forgot he was sick.

"My father spoke very fondly of Freedomland, and although it was long gone before I was born, I remember him pointing out the last few remnants of it whenever we drove past the location on our way to visit family in Brooklyn."

Entertainment definitely is in the Heckler family genes. Al's grandfather, Professor William Heckler, was the veritable Barnum of bugs. The professor and his son, Professor Roy Heckler, ran the flea circus at Hubert's Museum that was located at 228 West 42nd Street from about 1923 until 1957.

"When my father was a young boy," added Victoria, "his grandfather would pay him for each flea he'd pick off his dog and bring to him for his circus. So I guess my father always had a bit of showman in him!"

Bob Oran (Cowboy)

Stocky New York-based stuntman Bob Oransky, professionally credited as Bob Oran, was a former boxer and barnstorming professional wrestler known as both the Cowboy and the Masked Marvel. The late stuntman appeared at Freedomland as a cowboy and can be seen in some of the pictures with children that survive in family albums.

A veteran of World War II, Bob performed as Black Bob in Wild West shows. During his career, he was a Brahma bull rider and a private investigator. He also became known in the film industry as a masseur to the stars.

Bob worked as a stuntman on films such as *Saratoga Truck* (1945), *Mister Universe* (1951), the Kirk Douglas/Eli Wallach film *A Lovely Way to Die* (uncredited, 1968), and on television shows such as *NYPD*, *Coronet Blue*, and in an episode ("Ticker Tape," February 24, 1959) of *Naked City*.

During rehearsals of *Mister Universe*, a romantic comedy about the wrestling business, a number of stuntmen, including Bob, suffered injuries. While demonstrating the art of falling out of the ring to actor Vince Edwards (later television's Dr. Ben Casey), Bob caught his foot in the rope, fell on his face, and suffered multiple contusions.

Bob appeared as an actor in a few of Doris Wishman's soft-core films of the late 1960s such as *My Brother's Wife* (1966), *Another Day, Another Man* (1966), and *Too Much Too Often!* (1968). He had one executive producer movie credit, as Robert Oran, for the 1966 adult film *The Girl from S.I.N.* He also appeared in the film but is uncredited.

Madeline Joyce "Joy" (Eichler) Robichaud (Young Annie Oakley)

She claims to have been a shy girl, but this young version of Annie Oakley from Bathgate Avenue and other Bronx locations certainly matured and "got her guns" with a unique acting experience at Freedomland.

Madeline Joyce "Joy" (Eichler) Robichaud was about 13 when Freedomland opened. She visited the park that first year with her mother and a good friend.

"I was interested in theater and shows and I had performed in children's theater," recalled Joy. "My interest in acting increased after winning a newspaper essay contest and meeting Patty Duke and Suzanne Pleshette backstage during the Broadway run of *The Miracle Worker*. When we visited Freedomland during the 1961 season, I met Margie Walker. She was a western performer, having taken over the Annie Oakley role through the 1962 season and appearing on stage in the Opera House. Her wardrobe included jeans, red shirt, tan cowboy hat, and short black boots, and her hair was in pig tails. She was one of the many stunt and other actors hired by the park. I remember that she also was a hand model."

Joy loved the Freedomland experience. She collected autographs (including Paul Anka, Harry James, and Captain Jack McCarthy) and was interested in working at the park. But, she was too young.

"Margie told me that everyone, including cowboys Bob Oran and Sam Stewart, liked having me around," said Joy. "I told them I was older than I actually was. They believed me and Margie suggested that I meet them at 8:30 each morning at the employee entrance. I would dress in my own western clothes. They taught me some of the stunts and I was an actor in training. They taught me how to shoot the rifles with blanks and how to jump off the roofs of the buildings and land in cardboard boxes."

Joy eventually discovered an opportunity to make some money by working in Freedomland's Wild West through the final season.

"I was told to see Elmer Attean, better known as Chief Black Hawk," said Joy. "Freedomland hired actual Native Americans from the Penobscot Tribe in Old Town, Maine, for its Indian village. Elmer was accompanied by his daughter, Rene, and son, Brian. They were wonderful people. Park guests would have pictures taken, those instant Polaroids, with the Atteans for a few dollars. To make the photographs more authentic, they asked me to be in many of the pictures as Annie Oakley and I was joined by my friend who had become an Indian girl. For a time, I was living near the park with her and her family. On one busy day, we made so much money from the pictures that we decided to take a cab to work the next day.

"I worked from dawn to dusk at the park," continued Joy. "Since I was not employed by Freedomland but did much more than just appear in pictures, a handful of actors were very kind to chip in $20 each per week from their earnings to provide me with about $120 each week."

As an aspiring actress, Joy sang at the park's Opera House as the Annie Oakley understudy for Margie. While exploring other areas of the park, Joy also came across opportunities that were not common among 1960s Bronx teenagers.

"The Flying Wallendas performed at Freedomland and they taught me how to walk a tight rope and swing by my feet from a trapeze," laughed Joy. "Ann Williams, who was the elephant trainer, taught me how to ride the elephant. I would meet her often for dinner and we would just talk. I learned so much about her life as an elephant trainer."

Other memories recalled by Joy involved a famous singer and a popular park store. During an appearance, Pat Boone presented her with an airline promotional ring. ("I still have it," said Joy.) She remembers, also, that her favorite shop in the park was the glassblowers' store in Little Old New York.

"Each payday, I would get a new animal and I had about 20 pieces," said Joy. "I then had an interview to appear in the off-Broadway production of *The Glass Menagerie* and I brought the collection with me. It helped me get the part. The animals were used in the production, but all eventually were destroyed accidentally. I still have a little teddy bear from the shop that was given to me by Mike McGlinn, who worked in the hat shop at the time."

During the last year of Freedomland, when many of the character actors were told not to return, Joy and her friend continued to find work at the park.

"During the previous years, since we were younger than 16, we often hid in the dressing rooms whenever the labor department paid a visit," said Joy. "In that last season, we again took matters into our own hands and during down time we would do some unusual things in the park. One involved the Northwest Fur Trapper ride and specifically the saloon that contained all the cowboy skeletons. We would get into that area and come up with some antics. The people on the ride did not know if we were real or not."

Joy and the other performers were heartbroken when Freedomland closed.

Billy the Kid and Annie Oakley. Billy Collins and Madeline Joyce "Joy" (Eichler) Robichaud take a picture in a Freedomland photo studio. Courtesy Billy Collins/Madeline Joyce "Joy" (Eichler) Robichaud.

"My friend and I walked right in after it closed and took some souvenirs," recalled Joy. "It was the most wonderful adventure. It was a four-year show for me. The summers were special and my family came to see me. I grew so much in those few years."

Since her Freedomland days, Joy has been a photographer for the *Hartford Courant* in Connecticut and also a personal trainer for people with physical challenges. She now lives in Arizona and teaches improvised dance to children.

"I recall fondly one woman years ago in Connecticut who I was helping when I was a trainer," said Joy, "and one day she asked me to retrieve several stored photo albums for her. One book contained pictures from Freedomland. While looking through the albums with her, to our surprise there was a photo of her son—and I was in the picture!"

Ben Rossi (Cowboy, Entertainer, Producer)

While young Freedomlanders may not recognize the name of Ben Rossi, he created a considerable amount of entertainment for park guests in the Bronx and at parks around the world.

As early as five years of age, Ben was performing at carnivals and fairs. He was a trick roper and then became a trick rider and circus acrobat when he reached seven. Ben first came to Freedomland at the age of 21 to appear in the 1961 "Colossus" show. He portrayed an American cowboy in the show's "Greatest Horsemen in History" segment. He also performed stunts as a Roman. The stunts included acrobatics, vaults, cartwheels, and shoulder stands atop Navajo, his palomino. His new bride, Vickie, portrayed Lady Guinevere in the medieval jousting part of the show.

Ben returned to Freedomland as the sheriff for the 1963 and 1964 seasons. Park executive Art Moss, who supervised the park's publicity and shows, also asked Ben to appear as a park performer with his horse and as a show producer.

Following Freedomland, Ben became an entertainment director at several small amusement parks in Florida; directed action scenes and sequences for television commercials, television programs, and films; and joined Walt Disney World and its various venues to create shows. He left Disney during 1984 to form his own entertainment company that produced live cowboy shows for the Disney park and other parks like Six Flags Over Texas, Marine World in California, and locations in Germany and Taiwan.

When he arrived at Freedomland for the first time, Ben said that he drove into the most magnificent place he had ever seen. A security guard escorted him and Navajo to the stables. He appreciated everything about Freedomland, from the attractions to the guests to seeing the well-known entertainment stars who performed at the Moon Bowl. He and his wife enjoyed the Brass Rail steakhouse along with many of the attractions, including the dark rides and the Tucson Mining Company ore buckets.

For the scaled-back last season, when most of the costumed entertainers were not retained, Ben was asked to generate income as an independent contractor for the park. He and several other performers proposed charging admission for daily shows in the Santa Fe Opera House and Saloon. Ben earned more from these shows than his Freedomland contract had provided him in the previous years.

Ben loved Freedomland. When comparing parks of the day, he ranked Freedomland at the top ahead of Disneyland. He cited the larger size of the Bronx park, the theme of American history versus Disney fantasy, that it had some of the most creative minds behind it, and that it attracted leading entertainment.

Until a few years ago, Ben maintained a website that featured his career in the entertainment industry. He had included this memory on the Freedomland section of the site:

> Of all the theme parks with which I have been associated, including the fabulous and remarkable Walt Disney World, none has left me with nostalgic recollections as treasured as those of Freedomland USA, because of the park's straightforward celebration of America, and her illustrious history.

Other Freedomland Actors And Entertainers

Many actors were scattered throughout the Freedomland themed sections and a significant number of them maintained Broadway, television, and other credits.

John Conant, as previously mentioned, was the singing sheriff in the west who also made more than 1,000 appearances in a variety of musicals as a member of stock companies. According to one cowboy actor at the park, John was perceived as aloof and never interacted with the other employees.

Nick Navarro, of Cuban heritage, portrayed a Pancho Villa-type character. He rode a burro named Rosie because she carried a large rose on her reins, and he played guitar, but no additional information is available about him. Frank "Tex" Shuwahe was a cowboy who often wore the deputy sheriff badge. Mel Tyler portrayed the old-time politician who walked through the streets in Little Old New York. He was a comic who appeared in night clubs, stock, burlesque, and vaudeville.

Actors also arrived from other venues, including several from Pleasure Island, Freedomland's sister park in New England. These performers included Ormond Davis, Charmaine Harma, and Clyde V. "Buddy" Farnan, Jr.

Ormond played the Old Prospector and joined Freedomland for the 1960 season. A singer, songwriter, and actress, Charmaine performed at New York City nightclubs, at the Pleasure Island saloon, and then at the Freedomland saloon for the opening season. Buddy hailed from Buffalo, New York. He became a magician, actor, and a song-and-dance man. He was the first general manager at Buffalo's Fantasy Island and he worked at parks in Atlanta and Chicago. Along the way, he made the transition into television, radio and advertising.

Many stuntmen and horse riders worked the Freedomland "Colossus" show during the 1961 season. Personal appearances to promote the park included the clowns Buttons & Bows (Hal and Rheba Malvey) along with Ben Rossi and Navajo. One such appearance occurred at the Roosevelt Field Shopping Mall on Long Island. During the early seasons, one of the stage coaches filled with park performers often took to the streets for parades and other local events that included appearances in the Macy's Thanksgiving Day Parade.

CHAPTER 12

San Francisco: 1906

*Welcome to San Francisco, where life is lived
to the hilt—at the earthquake's edge.*

—Freedomland's 1960 Complete Official Guide with Maps

The west coast of Freedomland featured San Francisco of 1906. On April 18 of that year, the ground shook violently. Fifty years later, the park re-created the quake with a dark ride.

One of the two stops on the Santa Fe Railroad was located here. From the station, guests descended stairs to Montgomery Street, Grant Avenue, and Pacific Street that featured Chinatown and its shops, Seaman's Hall, the Barbary Coast of carefree entertainment, and Fisherman's Wharf, where old salts mended their nets and told fish tales of Pacific sailing days.

Just a bit north into the Pacific Northwest, guests piled into bullboats for a trip along the Columbia and Snake rivers, passing a menacing moose, an Indian Trading Post, and a ghost town where the residents, including the horses, were bare bones.

Main Attractions

- Barbary Coast showcased the city's glittering entertainment district.
- Chinatown and Oriental Bazaar featured the Chun King Restaurant.
- Earthquake attraction (dark ride) simulated the catastrophe.
- Fisherman's Wharf with its group activities.

- Hollywood Arena (added 1961) featured music, circus, and other shows, the 1961 "Colossus" spectacle, and the Dancing Waters.
- Horse-drawn surreys to the Old Southwest.
- Little Pizza Restaurant and an Italian gift shop.
- Northwest Fur Trapper boat ride with nearby Indian Trading Post.
- A&W Root Beer Stand (added 1962).
- Santa Fe Railroad (San Francisco Station).
- Seal Rock with Pacific seals.

The official description for San Francisco read:

This is San Francisco—the Gold Rush days are still a living memory, the vigilantes are now some of the town's most respected citizens, the wild youth of the city has passed—but not quite. 'Frisco in 1906 is still something of a boom town, with all the raw vigor and generous excitement of the old Far West. Welcome to San Francisco, where life is lived to the hilt—at the earthquake's edge.

On April 18, 1906, the ground fell from under San Francisco's feet. You will safely see the San Francisco earthquake and fire re-created in harrowing detail. You will ride past buckling sidewalks, open fissures and collapsing buildings. You will see houses slide sideways and crack in two, then burst into flames. These thrills are yours in FREEDOMLAND's San Francisco Earthquake ride.

San Francisco is America's golden gateway to the Orient, and you'll find a corner of the Far East in FREEDOMLAND's Chinatown. Visit the colorful Oriental Bazaar, and dine on oriental delicacies at the Chinese restaurant. This is Chinatown as it really was— before San Francisco tumbled down and put itself back together again.

—Freedomland's 1960 Complete
Official Guide with Maps

Chinese Junks and Harbor Seals

The two Chinese junks in San Francisco Bay were built in Hong Kong. They were not billed as attractions but rather placed in the artificial bay to convey the authenticity of the themed area. The junks did not offer rides and guests were not allowed on board.

The seal pool featured Pacific harbor seals. Guests were able to purchase fish to feed to the seals. Unlike all the other animals in the park, the seals remained at Freedomland during the off seasons. During the winters, heaters were floated in the water. Park personnel regularly would check on the seals and break any ice. When necessary, the pool was drained, cleaned, and refilled. While the junks did not cause any trouble for park employees, the seals were a bit more rambunctious.

"Two seals turned up on roadways in the Bronx Thursday night and snarled traffic until they were taken in tow," reported an Associated Press news story that appeared in the December 28, 1962, issues of newspapers across the country. "The first one reported was a tan 100-pound female. The second was a 300-pound black bull about six feet long. The seals had escaped from the Freedomland Amusement Park in the Bronx."

The lady seal was loaded into a radio police car. Arthur Thornton of the American Society for the Prevention of Cruelty to Animals appeared with a truck and a lasso to capture the male. The seal, though, simply jumped into the truck.

Earthquake

While waiting on line for this dark ride, park guests listened to a recorded commentary about the devastating quake. A painted mural at the ride's loading area featured the ruined skyline of the city.

The Arrow Development attraction (eleven cars that each seated four passengers) took guests on a wild ride of very sharp turns through the streets of San Francisco. Prior to the quake, people were seen dancing at parties. From a safe distance, riders then witnessed houses that split and burst into flames, sidewalks that buckled, huge fissures that opened in the streets and then a person who popped his head out from a trash can. For effect, what appeared to be a rotating drum was suspended from the ceiling inside the attraction. The drum was filled with objects that added the sounds of breaking glass and falling masonry.

> Guests were transported in antique automobiles. Once inside, you found yourself "driving" on the streets of San Francisco, the evening before the disaster. People could be seen dancing the night away; oblivious to their fate. Your route travelled thru Chinatown and along the Barbary Coast, where an errant sailor was tossed from the waterfront saloon into the path of your horseless carriage. Suddenly, buildings began to shake and quiver. A two-story house slid off its foundations, right towards you. Frightened residents could be seen in the windows of the collapsing buildings. It was a thrill to be the "driver" during this adventure as you "steered" around buckling sidewalks and falling debris. Painted murals illustrated the destruction in graphic detail. At the climax, the great fire was depicted by the use of flickering orange lights and silhouettes of burned out buildings.
>
> —A childhood memory shared in *Building Disney's Dream: Arrow Development: The Little Company That Could* by Dexter Francis

Northwest Fur Trapper

Moving into the Pacific Northwest, an adventure-packed ride on a bull boat (sometimes spelled as one word by the park) occurred along the Columbia and Snake rivers. Passengers were taken on a narrated journey that featured a number of special effects as the Northwest Fur Trapper attraction relived the perils and the thrills of an expedition of the 1820s. The land featured the industrious (beavers building a damn), calm (a bull moose grazing on the shore), and dangerous (a cougar) animals, along with warlike Indians.

"Everybody down!" exclaimed Freedomland promotional material. "It's an ambush by Totempole Indians, and they're firing at 'you!' Look out! That cougar almost leaped in the boat. Careful of that falling tree! Duck, you're right under a collapsing bridge! Thrill follows thrill, but every risk is a calculated one—calculated to give you the time of your life, controlled to bring you through in absolute safety. You'll relive every danger of the old trapping days, but you'll be harmed by none."

At the entrance to the attraction was a 20+-foot cutout figure of Paul Bunyan. After Freedomland closed, the figure spent time in an architectural wreckage business in Stamford, Connecticut. It was sold during the 1970s or 1980s, but the company's records did not identify the buyer.

The attraction's thirty-two-and-one-half-foot fiberglass boats were constructed from a mold and built by the Minneford Yacht Yard on nearby City Island for $38,000. The nine boats (each carried 35 passengers) replicated the bull boats used by the explorers of the Northwest Passage.

Freedomland hired Winfield H. Hubbard's Denver company, Special Effects, to design the animation. Originally from the movie industry, specifically MGM, he supervised special effects for Magic Mountain in nearby Golden and later

Bull Boat. Park guests enjoy the dangerous guided boat tour through the Pacific Northwest. Courtesy Billy Collins.

he was associated with Six Flags Over Texas. Freedomland purchased Hubbard's animation for $95,000. The company also charged $2,395 for nine vintage guns and $1,475 for five cannons used on the ride. Records prior to the opening of Freedomland indicated that the total budget for the attraction was $426,000.

An infrared light triggered the props that interacted with park guests. The collapsed bridge narrowly missed the boat. A family of bears proved threatening until the guide fired his pistol. The Indian village included canoes, totem poles and teepees, and a shootout between the tribe and settlers placed boat passengers in the middle of the skirmish.

The attraction included an actual Boot Hill cemetery with a large pair of cowboy boots placed among the headstones. The moose once was real and cost the park about $10,000. The Skeleton Town saloon scene included skeleton gunfighters, a dude hanging from a tree, another guy fishing and catching a fish of just bones, and a horse that also was bare bones. Remnants of the ride, including the wood pilings, cement dock, and foliage could still be seen when the housing complex rose farther north on the property.

Many Freedomland employees considered the role of boat captain on this attraction to be one of the coolest jobs in the park. They were dressed in buckskins or other clothes of the period. The park's cowboys also sometimes became involved with this attraction. Between their shows, the cowboys would sit among the scenes of stationary figures and pull their hats over their eyes. As the boats moved close, they would leap up and run toward the boats to frighten the passengers.

The Hollywood Arena

The Hollywood Arena was added for the 1961 season. The first major event was "Colossus," a spectacular production created exclusively for Freedomland. The show primarily is remembered as a Roman gladiator spectacle, an odd addition to an American history theme park. Besides chariot races, gladiators in mortal combat and king Arthur's Knights in a jousting tournament, the show included the Three Musketeers, the Charge of the Bengal Lancers, Russian Cossacks, Argentine gauchos, and a portion referred to as the Greatest Horsemen of History. The cast included about 25 people and several dozen horses.

The show explored the history of horsemanship through the centuries and incorporated a variety of difficult stunts that resulted in a number of injuries, from twisted limbs to wounds from swords and jousting poles. Some of the talented horsemen fell off the horses. One of the most serious accidents involved a horse maneuver known as a weave in which horses from opposite sides of the arena galloped toward each other with each horse crisscrossing past the others. The sequence was for eight horses, but one horse was removed when its rider suffered an injury. With only seven horses to produce the weave, confusion occurred and two horses reportedly collided and died.

The 30-minute show was staged four times daily through the summer. It was produced by Sandy Howard, a Bronx native who lived in nearby Yonkers. He entered show business as a teenage publicist for Broadway shows, going on to direct the *Howdy*

Chariots race across the Hollywood Arena. Behind the park sign is the Hutchinson River Parkway. The open land immediately past the parkway later would become the final section of the Co-op City housing complex.

Doody Show and *Captain Kangaroo* on TV. He also produced radio talk shows and 72 films, including *A Man Called Horse*.

Other performances at the arena included elephant, tiger, and chimpanzee acts; the Hamid-Morton Circus with its clowns and daredevil performers that included the plunge of Suicide Stanley; aerial acts and acrobats; trick-car exhibitions; and musical entertainment that hailed from Munich, Paris, London, and elsewhere. Several of New York City's hosts of television kids shows—Office Joe Bolton, Sonny Fox, Claude Kirchner, and Fred Scott—appeared at the venue. The Hollywood Arena also was the site of the Dancing Waters, an array of fountains brilliantly and colorfully lit as the water soared upward in time to music.

CHAPTER THIRTEEN

The Old Southwest: 1890

FREEDOMLAND rolled three of Arizona's and New Mexico's most ornery towns into one: Tucson, Tombstone, and old Santa Fé.

—Freedomland's 1960 Complete Official Guide with Maps

By the time park guests arrived in the Old Southwest of 1890, the Pony Express rider already had delivered their messages to the local express office. The Tucson Mining Company soon would carry them high over the dry gulch in ore buckets to provide an aerial coast-to-coast view of the park. The Burro Trail was another mode of transportation. Eight mules moved as a pack to scale the Bronx version of the Rocky Mountains. The park planned for 10 packs of mules for the opening season and the weight limit of riders was 160 pounds.

To see the activity in the mines, the Mine Caverns dark ride employed train cars. Park guests rolled underground and darn close to the caves and bubbling lava pits that were home to giant bats and beetles, and spine-chilling cave monsters. After this experience, it was time to get back above ground and visit one of the few houses in the territory. But, Casa Loca was not a typical house. In Freedomland's version of a tilt house, everything was topsy-turvy.

Finally, a place to relax with a bit of eats and sarsaparilla could be found at the Opera House and Saloon, also known as the Music Hall. Silent films sometimes entertained guests. At other times, a play similar to those that entertained Americans on the frontier would command the stage. *Go West Young Man* might be on the bill, or audiences would enjoy a cabaret show with a band, singers, and a comedian.

"It's the sort of lively, hilarious fun that brought the prospectors in from miles around," according to Freedomland's promotional description. "*Every* night is Saturday night in *this* old mining town."

While more than a one-horse town, only a couple of roads—the Alameda and Quadalupe Street—raised the dust. The Chihauhua Trail led folks out of town and on to New Orleans.

Main Attractions

- Burro Trail across the Rockies.
- Casa Loca, the house where everything stood on its head.
- Libby's Hacienda, or Libby's Frito House restaurant.
- Mexican Market featured shopping.
- Mine Caverns (dark ride) showed guests the mysterious world under the earth.
- Pony Express Station with mail service to Fort Cavalry.
- Santa Fe Opera House and Saloon also became known as the Western Saloon and Opera House, the Music Hall, and the Red Garter Saloon; it was the Wild West show palace.
- Santa Fe Railroad Station (not a stop, but a small building for storage and usually where bandits boarded the train).
- Tucson Mining Company sent guests high above Freedomland in an iron ore bucket.
- Western Trading Post featured more shopping.
- Texas Longhorn herd (Louis Pasteur was the park's director of livestock), gunfights, meeting with the Old Prospector and wranglers.

Casa Loca

From the early 1900s through the 1980s, walk-through crooked houses were popular attractions in the U.S. Each house took on the appearance of a regular house or cabin until a person ventured inside. The attraction was known by a variety of names over the years, including Mystery House, Tilt House, Tipsy House, Whacky Shack, and Slanty Shanty. In the Bronx, you entered Casa Loca.

The Trick House was created during 1904 with tilted floors. Functioning windows did not exist, preventing a view of the outside world that would destroy the illusion. During 1923, the Amusement House added new features such as objects that seemed to roll uphill. The Amusement Structure of 1924 added multiple rooms. A few years later, flowing water defied gravity. Originally designed as individual attractions, many crooked houses became part of park funhouses. On a rare occasion, the concept was incorporated into a park dark ride.

The effects of disorientation manifested itself at Freedomland. According to promotional material, Casa Loca is "a house where you'll find that water runs uphill, rooms turn upside down and former tenants come popping out of the wall, all in obedience to strange magnetic forces."

The attraction showcased a façade that allowed Casa Loca to blend into the Old Southwest landscape. On the roof, a small spinning cabin replica was used to draw the attention of park guests. After waiting on line, guests entered the small shack that maintained two walkways, with one slightly higher and behind the other.

Casa Loca, according to the Freedomland story, was owned by an old miner. He dug for gold and sat by the table drinking cans of beer. To get rid of the empty cans, he would lay a can on its side and watch it roll up the table and out the window. In the second room, the pool table featured an uphill ball feed mechanism to place the balls on the table. When you hit a ball on the table, it rolled into the least anticipated pocket.

In this section of the park, the restrooms were located near the attraction. Possibly Freedomland's planners figured that, after exiting the crooked house, personal matters might be a little disoriented and require immediate attention.

Mine Caverns

According to Dexter Francis:

> There were two levels, one of which was underground. The first scene was a family of cave dwellers engaged in petrology. A caveman menaced intruders with a huge boulder. Dragons stuck their heads through crevices in the cave walls. Directly ahead, the path appeared to be

blocked by a pile of rocks, which were pushed aside by your mine cart, revealing a vast subterranean cavern inhabited by giant insects and other strange creatures which defied description.

—A childhood memory shared in *Building Disney's Dream: Arrow Development: The Little Company That Could* by Dexter Francis

Fourteen mine cars on tracks were used, with four passengers allowed to ride in each car. The tracks descended and ascended to simulate actual rail haulage in a mine. Besides the insects and creatures, the caves were filled with stalagmites and stalactites. A miner could be seen exploding TNT. At the end of the ride, lights would brighten the mine, a horn would sound, and another mine car with a fictitious family on board headed out of control in the direction of the car carrying park guests. The rogue car would stop before causing a collision as the guests pushed through to daylight.

Santa Fe Opera House and Saloon

The Santa Fe Opera House and Saloon, later to be called the Western Saloon and Opera House, the Music Hall, and the Red Garter Saloon, was the Old Southwest's biggest entertainment palace. The venue hosted original western shows and, at times, welcomed modern-day electronics in the form of live broadcasts for New York City radio shows. Radio personalities Scott Muni and Jack Sterling broadcast from the opera house that was sponsored by Pepsi-Cola.

The first western show on the park's opening day was an original western dramatic and comic opera in four acts and five scenes: *Go West Young Man, or The Adventures of Johnnie Freedom and Buckskin Joe, or The Conquests of San Francisco Frankie.* The production was written and produced by Hal Adelquist, who primarily is known for creating and producing television's *The Mickey Mouse Club.* He left Disney's employ sometime during 1956 and was hired by C.V. Wood for Freedomland.

The stage manager for this performance was John Morris, who later became a rock music production manager for the first European and American tours by Jefferson Airplane. He also was the director of production for the 1969 Woodstock Festival and the developer of the Rainbow Theatre, London's first permanent rock auditorium.

Other members of the crew were either Freedomland employees or contract workers. They included carpenter J.V. Towers, engineer and gas man (possibly for lights or special effects) John Vitelli, machinist Eli Levy, barker and prop man Eddy Strembel, costume director Gordon Weiss, and extemporaneous impresario Jimmy McKoy.

The stars were Don Crabtree as "Johnny Freedom," Charmain Harma as "San Francisco Frankie," and Buddy Farnan as "Buckskin Joe of the Bronx." The remainder of the cast included Jo Anne Leeman as "Sweet Sue," Margie Walker as "Hard Headed Hanna," Connie Warner as "Giddy Gertie," and Monika Erickson as "Sophisticated Sal."

The Tornado Trio (Mark Donald as conductor/pianist, Billy Norman playing violin and guitar, and Bob Roth on drums, cymbals, and effects) provided the music. Another contributor to this show was Tom Adair, who penned some of the lyrics. Adair's career included the composition of many popular songs for movies and Broadway (including the lyrics for *Let's Get Away from It All*), working for Disney television programs, and then writing scripts for many television shows.

The Tucson Mining Company Sky Ride

The Freedomland sky ride, in the shape of ore buckets for the Tucson Mining Company, likely was the first time that many people rode a skyway at a park.

During the building of Disneyland, Freedomland creator C.V. Wood became acquainted with the Von Roll company. The first Von Roll VR 101 sky ride in the U.S. opened at that park before Disneyland's first anniversary. The Swiss company, which traces its roots to 1803, then manufactured the conveyance system of the Freedomland sky ride. According to Rob Von Roll, a sky ride historian, the Freedomland ride was the company's first Double Von Roll VR 101 sky ride.

Freedomland was the first and, for a long time, the only park to have what appeared to be four cables on a sky ride. Actually, the ride incorporated two extended cables, but the eyes of park guests visualized four cables with two traveling in one direction and two others traveling in the opposite direction.

The height for a portion of the ride possibly reached 70 feet, judging by the height of the towers, though initial promotional material indicated a height of about 40 feet. The excursion was a round trip between the Old Southwest and Old Chicago during the first two seasons. During 1962, guests were permitted to board at the turnaround house in Chicago. They were able to enjoy a one-way trip in either direction, or return to the site of departure. On July 4, 1960, the Tucson Mining Company carried 9,441 riders.

Gangloff Cabins, another Swiss company, manufactured the gondolas. A *Minneapolis Star Tribune* article from the time of the park's grand opening indicated that the ore buckets (towers/machinery not confirmed) were purchased from the Brussels World's Fair (Expo 58). Sixty-four gondolas were operational on the Freedomland ride, with 32 traveling in each direction at peak times. During the 1920s, Gangloff manufactured the first cable railway car cabin. Today, the company remains a proficient partner for custom–made cabins and cars for all conceivable kinds of railways, lifts, trams, and other conveyance.

The ore buckets were not perfectly round or square, as with most sky ride cabins. The buckets were oval in shape as was common with other two- and three-passenger Von Roll sky rides. The Freedomland ore buckets originally were a rust or brown color. After a couple of seasons, a painting project converted the buckets to multi-color cabins. Children often commented that the buckets were as colorful as M&M candies.

Sky ride fans still can enjoy one of 11 classic Von Roll sky rides in the U.S., including the attractions at the San Diego Zoo, Sea World San Diego, Six Flags Great Adventure, and Cedar Point.

CHAPTER FOURTEEN

The Freedomland Record Album

Hats off to Johnny Freedom…That's our boy.

—Music by Jule Styne / Lyrics by George Weiss

De Vol, Styne, Weiss Collaboration

The Freedomland U.S.A. record album, issued by Capitol Records, was touted as "the official re-creation in music of the most famous actual and fictional events that represent Americana from its birth to its future." The tunes were written to capture the spirit of the themed areas of the park and to play continually in each of its sections.

The music was created by Jule Styne with the lyrics by George Weiss. The album was arranged and conducted by Frank DeVol. According to Freedomland promotional material:

> Jule Styne and George Weiss were signed by Ted Raynor, president of Freedomland, to write the score for its musical album. Styne was in Florida where he worked on the score and wrote 20 songs. As in their last collaboration, on the highly successful "Mr. Wonderful," Styne wrote the music and Weiss the lyrics. … Styne and Weiss have written a tune called "Johnny Freedom" which has all the earmarks of becoming a hit.

Styne is famous for his movie and stage music, including *Three Coins in the Fountain, High Button Shoes, Gentlemen Prefer Blondes, Peter Pan, Gypsy,* and *Funny Girl*. Weiss was a songwriter and arranger whose famous songs included *Lullaby of Birdland, The*

Lion Sleeps Tonight, and *What a Wonderful World*. De Vol (sometimes DeVol) wrote arrangements for the studio recordings of many top singers, including Nat King Cole, Ella Fitzgerald, Sarah Vaughan, Tony Bennett, Dinah Shore, Doris Day, and Vic Damone. Several of them performed at Freedomland.

Frank's single most famous arrangement may be the string and piano accompaniment for Nat's *Nature Boy*. He also wrote the scores for many Hollywood movies, receiving Academy Award nominations for *Pillow Talk*, *Cat Ballou*, and *Guess Who's Coming to Dinner*. His television theme tunes included *Family Affair*, *Gidget*, *The Brady Bunch*, and *My Three Sons*. He also appeared in front of the camera, as the bandleader Happy Kyne on the talk show parodies *Fernwood 2 Night* and *America 2-Night*, and in episodes of *I Dream of Jeannie*, *Bonanza*, *Petticoat Junction*, and *Get Smart*.

The Performers

Jill Corey

Jill Corey's demo tape came to the attention of Mitch Miller at Columbia Records. She appeared on the *Dave Garroway Show* and became the youngest star ever at the Copacabana nightclub. She was the last featured singer on *Your Hit Parade* and her biggest song was "Love Me to Pieces."

Richard Hayes

Richard Hayes appeared as an actor, singer, game show host, and disc jockey. Between 1948 and 1953, he garnered 14 top-25 hits. His most successful record was his rendition of "The Old Master Painter." He appeared on many programs and was a regular on Arthur Godfrey's television and radio programs from 1958 until 1972.

Johnny Horton

Johnny Horton sang country and rockabilly music. He was known for historical ballads including "The Battle of New Orleans," "Sink the Bismarck," and "North to Alaska." His rendition of "Johnny Freedom" reached 69 on the charts.

Jimmy Rushing

A blues shouter, balladeer, and swing jazz singer, Jimmy Rushing was the featured vocalist of Count Basie's Orchestra from 1935 to 1948. Known as "Mr. Five by Five" due to his rotund build, he was the subject of the 1942 popular song of that same name. Among his best-known recordings are "Going to Chicago" and "Harvard Blues."

Charley (Charlie) Weaver

This was the character created by Clifford Charles "Cliff" Arquette, an actor and comedian, initially known in the midwest rather than nationally. Cliff appeared on radio, in theatre, and in movies, and was credited with performing on 13 different daily radio shows at different stations in Chicago. When Cliff accepted television talk show host Jack Paar's invitation to appear on the *Tonight Show*, he created "Charley Weaver, the wild old man from Mount Idy." He would bring and read a letter from his "Mamma" back home. This characterization proved so popular that Cliff almost never again appeared in public as himself. As Charley Weaver, he wore a squashed hat, round glasses, rumpled shirt, broad tie, baggy pants, and suspenders.

Earl Wrightson

Earl Wrightson was a singer and actor best known for musical theatre on radio and stage, concerts and television performances. He also appeared on television talk and variety programs. He recorded many albums, including more than a dozen musicals and operettas.

Album Liner Notes

The liner and selection notes from the album did not completely compare to the visual Freedomland. Before the park opened, some attractions were altered.

> Freedomland U.S.A.! This fabulous re-creation of the United States occupies eighty acres in the Baychester section of the Bronx in New York City. Reproduced at Freedomland is the geography and topography of our

country, beginning with the very shape of the entertainment center which is that of the United States. More than $65 million has been spent to establish such areas as "Little Old New York," a Civil War battlefield, Western mining towns, the Great Lakes, Chicago at the time of its Great Fire, San Francisco of the Barbary Coast period, Mardi Gras in New Orleans, Hollywood in the Twenties, a present-day satellite base, and other exciting mementos of our past and present.

Freedomland is even larger than the fabled Disneyland with some thirty-seven different rides. Costumed attendants and actors re-enact moments in history, with carefully detailed reconstructions as the background. Each ride takes spectators into the heart of the age, and each section is minutely planned to evoke the excitement and color with thrilling authenticity. And throughout Freedomland rings appropriate music, especially composed by July Styne with lyrics by George Weiss, to underline the panorama of America that unfolds.

—Freedomland U.S.A. Record Album

The Music

Explanations of the songs from the album cover.

"Overture" (Frank De Vol and his Orchestra) / Little Old New York (Richard Hayes)

In Freedomland, Little Old New York is a masterpiece of authentic re-creation, bringing back an era covering about 1850–1895. Everything about it is calculated to make you feel you are really there, including operating shops, entertainment of the period, even a street corner politician.

"Satellite City" (Earl Wrightson)

Satellite City in Freedomland is a thrilling glimpse into the future. Here, you may drive a futuristic car over an ultra-modern ribbon highway, or take a ride around the world in a spaceship, an exciting contrast in this world of yesteryear.

"Danny the Dragon" (Charlie Weaver aka Cliff Arquette)

Our friend Danny is a feature of Freedomland that is designed for the enjoyment of the younger set. Located in the Mardi Gras area down in old New Orleans, this dragon is a unique departure from the old roller coaster. Here, you ride on Danny's back as he twists and turns over a thrilling course. He is just one of the many happy events of the Mardi Gras.

"The Jalopy Song" (Jill Corey and Richard Hayes)

Just northeast of Little Old New York lies colonial New England, just as it used to be, complete with a New England fishing village. To make the trip through this charming area complete, you may take a drive-it-yourself car...a 1903 Cadillac. You take the wheel for a spin over hill and dale, under a covered bridge and past the scenery and homes of the period.

"Pine Country" (Earl Wrightson)

Probably the most elaborate and exciting ride at Freedom land (sic) is in a fur trapper's boat through the old Northwest. This trip takes you through uncharted waters and lonely pine country past Indian villages and a fur trapper's cabin. You'll see all sorts of wild life and, before your very eyes, a savage Indian war.

"Johnny Freedom" (Johnny Horton)

Johnny Freedom is the embodiment of the spirit of Freedom, the American spirit, just as Freedomland is a symbol of the United States itself. It is particularly apt that the song "Johnny Freedom" was inspired by Freedomland.

"On the Showboat" (Jill Cory)

Plying Freedomland's Great Lakes Region are two stern wheel (sic) steamboats, reminiscent of the showboat, so familiar on the old Mississippi River. With a capacity of 270 passengers, these stern-wheelers are one of the park's favorite rides. And down river at New Orleans, a real showboat is tied up at dock and, just as in the old days, there is a happy minstrel show to entertain the guests.

"San Francisco Fran" (Richard Hayes)

Another monument to the old days is San Francisco around the turn of the century. There you will see Chinatown, the great San Francisco earthquake, and the "wicked, wicked" Barbary Coast.

"The Chicago Fire" (Earl Wrightson)

The great Chicago fire of 1871 is re-created in Freedomland complete with hand pumpers and volunteer firemen. Every twenty minutes in a desolated block of "old Chicago," flames spring up and begin to lick at beams and shingles. The alarm bells ring and out of the city's fire station rushes a hand-drawn, hand-pumped fire engine. With assistance from civilians standing nearby, a 200-foot spray is directed on the blazing buildings until the fire is quenched…for the next twenty minutes.

"So Long, Ma" (Jimmy Rushing)

New Orleans in fact and at Freedomland is known best for Mardi Gras. The difference at Freedomland is that Mardi Gras is season-long and twice the fun. This area will appeal especially to the children for there is not only Danny the Dragon to entertain them, but a mirror maze, carrousel, and many other exciting rides. Further on in New Orleans you'll also see a pirate hide-out and take the thrilling "pirate ride."

Old Chicago. From the train station, Old Chicago of 1871 came into view. On the right is the Hallmark store. On the left is the Brass Rail Steak House. The center features the Relic House souvenir store and beyond it is the Chicago Fire. To the right of the attraction is the dock for the sternwheelers and to the upper left of the building is the turnaround house of the ore bucket sky ride.

Other Record Albums

The official park record album was not the only Freedomland record. At least two more albums are known to exist.

Piute Pete conducted square dancing lessons in the Fort Cavalry area of the park and from this an album was created: *A Child's Introduction to Square Dancing—Piute Pete and His Famous Freedomland Band.* Pete called square dancing regularly at the Village Barn in New York City. He also appeared at the city's Stork club and was the president of the New York Square Dance Callers Association. He appeared on radio and television shows, and in movies.

The album was produced by Wonderland Records and the liner notes included:

> But his foremost specialty is introducing young children and teenagers to the vigorous pleasures of this form of dance. As official caller at "Freedomland, U.S.A.," New York's celebrated amusement areas—and at many other places—his happy singing and calling has taught many thousans (sic) of youngsters the fundamentals of the square dance.

Another album referencing Freedomland was part of the massive collection of Boris Rose, a Bronx resident who was a well-known jazz archivist with a private collection of recorded tapes and acetates. He pressed his own albums from recordings he made at live performances that he attended or from live radio broadcasts.

Boris also was a prankster. He created an array of fake label names (including Titania, Ambrosia, Caliban, Session Disc, Ozone, and Chazzer Records), many of which he tried to pass off as European imports. Most of his albums bore an address on the front, such as "A Product of Stockholm, Sweden." Often, on the back, he would include "Manufactured in Madison, Wisconsin" or something similar in small type.

One album he created was from a performance by Stan Kenton and his Orchestra at Freedomland on July 28, 1962. A note with the album indicated it was Stan Kenton from his Freedomland July 28 and October 19, 1962, performances. While the first date is correct, the second date may be an error. Some of the songs on the album were broadcast live at Freedomland. Others may have been broadcast live from the studio at WNEW-AM.

The song "New Twist" on this record label actually should have been "WNEW Twist" after the New York radio station that frequently broadcast jazz from Freedomland. Other selections on the album include "It's Alright with Me," "Maria," "Waltz of the Prophets," "Blue Steam" (should be "Warm Blue Stream"), "Fitz," "Malaguena," and "All the Things You Are."

New Orleans and Mardi Gras

*New Orleans, with its French and Spanish past, throws
the biggest carnival in America, and you can take part in it
every day at FREEDOMLAND'S perpetual Mardi Gras.*

—Freedomland's 1960 Complete Official Guide with Maps

The New Orleans-themed area of Freedomland was a party
town that also had its dangerous side.

The celebration included a ride on the King Rex Carrousel
and on a turning table known as Spin-A-Top. The Crystal
Maze, as the world's first glass-walled house of mirrors, confused participants. Park guests watched from the outside as
people on the inside lost their way. The kids enjoyed riding
on the tail of Danny the Dragon, the fire-breathing friendly
monster with a heart of gold. The fun continued even when
a guest encountered a Freedomland pirate, who would sweep
people away on an adventure through Jean Lafitte country and
a battle between two pirate frigates.

New Orleans also recalled the rough times witnessed by
so many in this city and other parts of the country. Disaster
struck when the Tornado dark ride provided the experience of
a real twister. The landscape further was ruined by America's
Civil War. Under a flag of truce, park guests became immersed
in the fight of Billy Yank and Johnny Reb.

The attractions at Freedomland were found on Basin Street,
Bourbon Street, Rampart Street, and Beauregard Street.

Main Attractions

- Buccaneers (dark ride) was a thrilling pirate adventure.
- Carousel Toy Shop was located next to the Civil War ride. Notice the spelling of the word "carousel" for the toy shop; the word was spelled with an additional "r" for the King Rex Carrousel.
- Civil War attraction brought guests between the lines. The Charley Weaver Civil War Museum was located near the attraction.
- Danny the Dragon travelled through a world of wonders.
- Jesse Jewell Plantation House Restaurant was known for its fried chicken.
- Kandy Kane Lane for children focused on a toy fair (which could be a reference to the Carousel Toy Shop), swan boats, helicopter ride, and sand pile.
- King Rex Carrousel was an early 1900s Dentzel.
- Mardi Gras Sidewalk Café and other eateries.
- Pirate Gun Gallery was another place to practice target shooting.
- Popeye Museum (1962 season) featured the popular cartoon character.
- Spin-a-Top ride featured 18 tops on three turntables.
- The Crystal Maze was a baffling house of mirrors.
- Tornado Adventure (dark ride) simulated a twister in Tornado Alley.
- Wax Museum (1963 season) arrived from the Seattle World's Fair.

Buccaneers

A dark ride created by Arrow Development, the Buccaneers (sometimes referenced as the singular Buccaneer) attraction appears to have its roots in the concept for Disney's Pirates of the Caribbean, which celebrated its 50th anniversary in 2017.

A story that often has been repeated indicated that a former Disneyland employee worked on the early specifications for

Disney's attraction and then joined Marco Engineering. The designer reportedly recalled the concepts during the development of Freedomland's Buccaneers and possibly became embroiled in a legal matter over Disney intellectual property.

One storyline is that it was considered for Disneyland earlier than its 1967 debut. But, after Walt Disney and C.V. Wood parted ways, Walt put this attraction on hold as the pirate ride opened at Freedomland. The original Disney attraction was to be

The Buccaneer Ride. Later billed as the plural "Buccaneers" on the canvas attraction sign. The exterior of Arrow Development's dark ride during July 1960.

a walk-through wax museum. When the Freedomland ride was created as a multiple person ride-through attraction, Disney may have adapted the boat ride concept.

Another storyline is that the walk-through concept was discarded due to the advancement in audio-animatronics. Among the many unanswered questions: Did the Freedomland attraction contribute to the changes made to the Disney ride? Did Buccaneers delay the introduction of Pirates of the Caribbean until Freedomland closed its gates?

On the outside, Buccaneers had a pirate hanging from high up on the crow's nest. Its 11 cars shaped as mini pirate ships traveling on a track, with four passengers per car, encountered various scenes that included two waring pirate ships.

> ...the method of travel was a boat, with a skull serving as a hood ornament. Traveling through the opening pub scene lent a feeling of foreboding, as the pirates all had threatening, dangerous looks on their faces. More scenes of pirates followed, sailing by lighted buoys, digging for treasure beneath palm trees, and on various islands. The action exploded as skeletons frolicked about while a hapless pirate was hung (sic). For the windup, a sea serpent reared it's (sic) ugly head, emitting a bone-chilling shriek. Just when you thought you were safely past the menacing buccaneers, you found yourself sailing between dueling pirate ships, complete with cannon fire and explosions.
>
> —A childhood memory shared in *Building Disney's Dream: Arrow Development: The Little Company That Could* by Dexter Francis

Civil War

Freedomland opened during the centennial commemoration of the American Civil War. Though Civil War battles were not fought in the Bronx, the park's creators realized that this period of America's history would receive significant national attention through 1965. Many young boys and girls became interested in the war after experiencing this attraction. As adults, many joined Civil War history organizations, such as the Civil War Round Table of New York, and re-enactment regiments.

"Civil War" is FREEDOMLAND's intensely realistic re-creation of the great War Between the States. We think of the Civil War as taking place an age ago, but it really isn't such a long time past—the last veteran of those terrible battles died in 1959. On the Civil War ride in the New Orleans area, you will see and experience what the men in Union blue and butternut gray actually went through. FREEDOMLAND has taken scenes from several of the most crucial battles of the war, and brought them vividly to life.

Since you're a noncombatant, a war correspondents' wagon is your transportation on the battlefield, the kind the newsmen and sketch artists of both sides used to cover the fighting front. You pass a blockhouse, a derailed train, a tent camp, and burning houses. Suddenly you're trapped by cannon cross-fire; blue and gray are slugging it out—and you're caught in the middle! But you come through unscathed. You cross over a pontoon bridge, and drive past the house where General Lee shook hands with General Grant, to bring America's most momentous war to an end.

—Freedomland's 1960 Complete
Official Guide with Maps

The attraction was created during the dawn of modern audio-animatronics technology that had originated with Disney. Hollywood special effects experts had been hired by Marco Engineering to create the "soldiers" that moved and fired the guns.

Lines always were long for this attraction. Freedomland's pre-opening publicity material indicated that the park was prepared for the crowd with nine wagons that each would carry 27 passengers. During the first year, wagons were hauled by mules. To increase ride capacity and reduce wait times, several wagons were hitched together. After a few seasons, the mules were displaced and the correspondent's wagons were pulled by tractors modeled as steam engines. By eliminating costs associated with horse or mule power, the park reduced expenses during succeeding seasons. One park guest recalled that cars from the Horseless Carriage ride were used to travel between the battle lines during Freedomland's last season of operation, and that the park had silenced all explosions and gunfire.

Children decked out in Civil War Union and Confederate hats and souvenir toy swords were a common sight at the park.

A building near the Civil War attraction housed a small museum, Charley Weaver's Civil War Museum and Photo Gallery. Guests posed for pictures while wearing Civil War uniforms. A fan of American history, especially American Revolution and Civil War history, Charley already operated a popular museum in Gettysburg. The Charley Weaver Museum (later renamed the Soldier's National Museum and closed a few years ago) housed miniature Civil War dioramas created by Charley.

After Freedomland closed, Charley moved a number of the non-audio-animatronic figures from the attraction to his Gettysburg museum. A few were placed inside the museum and others were placed outside in the rear yard.

"The original Freedomland figures were molded out of some kind of material like fiberglass (including the uniforms), and were a bit smaller than life-size," said Freedomland fan and Civil War historian Bill Finlayson. "The actual Freedomland figures were painted, because they were meant to be outside in the elements. When I was there (just before the Gettysburg museum closed), I noticed just a few of these molded ones left, part of some interior dioramas on display. What I really want to know about is what happened to all the Freedomland figures that used to be displayed there at the old Charley Weaver Museum. They used to have quite a few more of these figures set up in the outdoor courtyard, many more than the few that were on display inside the museum."

When the museum closed, all the contents were auctioned without a forwarding address for the Freedomland soldiers.

Danny the Dragon

Created by Arrow Development for $47,000, Danny the Dragon was beloved by children. Freedomland had two Dannys, one green and one red. Each 74-foot-long train held 48 adults and children in cars that served as the dragon's tail.

To operate the attraction, Arrow synchronized the train with a wire buried in the roadway. Freedomland promotional material explained that guests weaved "through a world of wonders where storybook characters will live again along the way as Danny carries you through glorious gardens."

Danny was not unique to Freedomland. Several Dannys had been created for parks across the country. One refurbished Danny can be found today at a park in California.

King Rex Carrousel

The King Rex Carrousel reportedly was purchased from W.F. Rankin for $3,500. Research has not discovered any information about Rankin, the purchase, or the early history of the attraction.

This carrousel was not built specifically for Freedomland. It was created by William H. Dentzel and dates to the early 1900s (circa 1910). William was the son of carrousel pioneer Gustav Dentzel and he carried on the family business through the 1920s.

The original name of this carrousel, if it had a name, remains lost to time. The name Freedomland fans remember is believed to have originated with its installation at the park. Rex (founded 1872) is a New Orleans Carnival Krewe that stages one of the city's most celebrated parades for Mardi Gras. Rex is Latin for "King," and Rex reigns as the "King of Carnival." The carrousel was appropriately named not just for its role in the park but for its ultimate status as the last known half-standing, half-jumping, four-row, two-level Dentzel.

The carrousel's 72 menagerie figures were situated on a two-level platform. The ride, with a diameter of 54 feet and circumference of 132 feet, consisted of two rows of standing animals on the lower level and two rows of leaping animals on the upper level. The ride also included three chariots, or stationary coaches. This carrousel is considered highly unique when compared to others created by the Dentzel company, which sold new four-abreast attractions for as much as $24,000 during the early 1900s.

A 2017 article by managing editor Daniel Robinson in *Merry-Go-Roundup*, the publication of the National Carousel Association (NCA), indicated that the Freedomland attraction was similar to Model No. 108 in a William Dentzel catalog. The description for that model closely matched the specifications for the Freedomland carrousel. The description also indicated that Model No. 108 contained 20 sections and four chariots.

The upper platform of leaping figures included four each of rabbits, cats, pigs, ostriches, and, according to the NCA, very rare smiling bears. The lower platform of standing figures included an eagle/flag horse, a lion, and a tiger. Some figures were in matching pairs on the first and second rows. "It appears that many, if not all, of the horses on the second row were prancers," according to the article.

Popeye Museum

For the 1962 season, Freedomland opened a museum in New Orleans that featured the cartoon sailor Popeye. Prepared by King Features Syndicate, the owners of Popeye and distributor of the 220 made-for-television cartoons, the museum was conceived by Gene Plotnik, the syndicate's director of creative services. He also produced the live show to promote physical fitness that accompanied the opening of the museum.

The show, held in the Hollywood Arena in the San Francisco area of the park, opened on May 26 and lasted 12 days while the museum remained open until the end of the season. Actor Herb Messenger portrayed the sailor man and actor Brett Pearson was Brutus. The plot focused on Popeye, who arrived in town to be crowned king of the park. Brutus challenged the title. Herb and Brett staged a real knock-down, drag-out battle on stage. Popeye was floored four times during each show, but he emerged victorious each time at the end. By the last performance, Brett featured a split lip.

New York's WPIX-TV Channel 11 and its advertisers on the *Popeye* program were featured in the shows, which were hosted by children's show celebrity Captain Jack McCarthy.

The museum featured the history of *Thimble Theatre*, the newspaper comic strip that began during 1919. The sailor man made his debut in the strip 10 years later and, eventually, the strip bore his name. Six wall panels provided an illustrated history of Popeye. The museum also showcased six displays that explained the creation of a specific Popeye cartoon. The step-by-step process was featured along with the actual tools used by the artists: story boards, drawings, cels, and sound tracks. The museum screened the completed cartoon.

When Freedomland closed for the season, the exhibit traveled to the Mid-South Fair in Memphis, Tennessee.

Tornado

The Tornado dark ride created by Arrow Development was C.V. Wood's favorite attraction at the park. He called it the cyclone ride as it reminded him of his roots in Oklahoma and Texas. Eleven Model T style vehicles with four passengers per car drove guests through the storm that struck a midwest town. The winds were created by large fans.

> The Tornado Ride...sought to re-create the experience of being caught up, Dorothy like, in a real twister. ... Riders were transported in Arrow's antique autos. ... A strange whistling noise was heard while boarding, and signs warned you to hold onto your hats. Entering the darkened chamber, the car would execute a sharp U-turn, revealing a tranquil farm scene. Suddenly, a gusty wind hit riders in the face as the dreaded tornado was about to strike! Houses spun on end, their terrified residents visible through the windows. Various objects flew by as you approached the spinning funnel dead ahead. The car veered off into a rotating barrel as the wicked cyclone got you in it's (sic) clutches! Next, you found yourselves inside a barn. The din was earsplitting, with cackling chickens, mooing cows, and horses whinnying up a storm of fright. Helpless cows floated overhead, and a huge bale of hay threated to suffocate riders just before departing the scene of Mother Nature's wrath and chaos.
>
> —A childhood memory shared in *Building Disney's Dream: Arrow Development: The Little Company That Could* by Dexter Francis

Wax Museum

Tornado was sold to Kennywood Park in Pennsylvania after the 1962 season. For 1963, a wax museum opened in the vacated

Tornado location. The exhibits, featured at the 1962 Seattle World's Fair, reportedly were secured by the organizers of the New York World's Fair. A deal was struck with Freedomland, possibly between Robert Moses ("master builder" of mid-20th century New York City and surrounding suburbs, and president of the fair) and William Zeckendorf, Sr., to first bring the entire Seattle showcase to the Bronx and then to move the Last Supper portion of the exhibit to the 1964–1965 fair in Queens.

The Freedomland exhibit featured an $800,000 price tag. An eight-page brochure was created with the front cover boasting "FREEDOMLAND WAX MUSEUM takes you into the past with its scenes inspired by history, art, literature and legend. The fantastic world of authentic drama is viewed in an elegant life-like setting."

The 17 exhibit scenes were Romeo and Juliet, Albert Einstein, Kublai Khan and Marco Polo, Sir Francis Drake, the *Mona Lisa* (with Leonardo da Vinci creating his painting), King Solomon and the Queen of Sheba, Joan of Arc at the stake, Roger Delivering Angelique (from the "Poem of Chivalry"), Richard the Lion-Hearted, Faust and the Devil, Nimrod the hunter, the Death of Leonardo da Vinci, the Last Supper, Peter Pan, the Landing of Columbus, Snow White, and Robin Hood and His Men.

CHAPTER SIXTEEN

Freedomland Collectibles

Greetings from Freedomland!

—September 17, 1960, postcard sent
from the Bronx to Pittsburgh

Merchandising is a major contributor to theme park revenues. Years ago, when the first parks were created, a souvenir shop, if a park had one, often would be located near the exit. Today, though, the shopping experience is everywhere within a park and it often dovetails with nearby attractions.

C.V. Wood made money from souvenirs and other merchandise in a different way than creators of earlier parks. He first introduced his merchandising concept at Disneyland and then he incorporated it into his parks. Woody contracted retailers to rent the space. Many of the items that were sold incorporated the names of the parks as part of the branding and promotion strategy. At Freedomland, the vendors were many and included nationally known companies, local retailers, and tradesmen.

Freedomland memorabilia included:

- At least nine different styles of ashtrays of porcelain, glass, and metal. One popular ashtray featured a brass patina and was shaped as the continental U.S. with the words "Freedomland USA" across the middle. The Santa Fe train appeared across the top.

- Cigarette lighters and matchbooks, all with depictions of Freedomland attractions.

- Beer-branded items included Schaefer Brewery visors and fans. Bottle openers contained artistic scenes of the park. Coasters depicted the Pony Express rider.

- Bumper stickers of several different kinds were peel-and-stick ready for cars. Luggage decals immediately could be placed on bags or on car windshields.

- Dishes, salt-and-pepper shakers, trays, decanters, drinking glasses, and a Chicago Fire shot glass.

- Plastic binoculars and other merchandise were manufactured exclusively for children.

- Pins, charms, and sweater clips were available for ladies and wallets for men.

- A large paperweight was created in the shape of the Space Rover.

- The stores carried a large variety of hats, scarves, and a child's Indian headdress.

- A jigsaw puzzle could be purchased that featured the Freedomland map with attractions.

- A miniature automatic pencil with refillable lead in the shape of a rifle contained a spring device to pull, load, and discharge.

Digger O'Toole Card. Actor John Fortna portrayed Digger O'Toole and regularly presented his calling card.

- Pocket and other knives were a popular "guy thing" during the 1960s. Several knives sold at the park contained the Freedomland name or logo. One included a compass.

Freedomland Board Game

The board game was manufactured by Pressman Toy Corporation of New York City, with offices in Manhattan and a factory in Brooklyn. Today's operations are in New Jersey. Among the company's many board games are Concentration, The Newlywed Game, Topple, and Othello.

The Freedomland game first appeared during 1960. It was sold in the park and also likely in retail outlets outside the park. It came with a "spin" board that featured Janie (Jane) and Johnny Freedom. Players would use the Pony Express, Santa Fe express, big sternwheeler, or the stagecoach "for a thrilling cross-country race" on the game board. The lower left side of the board contained a small slot to place "souvenir cards." The game also came with colored pieces, or tokens, that were used to represent each player. Two to four people could play the game.

Freedomland Pennants

Various colors, sizes, and graphics were featured on Freedomland pennants. Red and green were most common, but pennants appeared in brown, orange, white, and blue. A rare teal color pennant featured an image of an Indian with a full headdress.

The pennants were made from felt, which was common for pennants of schools, sports teams, and other tourist attractions. The pennants featured park attractions (Pony Express, the Chicago Fire, the Santa Fe Railroad, the Space Rover, the Civil War ride) and a variety of people and animals (a police officer, an Indian chief, a cowboy on a horse, a large bear). After a few seasons, the pennants featured the Freedomland cartoon kids found on park promotional material and even on the stage walls of the Moon Bowl.

The majority of pennants were 25 inches long and many contained ties on the left side. Some pennants were seven inches long and did not have ties.

Freedomland Slides

For a guest who forgot a camera, just didn't want to carry it, or didn't have one, memories of Freedomland were captured in a set of slides. The photos included several key attractions along with the concept artwork that was featured in the 1960 park guide and on park postcards.

The company name (Sawyer's Inc.) was printed on the left side of the cardboard borders. From Portland, Oregon, Sawyer's was a manufacturer and retailer of slide projectors, scenic slides, View-Master reels and viewers (a three-reel set featured Freedomland), postcards, and related products. Eventually, the company was purchased by GAF Corp.

Freedomland Tickets

Freedomland featured eight ticket booths with 16 ticket stations. Once past the 20 turnstiles, guests entered the park through the streets of Little Old New York.

Admission prices fluctuated from $1 to a $3.95 package deal during the five seasons. A number of different entrance tickets/coins and ride tickets were featured during the park's history. These included individual 10-cent tickets in a booklet, a park passport, and all-inclusive attraction tickets.

Tickets and prices changed from season to season and, at times, during a season. Some examples::

- 1960. Admission was $1 for adults, 75 cents for juniors (13–17), and 50 cents for children. Ticket books, including admission and nine attractions, sold for $3.50 for adults, $3.20 for juniors, and $2.50 for children. Eleven attractions cost 50 cents for adults and 35 cents for children. Six attractions cost 35 cents for everyone, another six cost 25 cents, and four attractions cost a dime. Free attractions included the Chicago Fire.

- 1961. A pay-one-price (POP) ticket at $2.95 was instituted with the cost including all attractions and shows.

- 1962. POP was $3.50. A "family vacation" evening price was $2.50 plus tax for anyone entering after

6pm. The price provided access to attractions, all shows, and exhibits.

- 1963. Admission was curtailed to $1. A large ticket card (economy ride ticket for $2.50) was printed in a variety of colors, including gold, white, red, yellow, and green. The date of purchase was stamped on the ticket.

- 1964. Admission again was $1, but some attractions charged a small fee.

Up to the final days of the park, ticket pricing remained in flux. During September 1964, an economy ride ticket of $2.50 plus tax was available along with a $1 general admission, or a guest could enter the park with a quarter book of Triple-S Blue Stamps. The stamps were offered by Grand Union Supermarkets, which regularly promoted the park in its stores and circulars in the greater New York City area.

Hallmark Cards And Decorations

As a park sponsor, Hallmark maintained its retail operation in the Chicago area of the park. The company sold a variety of its popular merchandise that included both generic and park-specific cards along with other decorative pieces.

For Freedomland, Hallmark created cards associated with park attractions. Hallmark also featured a set of six Freedomland placemats. The placemats could be used "as is," or, with its perforations, the U.S. map portion could be removed. Various park attractions surrounded the border. Color-coded and numbered, these also could be removed and positioned in the appropriate sections of the park. Another popular item was a cutout of the sternwheeler for table display.

A decorative collector packet of postcards was sold as a set. The cards showcased the artists' concepts of attractions created during the park's development stage and featured the Horseless Carriage, a Civil War correspondent's wagon, a bull boat of the Northwest Fur Trapper ride, a sternwheeler, the Tucson Mining Company ore bucket ride, the Borden farm, the Chicago Fire, the Chicago fire house, and the Space Rover.

The cards were packaged in a decorative sleeve that featured the Freedomland U.S. map of attractions. These cards would not be used to mail quick messages as the pictures did not have a glossy finish, the paper stock was not sturdy, and the backs were not designed for postal use. However, the sleeve in which all the cards were housed could be sealed and mailed.

Other individual postcards, some with the same images, were sold and could be mailed. The cards also featured pictures of park scenes, including the train, a shoot-out, the ore buckets, and one image that showcases the trolley, sternwheeler, and train (with the contemporary Bronx in the background). A larger set of postcards, measuring 6x9 inches, also could be purchased and mailed, or simply saved as a collectible item.

Some postcards that were mailed from Freedomland have turned up in recent years. Among the comments from more than 50 years ago:

- Greetings from "Freedomland" in the Bronx, where I rode in an old ore-bucket at the old "Tucson Mine," pardner, on a cable across the park.
- Mom—This is truly a fabulous place. You would just love it. We all rode on this iron horse.—Love J.B.

Souvenir Guide Book

Throughout this book, excerpts have been incorporated from Freedomland's 1960 and 1962 Complete Official Guide with Maps. The image that appears on the cover of the premier season's park guide (and on this book's cover) was the most popular and most recognizable of all the logos and artwork created by Freedomland. At the park, the guide book sold for just a quarter.

Unusual And Generic Souvenirs

One of the most unusual souvenirs associated with Freedomland was a turtle rattle. Made in Japan, as were many souvenirs of the time, it was constructed from papier-mâché. Beads within the shell created the rattle. With the stick, it measured 16 inches in length.

While many souvenirs were created for Freedomland, a number of others, including the rattle and a Round Up Rack, were generic and stamped, labeled, or tagged with the park name. The Round Up Rack was the perfect place for any young cowboy or cowgirl to hang a hat, along with Hopalong Cassidy or Annie Oakley guns, and place below a pair of Roy Rogers or Dale Evans boots.

Today's Souvenirs

Though Freedomland has not sold memorabilia for more than 55 years, original items can be located in antiques stores, flea markets, and online.

A few contemporary items, specifically model railroad cars and accessories with the Freedomland logo, have appeared during recent years. Though none of the model train cars of the time featured the park, a company recently created a Freedomland box car and a tanker car for "O" gauge tracks. To accessorize the model layouts, another company created a vintage-looking billboard sign with the Freedomland logo. The company also produced one for Freedomland's Pleasure Island sister park in Wakefield, Massachusetts.

CHAPTER SEVENTEEN:

Satellite City: The Future

FREEDOMLAND has taken you on a tour of America's past; in Satellite City, you can step right into the future, living it as you and your children will live it, seeing and hearing the sights and sounds of the coming age. And what an age! The age of space travel and of atomic power, of progress in science and technology that today's engineers can barely imagine. ... Satellite City, where tomorrow's dream becomes today's reality.

—Freedomland's 1960 Complete Official Guide with Maps

While the rest of Freedomland focused on America's past, Satellite City, at Canaveral Court, Star Terrace, and Space Circle, displayed contemporary America and the excitement about the space race and new technologies.

The Braniff Space Rover was a stratospheric cruiser roaring into space. The Blast-off Bunker was a reproduction of a Cape Canaveral rocket-launching blockhouse. During the 1961 season, NASA maintained a display detailing the American space program that included an official NASA film of the first U.S. missile shot and details about future space exploration.

The Satellite City Turnpike was a daringly designed cloverleaf highway. The Moon Bowl arrived during the second season as an outdoor stage for top musical entertainment and to provide guests with the world's largest outdoor dance floor.

Main Attractions

- Blast-off Bunker / Astronaut Training Center showcased the launching of a Cape Canaveral space rocket.
- Braniff Space Rover provided a round-the-Americas cruise through stratospheric space.
- Moon Bowl (added 1961) featured entertainers.
- Moving Lake Walk became the Moving Sidewalk when the Moon Bowl stage and dance floor replaced the lake.
- Spaceway: Satellite City Turnpike offered a drive in a modern sports car over the road of the future.
- Spaceport Refreshment Center was sponsored by Coca-Cola.
- Special exhibits promoted science, industry, and space travel as the wonders of tomorrow.
- Arcade and hobby shop.

Blast-off Bunker

From the bunker, park guests learned about America's adventure into space with the simulated firing of a rocket from Cape Canaveral. Guests walked into the control room to witness last-minute preparations and the count-down. Then, they were able to track the flight on screens and watch the retrieval of the rocket's nose cone.

Braniff Space Rover

The Braniff Space Rover (sponsored by Braniff Airways and with a seating capacity of 250) could be referred to as an illusion. It simulated a trip into space. The attraction, associated with Otis T. Carr, is believed to be one of two that were built. The other was promised but never delivered to Frontier City USA in Oklahoma City, Oklahoma.

As the creator of a company focused on "free energy," Otis has been credited as the developer of an "anti-gravity flying saucer." He was mentored directly by Nikola Tesla, the engineer and scientist who is best known for his contributions to the design of the alternating current electricity supply system. During the mid-1940s, Otis completed his plans for an interstellar spacecraft, the OTC-X1, with OTC representing his initials. This craft could power itself and fly to any destination in the universe. It was controlled by a person's thoughts and intentions. This was possible, according to Otis, through a perfect combination of sacred geometry, resonance coupling, crystals, and space-energy.

Supposedly, certain secrets of his "free energy" device were incorporated into his patent (2,912,244) for an object that resembled a conventional disc-shaped flying saucer. To obtain the patent for the design from a skeptical Patents Office, Otis claimed his invention was an "amusement device," a flying saucer ride that spun around. The patent, though, reportedly contains the hidden geometries that allow the craft to traverse space time.

"This invention," according to the introduction of the patent filing, "relates generally to implements in amusement devices, and more particularly to an improved amusement device of the type where the passengers will receive the impression of riding in an interplanetary spacecraft." The description of Otis' invention and work appears on several websites.

Anyone who ventured into the Freedomland space rover was treated to a flight over South America (Brazil, Argentina, Peru, Panama) and then back to the states to fly over Chicago, Dallas, and New York City. According to park information, Braniff captured these images by strapping eight cameras specially built by Kodak to the belly of a jet.

When it was not imitating space travel, the attraction featured radio disc jockeys and interviews with celebrity entertainers, including WWRL Radio's Hal Jackson with Paul Anka.

Moon Bowl

The Moon Bowl was added during the park's second season. The large reflection pond that was about one foot deep was replaced with a wooden dance floor and band shell. Its 15,000-square-foot open area was touted as the world's largest outdoor dance floor.

Benny Goodman has been given credit for the creation of the Moon Bowl. Freedomland executives, especially Art Moss, listened to him when he complained about performing in the Hollywood Arena, which he declared was for horses ("Colossus" showcase) and did not offer a dance floor.

The Moon Bowl provided free musical entertainment. It opened on a Thursday evening and drew a crowd of 9,000 teenagers. Benny's performance was so successful that Art, as the executive in charge of advertising, public relations, and lessee relations, pursued other entertainers, including Paul Anka. Art approached William Zeckendorf, Sr., and asked for permission to pay Paul a considerable sum for three nights. The Moon Bowl performances helped the park increase attendance.

Moving Sidewalk

When the park opened, Freedomland called this new phenomenon the Moving Lake Walk (brochure description: "cross Satellite City Lake on a traveling sidewalk"). The name was changed to the Moving Sidewalk (brochure description: "street of the future") by 1962. Originally, the "sidewalk" moved over a lake. The lake was removed to create the Moon Bowl dance floor, but the "sidewalk" remained a park attraction.

Moon Bowl 1962. The Moon Bowl and its dance floor were adjacent to the modern turnpike.

Satellite City Turnpike

According to a Freedomland official guide:

> You can drive a smart, streamlined sports car over the twisting Satellite City Turnpike, the cloverleaf highway of the future. You'll have full control of your vehicle as you glide around sharp curves and over challenging hills. It's tomorrow's road, driven by tomorrow's motorists, in tomorrow's cars.
>
> —Freedomland's 1962 Complete Official Guide with Maps

Arrow Development built the Spaceway turnpike's gasoline-driven cars for $80,000. Park employees helped slow the cars when they returned from the turnpike by jumping on the running board and pressing the brake pedal. Amoco (American Oil Company) was a sponsor of the attraction and maintained a petroleum exhibit in the area.

The famous Amoco tagline ("You expect more from American and you get it") was featured at the turnpike. A park description for this car attraction stated:

> Those who are four feet and taller will be able to drive the sports car of the future over a futuristic freeway, which will take them all around Satellite City. There will be 40 cars, 20 on each of the two separate roadbeds.

CHAPTER EIGHTEEN

Musical Entertainment at Freedomland

*So, this 19-year-old kid gets to conduct those
monster musicians. What an experience!*
—Bronx guitarist John Falbo

For Freedomland to attract audiences of various ages whose interests reached beyond history, management booked top-line singers and musicians during each season. Lionel Hampton was the opening day headliner. The talent budget for the 1963 season was $1.2 million.

Through its five years of operation, Freedomland featured more than 150 celebrity entertainers. Most of the singers and musicians performed in the Moon Bowl in Satellite City, with swing bands from the 1940s and contemporary pop and rock stars attracting older teens and young adults to the park. Other performers appeared in the Hollywood Arena in San Francisco or in the Old Southwest Opera House and Saloon.

Singers

Paul Anka

Paul Anka appeared at Freedomland more often than any other entertainer. Anka maintained a prominent relationship with Freedomland. His manager, Irvin Feld, booked him for the fantastic sum of $100,000 for one weekend of performances. This was considered the highest amount an artist ever had been compensated with up to that time. According to the singer, his talent agency thought the amount was an error and created the contract for $10,000.

Irvin owned a chain of record stores in the northeast and he financed rock-and-roll shows at various venues. He also produced other music artists who appeared at Freedomland.

A 28-minute documentary (*Paul Anka, Lonely Boy*) is available online. About six minutes of the film features Paul at Freedomland, with footage from behind the scenes and during a performance. A series of publicity photographs from 1964 show him and Freedomland staff member Janet Hannigan cutting a huge birthday cake to serve 3,000 people who celebrated the singer's 23rd birthday.

> The swingingest part in these parts this summer is the Moon Bowl in that sprawling entertainment complex in the Bronx known as Freedomland.
>
> Name the popular vocalists and bands of the moment, and chances are you'll find them in this U.S.-shaped and historically oriented amusement park. ... Anka will be host for the park's most unusual event of the season, "Swing Night," dedicated to giving an around-the-clock, "locked-in" night of entertainment for thousands of high school graduates.
>
> The date is June 21, and the idea, according to Art K. Moss, [Freedomland] managing director, is to provide a place where exuberant graduates can let off steam safely without the traffic and other risks involved in the usual unregulated round of graduation hijinks.
>
> There will be continuous music for dancing through the night, various contests, access to all rides and other standard attractions of the park and serving of breakfast from 2 a.m. until dawn. The only adults allowed in the park will be the chaperones of the respective groups.
>
> —UPI, 1963

Paul frequently was heard on the radio on Freedomland commercials. He sang this jingle in one of the ads:

> Come on out to Freedomland
> For the greatest time you've ever planned.
> Fun and thrills go hand in hand
> At exciting Freedomland.
> Bring along that special date,
> Come out early, stay late.
> You can dance in the pale moonlight
> On a riverboat every night.

According to park photographer John Wagerer, one of the many park promotions involved Paul and the slippers of his female fans. The promotion asked girls to send in one of their slippers along with a photo before Paul would make an appearance at the park. He selected a slipper and then he and the young lady enjoyed a date.

Cecile Ferraro Ross has known Paul since those Freedomland days, attending a countless number of performances at the Moon Bowl. Cecile became the first president of the singer's fan club and has remained close friends with him all these years.

Bobby Darin

Walden Robert Cassotto, better known as Bobby Darin, was raised in the Bronx not too far away from Freedomland. He was sickly as a child from rheumatic fever, and this led to life-long heart issues.

Darin was booked to perform for a week (Friday, July 19, until Thursday, July 25) during 1963 at the Moon Bowl, accompanied by conductor and arranger Richard Behrke. At least one performance on July 23 was held during heavy rain on an extremely hot day. Darin became ill backstage and collapsed. He needed oxygen and was taken by ambulance to Mount Sinai Hospital, where he spent two days undergoing tests. His doctors advised him to rest for six to eight weeks and to curtail any type of strenuous activity.

Publically, Darin's collapse was attributed to exhaustion. Privately, it was believed at the time that he had suffered a heart attack, although an official diagnosis never became public. An Associated Press story erroneously reported that he collapsed on his way to a performance at Freedomland but did not require hospitalization.

After the incident, Darin took a train to Hollywood and then traveled to his home in Palm Springs, accompanied by his wife, actress Sandra Dee. The couple had separated and had not officially announced that they were together again. Dee later was asked if her husband's health issue at Freedomland helped them reconcile.

"No truth to that at all," she said in a public comment. "Bobby and I are back together because we have always loved each other and because we never should have broken up in the first place."

Despite her denials, the Freedomland incident sparked a renewed effort by the couple to work on their marriage.

Johnny Horton

Country and rockabilly singer Johnny Horton sang the Freedomland U.S.A. theme song, "Johnny Freedom," that was created exclusively for the park. When the single was announced, a four-page advertisement appeared in the June 6, 1960, issue of *Billboard* magazine. The second page of the ad contained just a little bit of music hype: "destined to become the biggest record of the year."

The song officially was released on a 45 rpm on July 4, 1960. It rose to #69 at Billboard, stayed on the charts for four weeks, and was featured on the Freedomland record album issued by Columbia Records. Music industry personnel considered it the "B" side of the record with "Comanche" as the "A" side. But it was "Johnny Freedom" that was promoted on the music charts. "Comanche" never made it into the top 100.

> Johnny Freedom is the image of the American spirit. He was reared in America's past, he lives in America's present and his future will be fulfilled in America's dreams and aspirations. Johnny Freedom is the embodiment of Freedomland U.S.A. where all of America comes to life. At Freedomland, you'll explore waterways and wilderness in the picturesque Northwest. Tour futuristic highways to Cape Canaveral. At Freedomland you'll thrill

to 35 exciting rides such as stagecoaches, stern-wheelers and space ships. You'll live through 41 authentic historic re-creations including the Chicago Fire, the Mardi Gras in New Orleans, and a Civil War battle. Be sure to visit Freedomland, located in New York City...it's the thrill as big as America itself.

—45 rpm record jacket

Johnny sang the song on *American Bandstand* before the park officially opened and on *Jubilee U.S.A.* just after the park opened. He also sang the song on Eddy Arnold's show.

When he recorded the song for the park's debut, Johnny already had become a popular singer. His semi-folk "saga songs" that started the "historical ballad" craze included the 1959 hit "The Battle of New Orleans." The song was awarded the 1960 Grammy Award for Best Country & Western Recording. Among his other successful songs were "North to Alaska" and "Sink the Bismarck."

Johnny Horton Day at Freedomland was held on July 16, 1960. The celebration was the final touch to an essay contest conducted by Columbia Records and Freedomland. Winners of the contest, based on a 50-word essay that explained "What Freedom Means to Me," traveled to New York to participate in events at the park.

Just four months later, on November 5, 1960, while "North to Alaska" was climbing the charts, Johnny Horton was killed in an automobile accident in Milano, Texas. Traveling with several others after an appearance in Austin, Johnny was behind the wheel heading to Shreveport, Louisiana. According to a survivor of the accident, Johnny was driving too fast. About 2am, near Milano, the car was crossing a bridge when a truck approached from the opposite direction. It hit both sides of the bridge before ramming into Johnny's Cadillac. Johnny had practiced avoiding head-on collisions by driving into ditches, but the narrow bridge became a trap. He was breathing when he was pulled from the car, but he died on the way to the hospital. The 19-year-old truck driver was intoxicated.

The following provides additional insight about the recording of "Johnny Freedom." Freedomland is referenced as an "exposition" and, though unconfirmed, this public information indicates Johnny appeared at the park on opening day.

On the 10th [March 10, 1960] he [Johnny Horton] cut two more [Leon] Payne songs, the atmospheric homage to Jim Bridger and "The Battle Of Bull Run," a "Battle Of New Orleans" soundalike, even down to the drums. To complete a day of historical remembrances, he laid down Snow-Shoe Thompson and Jimmy Driftwood's "John Paul Jones." [Driftwood's real name was James Corbitt Morris]. The theme continued the next day when over two sessions they remembered "Comanche" (The Brave Horse), "Young Abe Lincoln," "O'Leary's Cow," and "Johnny Freedom." "Johnny Freedom" was recorded on the insistence of Columbia president Goddard Lieberson to help push the opening of the Freedomland USA Exposition in the Bronx, New York, on 19th June 1960. Apparently, Gordon Stoker of the Jordanaires helped out on the vocals as Horton was struggling with it. They needn't have bothered as the song was rubbish, sounding like a poor Elvis movie soundtrack. The single and an album of the other recent cuts called *Johnny Horton Makes History* were issued and Horton appeared at the Freedomland opening, together with other appearances, linked to the launch.

—Rockabilly Hall of Fame Website

Little Peggy March

Margaret Annemarie Battavio from Lansdale, Pennsylvania, was 13 years old and just four-feet-nine-inches tall when she recorded "Little Me." At that time, the producers learned that her birthday was during the month of March and she became Little Peggy March.

On April 24, 1963, "I Will Follow Him" rocketed to number one on the U.S. music charts. The song had been recorded during early January and released on January 22. Little Peggy March became the youngest female artist with a number one hit. It also reached the top of the charts in Australia, New Zealand, South Africa, Japan, and Scandinavia.

Soon after her song reached the top, she appeared at Freedomland's Moon Bowl. An entertainment tidbit in newspapers during June 1963 reported:

> "Little Peggy—June 8–9, 15-year-old recording star Peggy March at Freedomland (amusement park with historic background); also The Chordettes, Arthur Godfrey's old vocal quartet.

The last song recorded by the Chordettes, "Never on Sunday," was issued June 1961 and the group broke up some time after that song hit the charts. It is not known which members went their separate ways nor which members—Lynn, Jinny, Janet, Carol—performed at Freedomland.

Other Singers

The following is a partial list of other popular singers who appeared at Freedomland. The accuracy of the dates and venues for the singers, along with the groups, orchestras, and musicians featured throughout this chapter is dependent on a variety of sources published at the time or years later.

Moss, Herman, Bennett. Freedomland executive Arthur K. Moss (left) is backstage at the Moon Bowl with musician Woody Herman and singer Tony Bennett.

- Tony Bennett, Moon Bowl, July 1–7, 1963.
- Pat Boone and family cut the opening day ribbon and he returned to the park in 1962.
- Anita Bryant sang "Getting to Know You" while walking through the crowd, according to the memory of a park guest. Documentation has not been located for her appearance.
- Solomon Burke, Moon Bowl, May 16–17, 1964.
- Freddie Cannon performed with the Dick Clark All-Star Show on June 10, 1962.
- Chubby Checker, Moon Bowl, May 30, 1962. Some of the children twisted with him on stage. When he was asked to pose for pictures while twisting at Freedomland, Checker was quoted in an Earl Wilson celebrity newspaper column as stating, "Well I don't want to be typed..."
- Jimmy Clanton, June 6–7, 1964.
- Nat "King" Cole, Moon Bowl, 1963.
- Johnny Crawford of *The Rifleman* also sang and appeared during 1963.
- Joey Dee (of the Starliters), Moon Bowl, July 20, 1963, to appear on Clay Cole's television show.
- Dale (Houston) & Grace (Broussard), Moon Bowl, June 6–7, 1964.
- Jimmy Dean reportedly earned $5,000 for a two-day gig at the park on May 18–19, 1963.
- Dick and DeeDee (Dick St. John and DeeDee Sperling), Moon Bowl, Saturday and Sunday, June 13–14, 1964.
- Bo Diddley, Moon Bowl, 1963.
- Little Eva (Eva Narcissus Boyd) performed at the park during 1962 and appeared in publicity pictures with one of Freedomland's steam engines (Monson No. 4) to promote her hit song "The Loco-motion." Also appearing in the photographs were songwriters Carol King and Gerry Goffin and producers Don Kirshner and Al Nevins.
- Betty Everett, Moon Bowl, May 23–24, 1964.

- Connie Francis, Moon Bowl, 1962.

- Marvin Gaye, Moon Bowl, 1964, along with the vocal group the Spinners, which included Bobbie Smith, Edgar "Chico" Edwards, Billy Henderson, Henry Fambrough, and Pervis Jackson.

- Lesley Gore, Moon Bowl, May 30–31, 1964, only weeks after her 18th birthday.

- Lena Horne, Moon Bowl, with Duke Ellington and his Orchestra, August 1961.

- Brian Hyland appeared with the Dick Clark All-Star Show on June 10, 1962.

- Jack Jones, Moon Bowl, August 23, 1963.

- Kitty Kallen, who had a hit with "Little Things Mean a Lot," performed at Freedomland on the weekend of May 25–26, 1963.

- Abbe Lane appeared with her husband's orchestra (Xavier Cugat), Moon Bowl, August 1962, and again May 30 through June 2 in 1963.

- Steve Lawrence and Eydie Gormé, Moon Bowl, with Duke Ellington and his Orchestra, August 22–27, 1961. Tenor saxophonist Paul Gonsalves performed several solos during the show.

- Brenda Lee appeared with the Tommy Dorsey Orchestra, Moon Bowl, 1962.

- Trini Lopez, Moon Bowl, May 16–17, 1964.

- Garnet Mimms, with the Enchanters, Moon Bowl, in 1963, and again May 16–17, 1964.

- Ricky Nelson, Moon Bowl, July 3–4, 1962. The two-day engagement of several shows each day drew a crowd of more than 32,500. Guitarist James Burton played during the Freedomland performances and on the majority of songs during the first 11 years of Ricky's career. He has played with many leading singers, is a member of the Rock and Roll Hall of Fame, the Rockabilly Hall of Fame, and the Musicians Hall of Fame and Museum.

- Patti Page, Moon Bowl, May 20–27, 1962. During one performance, she introduced her new daughter, Kathleen Patricia, to the audience.

- Gene Pitney appeared during 1964.

- Poncie Ponce, Moon Bowl, June 1964 (with Diane Renay/ Bobby Rydell).

- Della Reese, Moon Bowl, 1963.

- Diane Renay sang "Navy Blue," Moon Bowl, June 1964.

- Bobby Rydell, Moon Bowl, June 1964. "Back in that time," Rydell recently recalled, "it was one of the many fabulous venues where we all performed."

- Neil Sedaka performed for an entire week beginning June 24, 1963.

- Dee Dee Sharp performed with the Dick Clark All-Star Show on June 10, 1962.

- Terry Stafford, Moon Bowl, May 30–31, 1964.

- Rufus Thomas, Moon Bowl, June 67, 1964.

- Johnny Thunder, June 6–7, 1964.

- Johnny Tillotson appeared during 1964.

- Conway Twitty performed with the Dick Clark All-Star Show on June 10, 1962.

- Jerry Vale, a Bronx native, sang at the Moon Bowl on several occasions. At least one appearance was with the Richard Maltby Orchestra.

- Rudy Vallee made a 1962 appearance at the Moon Bowl with the Broadway cast from *How to Succeed In Business Without Really Trying.*

- Sarah Vaughan, Moon Bowl, August 15–21, 1961, with the Jimmy Dorsey Orchestra under the direction of veteran jazz trumpeter and bandleader Lee Castle (nee Lee Aniello Castaldo).

- Bobby Vinton, Moon Bowl, September 28–29, 1963, and again with the Peter Palmer Orchestra, July 24–30, 1964.

- Dionne Warwick, Moon Bowl, May 16–17, 1964.

- Andy Williams, Moon Bowl, September 16–17, 1961, and again during 1963.
- Jackie Wilson, Moon Bowl, July 3–9, 1964.
- Little Stevie Wonder was 14 when he performed at the Moon Bowl during 1964.

Other singers who performed at Freedomland included Bernie Allen, Frank Fontaine, Kathy Keegan, Major Lance, Julius LaRosa, Johnnie Ray, and Harriet "Tina" Robbin.

Groups

The Chaperones

The group consisted of Tony Amato (lead), Roy Marchesano (first tenor), Tommy Ronca (second tenor), Nick Salvato (baritone), and Richard Messina (bass). Tommy and Roy went to Farmingdale High School on Long Island. Tony was from Deer Park and Nick was from Bethpage.

The group had a couple of different names prior to the Chaperones, including the Sharptones and the Fairlanes. The name "Chaperones" was given to them by Jubilee Records, because the term was popular at the time for school dances and proms. Nick attended college with Steve Blaine, whose father, Jerry Blaine, headed Jubilee Records. In 1959, the group was invited to record for the Josie record label, which was part of Jubilee Records. The song they recorded, "Cruise To the Moon," was written by Roy. The record was released during the summer of 1960, and landed the group a gig at Freedomland.

According to the group, they were part of a show in Frontierland, but this is a Disneyland term. At Freedomland, they performed in the Old Southwest section of the park in the Opera House and Saloon. The show on which they appeared was hosted by popular New York City disc jockey Murray the K. The exact date is not known nor are the names of the other singers/groups in the show.

Lennon Sisters

The Lennon Sisters were one of the most popular vocal groups during the time of Freedomland and today they continue to perform across the country.

The original group consisted of four—Dianne, Peggy, Kathy, and Janet—of the six sisters from a family of 11 siblings. From 1955 until 1968, the group appeared regularly on *The Lawrence Welk Show*. Of the sisters, Peggy, Kathy, and Janet appeared at Freedomland, as Dianne recently had retired to raise a family. They performed at Freedomland on two occasions. Kathy specifically remembers appearances at the Moon Bowl during the August 1962 and August 1963 seasons.

"In those summers, we would first appear at the Atlantic City Steel Pier and then head north to Freedomland," recalled Kathy. "We were California girls, and while we were comfortable with the hot weather, it was the humidity along the East Coast that sometimes got to us. In Atlantic City, we appeared indoors, but at Freedomland we were outside. In those days, we didn't have electric curlers or blow dryers backstage. Between shows, we would do all we could to get ready and to be presentable for the next show."

Kathy remembered that Richard Maltby and his band backed them at the Moon Bowl and they also had some experiences with Benny Goodman.

"We had performed with the Maltby musicians at other venues, such as state and county fairs. We knew Richard and he had a very good band. We also were backed by some of the musicians from the Benny Goodman Orchestra. Benny was tough on his musicians and many others. We were very impressed with his great talent, but often his ego took over. Backstage at the Moon Bowl, Benny complained about the size of his dressing room. We three girls had the larger one and he had the smaller dressing room. Our father offered to have us switch dressing rooms with him, but Benny eventually declined."

The Lennon Sisters loved Freedomland, enjoying the many attractions, the food, their fans, and the many people they met for the first time at the park. A 1962 Freedomland publicity photo features the sisters backstage with singer, musician, bandleader, and actor Rudy Vallee. He was at the park that day along with the rest of the cast of the Broadway show *How to Succeed in Business Without Really Trying*. The Lennon family photo album also includes pictures of the sisters on the Horseless Carriage, Danny the Dragon, and the train.

"Our favorite had to be the car ride," remembered Kathy. "Just by the pictures, you can see we were having so much fun laughing throughout the ride as the car moved back and forth. Freedomland was one of the greatest ideas for a park. We had so much fun and we couldn't believe it failed.

"We enjoyed Freedomland more than other venues for another reason. Following many appearances on the East ZCoast, after Freedomland, we were going home after all that

The Lennon Sisters enjoy the Horseless Carriage ride. From left: Kathy, Peggy and Janet. Courtesy the Lennon Sisters

time to see our mom and our younger siblings. Our younger brother, Billy, also got to enjoy Freedomland. We always would bring one of our younger brothers or sisters on the road with us. Billy was with us during our Freedomland stop during 1963 and he loved the park."

The sisters were fans of Patti Page and Kathy especially was fond of Connie Francis. Both Patti and Connie appeared on the same Moon Bowl stage during the 1962 season. After all this time, the Lennon Sisters continue to maintain a busy appearance schedule. Peggy retired awhile ago and younger sister Mimi replaced her to sing with Janet and Kathy. While many of their performances are in Branson, Missouri, they still tour the country. On Christmas Eve 2017, their 24th Christmas season in Branson, the sisters celebrated their 62nd anniversary at the Andy Williams Moon River Theatre.

During the early 1960s, one fan rode the New York City subways and another grabbed a plane from Detroit to see the Lennon Sisters sing at Freedomland.

"My father used to bring me to a lot of their concerts," recalled Mary Ann (Broome) Rosenthal. "He was a Lawrence Welk fan and he knew I loved the Lennon Sisters."

One season, Mary Ann believes it was 1962, she boarded a plane in Detroit by herself and met with a couple of Cleveland friends who had arrived in New York. They booked a Manhattan hotel and together ventured to the Bronx to see their favorite vocalists.

"We stayed for all the shows, from the first until the last," said Mary Ann. "We hung out backstage and talked with them until the next show. We didn't spend much time at the other park attractions. I had blinders on and just wanted to see and be with my favorite group."

Mary Ann met Eveline Marcello at the Moon Bowl performances and they still keep in touch.

"The Lennon Sisters and I were from large families," recalled Eveline. "I grew up in an old farmhouse in Flushing, one of the last in Queens, as the last of eight children. I was the adventurous one, and traveled across the country, often cutting school, to see Kathy and her sisters perform. I loved them from when I first heard them during 1961. I loved their sound and my connection with them helped me become a professional singer. My vocals are very similar to their sound."

Eveline's first visit to Freedomland also occurred during 1962 when she was just 15 years old. The purpose was not to see the park, but to see the Lennon Sisters. She returned the following year for their week-long engagement, taking the subway and recalling that a few times an older brother got her there and back home by car.

"I was in their fan club, which was located in California," said Eveline, "and I wanted to meet them. The club arranged for me to be a reporter and to interview them at Freedomland. I met their father and enjoyed a wonderful time backstage with all of them. After answering all my questions, they told me to put my pen down, because they wanted to know all about me. I spent that entire week watching their shows and then spending time with them backstage. I was a fan who became very good friends with them, remaining friends to this day."

Eveline has a number of photographs with the sisters backstage at Freedomland and one of the photos includes young brother Billy. While she maintains a vivid memory of those days at Freedomland with the Lennon Sisters at the Moon Bowl, she does not recall too much about the park. The reason is she did not see much of it.

"I wanted to see the performances and spend time with the Lennon Sisters, so I did not take too much time away to see the park. But I do recall playing an arcade game in 1963, the one where you use a water pistol to shoot water into the mouth of a clown. I couldn't loose and I gave all the prizes, including dishes, to Peggy Lennon for her hope chest as she was planning to marry. The vendor didn't like that I won so often and he told me not to return."

Eveline's memory of the arcade game during the 1963 season is consistent with the changes that occurred at Freedomland that season and then continued into 1964. Park management decided to invest more in amusement park attractions, games of chance, and celebrity entertainers as it downplayed the history-themed attractions. These changes, though, did not affect Kathy, Mary Ann, and Eveline. The wonderful memories created at the Moon Bowl developed into life-long friendships.

The Socialites

Also known as Lorraine & the Socialites for lead singer Lorraine Anthanio, the group experienced an interesting reaction during an afternoon performance. According to Lorraine, they were singing at the Moon Bowl and an exhibit nearby was planning to shoot a man from a cannon. Just as the ladies were getting to a key part in one of their songs, the cannon exploded and the audience scattered.

The Tokens

The Tokens released the hit song "The Lion Sleeps Tonight" during late 1961. Lead singer Jay Siegal said the group performed the next year at the Moon Bowl. The group sang this hit and the 1961 hit "Tonight I Fell In Love." It was "in the summer of 1962," he said. (More likely 1963 based on the information below.) "I won't forget that concert as we played with Dion and the Belmonts and Count Basie and his orchestra."

During 1960, Dion left the Belmonts for a solo career. He sang with other back-up performers and did not reunite with the Belmonts until 1966. At Freedomland, it is possible but not confirmed that the Del-Satins backed-up Dion. According to the memories of a number of fans, Dion did appear at Freedomland as a solo artist (July 26–31, 1963) with Bronx guitarist John Falbo and the Count Basie orchestra.

"Well, I've got a vivid memory of that appearance," recalled John. "As I pulled up to the stage entrance in my '63 Dodge convertible, who should pull in beside me but Count Basie in his four-door convertible Lincoln. He was in that sea captain's hat. With a wink and a nod, we entered the Moon Bowl. He had the hit 'I Can't Stop Loving You' and was on the same bill, and would be the band to backup Dion. So, this 19-year-old kid gets to conduct those monster musicians. What an experience!"

John now mostly works in Las Vegas but his roots are found in New York recording studios, Bronx nightclubs, and national and international tours.

Motown Review

During July 1964, Freedomland hosted a Motown Review at the Moon Bowl that included the Contours, Martha and the Vandellas, Smokey Robinson and the Miracles, the Temptations, Mary Wells, and Kim Weston. Each act performed about three songs. Mary was billed separately as having a one-week stand at Freedomland that began on July 14, 1964, but the information could not be confirmed if her appearance was part of the Motown Review or if she was featured as a separate performer.

Other groups that performed at Freedomland included:

- Bobby Comstock and the Counts (often backed up singers at the Moon Bowl).

- Gary Lewis and the Playboys, according to a 1966 California newspaper clip, auditioned at Freedomland. The group's first successful song, "This Diamond Ring," did not become a hit until February 1965, a handful of months after Freedomland closed.

- Jay and the Americans were on the *Clay Cole Show* that was broadcast from the park.

- The Angels, Moon Bowl, June 6–7, 1964.

- The Chiffons, Moon Bowl, June 6–7, 1964.

- The Everly Brothers, Moon Bowl, August 20–27, 1962.

- The Four Seasons performed the week of April 16, 1963, and headlined at Freedomland May 23–24, 1964.

- The Kingsmen, Moon Bowl, June 6–7, 1964.

- The Orlons, Moon Bowl, May 16–17, 1964.

- The Reflections, Moon Bowl, May 30–31, 1964.

- The Ronettes, Moon Bowl, May 23–24, 1964.

- The Serendipity Singers, Moon Bowl, August 7–13, 1964.

- The Shirelles, Moon Bowl, May 30–31, 1964.

- The Tymes, Moon Bowl, May 23–24, 1964.

- The Village Stompers, Moon Bowl, August 14–20, 1964.

The Dovells, the Duprees, the Emotions, the Majestics, the Mills Brothers, the Sat-lites, the Searchers, and the Shangri-Las also performed at the park.

A considerable number of Freedomland's music shows were hosted by comedian Danny Crystal. Not much is known about him. An article in a July 1950 entertainment magazine stated that "Crystal is loaded with talent and had the room [the Monte Carlo in Pittsburgh] rocking with stories, songs and impressions." It is believed that the same guy later became director of eastern operations for Pat Boone Entertainment.

Musicians and Orchestras

Louis Armstrong

Louis Armstrong appeared at Freedomland's Moon Bowl on several occasions that included eight days starting August 28, 1961, and again for four days over the Labor Day weekend in 1964.

Through the big band years, Armstrong performed and recorded in small band combinations while also working with his orchestra. He disbanded the orchestra during July 1947 and then formed a group under a number of names but generally known as Louis Armstrong and the All Stars. These ensembles appeared across the country, including at Freedomland, from August 13, 1947, until Armstrong's death on July 6, 1971.

During the 1961 Freedomland appearance, the All Stars included James "Trummy" Young on trombone, Joe Darensbourg on clarinet, Billy Kyle on piano, Irv Manning on bass, Danny Barcelona on drums, and Jewel Brown, a jazz and blues vocalist. For the 1964 performances, most returned but Russell "Big Chief" Moore now was the trombonist and Eddie Shu played the clarinet.

While performing in the Bronx during 1961, Armstrong received an August 28 Western Union telegram from a nearby resident.

LOUIS SATCHMO ARMSTRONG:

= DLR I MMY FREEDOMLAND BRONX NY =

=HELLO POPS GLAD TO KNOW YOU ARE SO CLOSE

TO OUR HOUSE WE ARE

=VERY HAPPY AND WILL DIG YOU REAL SOON
PLEASE CALL US OLINVILLE=33313=

THE FAMILY CLARENCE EVELYN AND SONNY. =

Armstrong's 1964 appearance at the park was the Friday through Monday of Labor Day weekend. Friday through Sunday performances were at 5pm, 8pm, and 10:25pm. On Monday, shows were 5pm, 8pm and 9:25pm.

> The Labor Day weekend found Freedomland looking more like a ghost town than anything else—with the exception of the Moon Bowl where the great Louis Armstrong held sway. These were four glorious days of music and Pops and old friends. There was Johnny Windhurst [trumpeter], Ruby Braff [trumpet/cornetist], Dan Morgenstern [writer/editor/archivist/producer], Danny [banjoist/guitarist] and Blue Lu Barker [vocalist], Dick Wellstood [pianist], Max Kaminsky [trumpeter/bandleader], Slim Thompson [possibly the 1930s film actor], Creole Pete [tenorman from Fats Domino's group], Kenny Davern [clarinetist], Nat Lorber [trumpeter], Charlie Gang Gang, Leon Vogel and Mr. and Mrs. Ernst Steiner and Mr. and Mrs. Klaus Napel from the Hot Club of Zurich.

> Too bad that when Pops finally is playing in NY at a place where the only admission is one buck and is fairly convenient to get too [sic]—only a handful of musicians came to dig.

> —*Coda*, October/November 1964 (Canada's jazz magazine, 1958–2009)

To celebrate International Jazz Day on April 30, 2013, the Louis Armstrong House Museum in Corona (Queens), New York, and the Jazz Journalists Association presented a lecture and listening session about Armstrong that included a rare recording of his 1961 performance of "West End Blues" at Freedomland. This song and other recordings from that engagement were donated to the museum by the son of Freedomland Moon Bowl sound engineer Peter Davis. The songs never were circulated, issued, or listed in jazz discographics.

Count Basie

Count Basie and his orchestra performed at Freedomland on several occasions: July 27 through August 1, 1961; during the summer of 1962 with the Tokens and Dion; July 26–30, 1963; and on the final weekend of September 12-13, 1964.

A media interview was conducted at Freedomland during 1963. Here is an excerpt:

> It was a hot and humid summer Saturday afternoon when we made our way from mid-town Manhattan up to the Bronx—to a place called Freedomland, known as a family entertainment centre, or the Disneyland of the East Coast. Here, Count Basie and his orchestra were fulfilling a one-week engagement in the outdoor ballroom at the amusement park.

> [Basie:] "This engagement at Freedomland is very nice. A chance to play locally and to be at home to play to all types of people."

> It was about four o'clock in the afternoon, the temperature was 98 degrees—yet a sizeable crowd had gathered around the stand as the Basie band swung into "One Mint Julep." This is one of the featured numbers from their album *This Time by Basie*, which is definitely receiving tremendous play on commercial radio stations throughout the United States.

> As I sat listening to the Basie Boys, it brought to mind the quotation from New York's popular disc-jockey, William B. Williams, who said of Basie's rendering of this tune: "When you listen to this, if you don't nod your head, snap your fingers or tap your feet—you're sick." By the looks of things around me, everybody was pretty healthy at Freedomland.

Rolf Ericson And Bill Crow

Rolf Ericson was a fluent and sensitive master of the trumpet and fluegelhorn, and his talent achieved a unique mix of credits with orchestras and singers. His Freedomland connection involved the Benny Goodman Orchestra. It is widely known that many of Goodman's employees found the King of Swing "strange." This included Ericson, who played in the orchestra for 10 days at Freedomland.

During a 1990 interview, Ericson said that "Benny had this excellent guitarist, Turk van Lake. Every time he tried to play, a solo or just rhythm, Benny would say, 'No guitar.' This cat just sat there all night long and it happened again and again. At the end of the 10 days he hadn't plucked a single note.'"

Popular jazz bassist Bill Crow performed at the park with the orchestra and confirmed the same incident in an online post years later and also in his book *From Birdland to Broadway*.

Curtis Ousley

Curtis performed under the stage name King Curtis. He was an American saxophone virtuoso known for rhythm and blues, rock and roll, soul, blues, funk, and soul jazz. Variously a bandleader, band member, and session musician, he also was a musical director and record producer. He was best known for his distinctive riffs and solos such as on "Yakety Yak," which later became the inspiration for Boots Randolph's "Yakety Sax" and his own "Memphis Soul Stew." His Moon Bowl appearances are recorded as May 30–31, 1964.

Other musicians and orchestras under the Freedomland spotlight at the Moon Bowl, Hollywood Arena, or elsewhere included:

- Ray Anthony (Raymond Antonini, trumpeter and band-leader) and Kellie Greene (jazz pianist).

- Danny Barker, a jazz vocalist and musician who played guitar and banjo, appeared on the sternwheelers and elsewhere in the park until, according to an undated and unnamed newspaper item reported that he "is no longer singing and playing at this amusement park, thanks to the non-musical ear of a newly hired efficiency expert."

- Billy Bauer was a jazz guitarist who played with orchestras and in small groups. He was a lead in the bebop movement. He performed with Benny Goodman's orchestra at the park. His father was in the audience during a September 9, 1961, show at Freedomland that also was recorded for broadcast. After the show, the father congratulated his son and reportedly said, "Gee, I'm sorry. I didn't know. I just didn't know." The guitarist recalled that his father wanted him to find a solid career and never thought the son would be so good a musician to play with Benny Goodman.

- The Jimmy Dorsey Orchestra under the direction of Lee Castle (Lee Aniello Castaldo) with singer Marilyn Mitchell and entertainer Donald O'Connor appeared in August 1963. In a Walter Winchell newspaper column published days later, O'Connor reportedly "quit Freedomland TV spot in huff because whole show wasn't devoted to him."

- The Tommy Dorsey Orchestra with singer Tommy Sands appeared on June 15, 1963.

- The Les and Larry Elgart Orchestra performed during the 1963 season. Larry played saxophone and Les played trumpet. During 1954, they recorded the song "Bandstand Boogie" that would become the theme for the long-running television dance show *American Bandstand*.

- Duke Ellington and his orchestra, Moon Bowl, August 22–27, 1961, and summer of 1964. Jazz double bassist John Lamb was a struggling musician in 1964 when he was invited, through a personal phone call from the band leader, to play with the orchestra at Freedomland. Lamb carried his base on two trains and in a taxi from Philadelphia to the Bronx.

- Lionel Hampton and his orchestra appeared on the evening of the park's first day. He also appeared at other times, including August 3–6, 1964.

- Harry James and his orchestra, Moon Bowl, September 29 through October 1, 1961. The orchestra appeared again on August 31, 1962, with Buddy Rich as drummer.

- Stan Kenton's 1962 performance at Freedomland included vocalist Jean Turner.

- The Richard Maltby Band with trumpeter Doc Severinsen who led the NBC Orchestra on *The Tonight Show Starring Johnny Carson*.

- Ron Metcalfe and his orchestra, May 25–26, 1963.
- Glenn Miller Orchestra under the direction of Ray McKinley.
- Buddy Morrow with the Dick Clark Caravan of Stars on June 10, 1962.
- Gerry Mulligan (Concert Jazz Band with jazz bassist Bill Crow).
- Les Paul and Mary Ford, Hollywood Arena, 1961.
- Tito Rodriguez and his orchestra, Moon Bowl, appeared on the same dates as Bobby Vinton (September 28–29, 1963). His orchestra also appeared at the Latin American dance contest at the Moon Bowl on August 25, 1964.
- Si Zentner (trombonist and band leader) and his orchestra appeared at the park July 12–18, 1963. His 1962 album *Up a Lazy River* won the Grammy Award for Best Pop Instrumental Performance.

Additional musicians who performed at the park included Cab Calloway, Warren Covington and his orchestra, Maynard Ferguson, the Gene Krupa Quartet, Woody Herman and his orchestra, Ralph Marterie and his orchestra, and Peter Palmer and his orchestra. Latin nights also were featured at Freedomland, with Jose Trudello and Rosita Pagano among the performers. A hootenanny was held at Freedomland during the 1963 season with Bud and Travis (a folk music duo from San Francisco; Bud Daishiell and Travis Edmonson), the Phoenix Singers (a trio of black folk singers; Ned Wright, Arthur Williams, and Roy Thompson), and Ian and Sylvia (a Canadian folk-and-country duo; Ian and Sylvia Tyson).

Drum Corps

Various drum crops were featured in parades, performances and contests.

Every weekend during 1962, local corps appeared at the park, including the Sea Battalion Midshipmen, the Bethpage (Long Island) Colonials, the Babylon Islanders, the Shoreliners

(Neptune, New Jersey), the North Hudson Girls, the Lawmen of the 122nd Police Athletic League, and the Bridgeport (Connecticut) Police Athletic League.

Other corps that appeared at the park were the Legionnaires Junior Drum and Bugle Corps (Oceanside, New York), the Bellaire Drum and Senior Bugle Corps (Bellmawr, New Jersey), and the Corporal Carroll Junior Drum and Bugle Corps (West Haven, Connecticut).

CHAPTER NINETEEN

Others Associated with Freedomland

There's a holdup in the Bronx,
Brooklyn's broken out in fights;
There's a traffic jam in Harlem
That's backed up to Jackson Heights;
There's a scout troop short a child,
Khrushchev's due at Idlewild!
Car 54, Where Are You?

—Lyrics by Nat Hiken and music by John Strauss

Stage, movie and television actors, along with comedians, professional athletes, and other popular personalities of the day, visited Freedomland to perform, for publicity appearances, or simply to visit and to be recognized by park guests.

The fashion industry also enjoyed the park landscape, with photo-shoots occurring regularly to promote the latest designer clothes and undergarments. Then, there were people who may not have been household names but were from various walks of life and forever will have a connection to the park.

Eddie Albert

Eddie Albert appeared on June 10, 1961. A park publicity photo features him befriending a cowboy bandit. A few years later, he would become known to baby boomers as Oliver Wendell Douglas in the television sitcom *Green Acres*. At the park, parents and grandparents already knew him from such films as *Roman Holiday*, *The Comeback Kid*, *Oklahoma!*, and *The Longest Yard*.

Johnny Coons

"Uncle" Johnny Coons narrated the 1963 Freedomland "Travel Time" film that was the popular promotional trailer for the park. Johnny was involved with early live children's television programming in Chicago. He also was one of the leading specialists for "voice" characterizations as the voice of Space Mouse on *The Woody Woodpecker Show* and Heap O'Calorie, a parody of actor Andy Devine, on *The Dick Tracy Show*.

Bob Cummings

Charles Clarence Robert Orville Cummings was an actor known for his roles in films (such as *Dial M for Murder*), and on stage, television, and radio. While in high school in Missouri, Bob was taught to fly by his godfather, Orville Wright. He became the first official flight instructor in the country and served in this capacity during World War II.

Most baby boomers remember Bob from his television work, including the first televised performance of *Twelve Angry Men* and the hit comedy *The Bob Cummings Show* that was renamed *Love That Bob* in reruns.

In a Freedomland publicity photo captured during July 1960, Bob is shaking hands/paws with the monkey of the park's organ grinder. He was one of the featured celebrities at the 1955 opening of Disneyland.

The Amazing Randi

To baby boomers, James Randi was known as the Amazing Randi, the magician who appeared on many television programs, including the *Wonderama* shows filmed at the park for WNEW-TV. He created a prop—a floating faucet with running water—for Casa Loca.

An online commenter recalled the prop:

> The first time I ever saw this illusion was in the early 60s as a boy in the Bronx visiting a now-defunct amusement park called Freedomland. ... They had one of these "floating faucets" illusions with water pouring into

a bucket. Casa Loca was very similar to the "Vortex" places that exist in a few locations around the country, which purport to "violate the law of gravity." I was corresponding with James Randi a few months ago about those Vortex tourist traps and I mentioned Casa Loca. Much to my surprise, he told me that he was the person who designed it for the amusement park.

The Three Stooges

Moe Howard, Larry Fine, and Joe (Curly Joe) De Rita appeared at Freedomland's Moon Bowl several times as they promoted their early 1960s films. Besides staring in several films, the boys enjoyed a cameo role as firefighters in *It's a Mad, Mad, Mad, Mad World*. They appeared at the park with their New York television friend Officer Joe Bolton.

Toody And Muldoon

Fred Gwynne and Joe E. Ross from *Car 54, Where Are You?* appeared at the park during the weekend of June 2–3, 1962. As reported in *Television Radio Daily* of Friday, June 1, 1962:

> *Car 54*'s Toody, Muldoon Booked for Freedomland—Joe E. Ross and Fred Gwynne, Toody and Muldoon of NBC-TV's *Car 54* series, will share the spotlight with Gene Krupa's Quartet at Freedomland's Moon Bowl this weekend."

The appearance promoted the show that aired originally from September 17, 1961, until April 14, 1963. The actors likely were filming episodes of the show nearby at the borough's Gold Medal Studios (807 East 175th Street).

Other Celebrities

The following is a partial list of other popular celebrities who visited Freedomland:

- André Baruch was an American film narrator, radio announcer, news commentator, talk show host, disc jockey, and sportscaster. For the 1961 opening week, he introduced the many celebrities in attendance.

- Chick Darrow owned Fun Antiques, a Manhattan store specializing in out-of-date toys and games that opened during 1962. A former vaudevillian, Chick appeared at shows at the Hollywood Arena.

- Actor Henry Fonda visited during the 1961 season with adopted daughter Amy.

- Singer and television host Merv Griffith appeared with a "sing-for-all" on the Sunday night of the 1961 opening weekend.

- Actor and singer Eddie Hodges of the 1960 film *The Adventures of Huckleberry Finn* appeared in 1963.

- Vaughn Meader was the comedic star of *The First Family* record album that received the 1963 Grammy Award for Album of the Year. He was featured on the *Clay Cole at the Moon Bowl* television show.

- Ventriloquist Jimmy Nelson with Danny O'Day and Farfel the Dog appeared on opening day (June 10) of the 1961 season.

- Actor Hugh O'Brien as television's Wyatt Earp appeared in character and rode a horse through Little Old New York and other areas of the park on Saturday and Sunday, September 10–11, 1960.

- Child actor Jon Provost as "Timmy" appeared with his television parents, June Lockhart, Hugh Reilly, and, of course, Lassie.

- Actress and singer Debbie Reynolds appeared on New York City's Park Avenue and 42nd Street on June 2, 1960, to publicize Freedomland and to accept an invitation to appear at the park's June 18 preview that benefitted the Children's Village Interfaith Chapel Fund and other youth charities.

- Johnny Roventini, the Brooklyn son of Italian immigrants, was the bellboy in Philip Morris advertisements who issued a "Call for Philip Morris" cigarettes for more than four decades. Under four feet in height, Johnny was a bellboy at the New York Hotel in 1933 when he was discovered by an advertising executive. Johnny reportedly could vocalize a perfect B-flat tone as he repeated the famous words over a million times during his career. He was described by Philip Morris personnel as a "living trademark." His park appearance included a car ride through the streets of Little Old New York.

- Allan Sherman, a comedy writer, television producer, and music parodist of "Hello Muddah, Hello Fadduh" fame performed his songs and comedy at the Moon Bowl.

- Herb Shriner, a humorist, radio personality, and television host mostly active during the 1940s and 1950s enjoyed the park with his children.

- Red Skelton, the popular comedian, received this line in a gossip column that appeared in a September 5, 1961, California newspaper: "Red Skelton will make a personal appearance at New York's Freedomland [wh]ere the nation's school kids start writing on their slates 'I love you so' this new school term." This information has been shared with several organizations that maintain the comedian's papers and collections, but documentation is elusive about the appearance.

- General James Alward Van Fleet was in attendance during the 1961 season opening week. A World War I U.S. Army officer, he served as a regimental, divisional, and corps commander during World War II. He was the commanding general of U.S. Army forces and other United Nations forces during the Korean War.

- Actress Monique Van Vooren cut the ribbon on opening day (May 26) for the 1962 season.

Other celebrity appearances at the park included Lucille Ball, Buster Crabbe, Troy Donahue with the Miss Teenage Fair competition, Dave Garroway, Peter Lind Hayes during opening week 1961, and the Otto Kunze Marionettes.

Broadway Connections

Freedomland maintained many connections to Broadway, including actors, dancers, producers, directors, musicians, and designers. Casts from Broadway shows regularly visited the park. These included members from *Bye Bye Birdie* and *How to Succeed in Business Without Really Trying*.

Jennifer Billings, a dancer in *Carnival*, was photographed checking, appropriately, the shoes of a horse during May 1961 and this publicity photograph to promote the opening of the season appeared in newspapers nationwide. Actress Lucienne Bridou performed in Freedomland's 1961 exclusive production of "Colossus." Soon after, she appeared in the Broadway cast of *A Funny Thing Happened on the Wary to the Forum*, portraying Panacea, from May 8, 1962, until August 29, 1964. She appeared in the movie of the same name, other films, and on television.

Michael Gifford (born Mary Michael Pollock) was a longtime New York City press agent. Her agency, Gifford-Wallace Inc., represented the musical *Hair*, Westinghouse Broadcasting, Fox Television, South Street Seaport, and Studio 54. She is credited with the sale of one million Freedomland tickets.

Actress Denise McLaglen was 34 years old when she was selected "Moon Bowl Queen" for the 1964 season from among 1,000 models and actresses. A daughter and niece in an acting family, by 1959 she had appeared in the Broadway musical *Gypsy* as a showgirl. Given her knack with animals, she also was responsible for the menagerie that enlivened a cast led by Ethel Merman. One night, a monkey in her care caused her trouble, escaping and then relieving itself on her. When Ethel saw her the next day, she said, "My dear girl, you look as though you've had a helluva night out."

Actress Mary Martin likely visited Freedomland since she was involved in its advance publicity as hostess of New York City's 1960 Sumer Festival. At the time, she was the star of the Broadway musical *The Sound of Music*.

Miles E. White was a leading costume designer of Broadway musicals for 25 years, including *Oklahoma!* and *Carousel*. For films, he received Oscar nominations for *The Greatest Show on Earth*, *There's No Business Like Show Business*, and *Around the World in 80 Days*. At Freedomland, the designer was involved with the park's 1963 Easter parade. Elsie the cow led the parade wearing a $1,250 Miles White spring outfit featuring a Victorian hostess gown. Elsie looked moo-velous.

Fashionable Freedomland

The park served as a backdrop for fashion shows and for photography for a number of designers.

Many fashion photo shoots at the time featured models showcasing furs, wardrobes for all seasons, children's outfits, and even the Maidenform bra and Raleigh clothing. Besides the contemporary fashions, the photographs for advertisements and the editorial spreads in newspapers and magazines featured the sternwheelers, the Jenny cars from the Horseless Carriage, Danny the Dragon, stage coaches, and trains.

One industry promotional event at the park featured the 1960 Miss Wool of America. A fashion newspaper columnist in the September 8, 1960, issue of *The San Bernardino County Sun* of California reported:

> A beautiful American girl has been selected as Miss Wool of America, a sort of an Ambassadress of Good Wool. At a fashion show in the famous Freedomland in New York, the models were all made of American wools and worsteds and it was interesting to learn that Miss Wool of America is Patti Jo Shaw. She was selected at the Powel County High School in Deer Lodge, Montana. Long ago I visited Deer Lodge and it wasn't a town from which I would expect a fashion representative to come, but fashion now is everywhere!"

Possible Sightings

An often-repeated story is that Burt Reynolds portrayed a cowboy during an entire park season when he was a relatively unknown stuntman. But, did he or didn't he appear at the park?

Ben Rossi, who administered park entertainment and served a couple of seasons as Freedomland's marshal, said that he had heard the same story, but did not believe that Burt was at the park for an entire season. Ben said the actor might have been at the park for a week, or even less, possibly over a long weekend. But, he wasn't sure if he actually worked there.

The actor's career highlights rule out that he would have been a season-long cowboy at the park. He already was an established actor, appearing in roles on various television programs, including *Riverboat, Pony Express*, and *The Blue Angels*. On *Gunsmoke*, Burt was portraying Quint Asper, the half-Indian blacksmith and "de facto" deputy.

So, if he was at Freedomland, he would not have appeared as an unknown stuntman in the western shows but as a rising Hollywood star. Possibly he was booked for a personal appearance to promote one of his television roles.

Mamie Van Doren has been connected with Freedomland for possibly turning down an appearance. Harvey Earl Wilson, a journalist, gossip columnist, and author published that she "requested 5Gs to work two nights at Freedomland; no answer yet" in an August 1962 column. No documentation has been located that the actress, model, singer, and sex symbol ever made the trip to the park.

The "Miss" Ladies

Miss Universe 1960 posed for a publicity photo at Freedomland. Linda Bement of Utah was the third Miss USA to be crowned Miss Universe. That year's pageant was the first Miss Universe competition to be televised nationwide. For a publicity photo in one of Freedomland's western sections, a noose was placed playfully around her neck and the rope was held by park cowboy Bob Oran.

Sherrylyn Patecell was 1960 Miss New York City. She took a publicity photo while aboard one of the bullboats of the Northwest Fur Trapper ride.

Penny Paulsen of New York City was named Miss Freedomland 1962. As a member of the staff of the Candy Jones Career Girls School, Penny provided makeup instructions for young ladies during the spring, fall, and winter. During the summer, she did the same at the school's summer camp on Long Island. At the time, Penny was a Hunter College student and she lived with her parents on 38th Street and Third Avenue. She wasn't a fashion model. Her work primarily focused on sports and recreation, teen fashion, and hair styling. Candy Jones was the fashion model. She also was a writer and radio talk-show hostess during the 1970s with second husband Long John Nebel.

Carolyn Wood (now Carolyn Wood Imbrie) entered the Miss High School of New York Pageant at Freedomland during her 1961 junior year. Her tap performance won the talent portion of the pageant. She became the original keyboardist for the musical group the Brooklyn Bridge.

Sports Celebrities

A number of athletes who were popular during the 1940s, 1950s, and 1960s appeared at Freedomland as celebrities or to participate in the sports clinics that were added to entice youngsters to visit the park.

Former players who visited were retired Brooklyn Dodgers Jackie Robinson and Roy Campanella. For the sports clinics that were held during the week of July 13, 1964, Johnny Blanchard, Jim Bouton, Clete Boyer, and Joe Pepitone of the New York Yankees, Tom Gola of the New York Knicks, and Richie Guerin of the St. Louis Hawks appeared at the park.

Several professional football players appeared at Freedomland a week earlier on the Friday, Saturday, and Sunday of the July 4 weekend as part of the WNEW-AM sports jamboree. The players were John Henry Johnson (fullback for San Francisco, Detroit, Pittsburg, and Houston, and later voted into the Pro Football Hall of Fame), Dick Lynch (defensive back with the Washington Redskins and New York Giants; later the commentator for the New York Giants' radio broadcasts and inductee to the Giants' Ring of Honor), and Abraham Woodson (cornerback and kick returner for San Francisco and St. Louis).

Golfer Arnold Palmer's name branded the mini-golf course at Freedomland, though it's unknown whether he visited the park.

Maryvonne Huet, the French figure skater who competed in ladies singles, appeared in a show at the park. She had won the gold medal at the French Figure Skating Championships during 1954 and 1955. At Freedomland, she was featured in "Ice-A-Rama" at the Hollywood Arena that presented four shows daily during the 1963 season. Also appearing in the show were adagio dance duo Roman and Dugan, comedy skater Johnny Melendez, trick skater Bobby Denard, and the chorus of Skating Lovelies.

CHAPTER TWENTY

Memories of Freedomland

During its inaugural season, Freedomland celebrated its one millionth guest. Two siblings represented this milestone.

—Eight-year-old Pamela Peters and six-year-old Billy Peters from Darien, Connecticut

The Peters children visited on August 23, 1960. Many children who were toddlers or teenagers at the time retain fond memories of Freedomland, whether their initial visit was during the inaugural season or the last year. Their impressions have remained vivid for more than 50 years.

Some women recall their first dates at the park. Men have shared boyhood stories about ditching bicycles and sneaking into the park through holes in fences. One hole brought a young boy to a location where he could jump onto the back of a sternwheeler and then leave the boat at the dock with the rest of the passengers.

Here are some more fond memories of Freedomland:

The Casa Loca had no exterior appeal whatsoever. In 1962, we were passing by and it, unlike the other attractions, had no waiting line. For that matter, it had no fancy lights, no people carts, and no electricity, either. We went in one end not knowing what to expect and came out the other amazed by what our senses told us was impossible. Simple disorientation and gravity created an illusion that had cans rolling up a table and out a window as well as pool table balls that went uphill. More than 50 years later, I thank Clark's Trading Post [Lincoln, New Hampshire] for re-creating what I consider to be the number-one Freedomland attraction.

—*John Bulakowski*
Queens Boy

It was during the start of the summer of 1960 that my father took my brothers and me to this unique theme park that re-created events in American history. The three parts of the park that I remember fondly are Little Old New York, Satellite City, and the Civil War. In Little Old New York, I recall seeing the Schaefer Brewery that showed how the beer was first brewed and how popular it became with the citizens of NYC.

The brewing process was created by a group of animated figurines that looked like little elves, which were enchanting. The figures were similar to Paul Ashley's puppets that would be appearing on *Laurel & Hardy* and *Let's Have Fun* shows on WPIX TV Ch.11 in NYC that fall. There was also the rocket launch at Satellite City, which my brothers and I saw on film on a TV monitor, and the wagon ride through the re-creations of the War Between the States.

I wanted to come back and see the park again the following summer, but my dad said "no." I was never able to see the kids' TV hosts/performers who appeared nor was I was able to see the Three Stooges or Fred Gwynne and Joe E. Ross, who played Police Officers Muldoon and Toody on *Car 54, Where Are You?*

Kevin S. Butler
—Freedomland Fan

My aunt, Betty Castelli, was an office clerk at Freedomland. She did come through with a lot of free tickets over the years, and in the later years, I purchased my own tickets when it was one price and free rides. With free rides as many times as you wanted, it was back to the Crystal Maze to test my skill against my brother, Eddie. I just purchased a stop watch, and I wanted to time myself from start to finish going through the maze. After about 10 to 12 runs, I was barred, due to the number of patrons I nearly knocked down during my runs.

Easter Sunday was April 18 in 1965 and Freedomland had been permanently closed since October 1964, but was still fun to visit, this time by bicycle. We had moved in 1963 from East 151st Street to East 233rd Street, a few miles from Freedomland. After it closed, I went on many hikes through Freedomland, exploring all the deserted buildings and rides. For some reason, the security guards welcomed me, since I was polite and was never a problem. Or, maybe, because I was still dressed in my Easter best. I never got to go on the burro ride in the Southwest hills of the Old West, but I wished I did, since the bike ride up and down the trail was great fun. My brother and I spent most of that day on the trail, until it was getting late. I led the neighborhood kids to one last visit in the late summer of 1965. Just about everything was completely boarded up or demolished. The only attraction available was a foot race around the empty track of the Horseless Carriage ride in Little Old New York. There were many boxes of documents, papers, and flyers all around, but sadly I did not think about saving them until many years later.

—*Thomas X. Casey*
President, Huntington Free Library (the Bronx)
Secretary, East Bronx History Forum
Secretary, Kingsbridge Historical Society

While growing up in the Bronx, I had fond memories of Freedomland. Riding on the horse-drawn trolley car of Little Old New York and seeing many of the stores and shops made me feel like I traveled back in time and was actually there. Observing the hand-blown glass shop gave me a real appreciation of the different shapes and colors of various glassware, not to mention the skill it took to blow and shape them.

The Civil War ride was one of my favorites, as I rode on a wagon from scene to scene listening to bullets being shot, cannons firing, and watching automated soldiers in their blue and gray uniforms. Taking a ride on the large sternwheeler really made me feel like I was going down the Mississippi River. You couldn't leave the park without visiting Elsie the cow in her Borden's house. I remember trying to walk across the tilted floor of the Casa Loca without holding the handrail but was not successful. Who could forget the pool table and the crooked cue sticks?

My fondest memory was getting the autograph of Connie Francis, the leading and most successful female vocalist of that time with such hits as "Vacation," "Lipstick on Your Collar," "My Heart Has a Mind of Its Own," "Stupid Cupid," "Where the Boys Are," and "Mama." After performing at the Moon Bowl, she was escorted off the stage by her bodyguards and she stopped two feet in front of me where I was able to get her autograph.

I often wonder how great a park Freedomland could have been had it survived. I believe the demise of Freedomland was largely brought about by the political and monetary issues in the building of Co-op City. It could have been an American historical and entertaining park all year round with land to expand and history updates as the years went by. In the winter months, part of the park could have been set up as a winter wonderland with sleigh riding, ice skating, skiing, and other winter activities. With good management, Freedomland had the potential of being an outstanding historical American amusement park famous throughout the country. Freedomland U.S.A. always will be a fond memory for me.

—Philip Centrone
A true Bronxite, born, raised, and still residing in the Bronx

My brother and I loved to ride in the Civil War wagons, but as far back as possible. We always got a kick of seeing the fallen trees and horses rise magically back into position behind us as they reset for the next group of travelers.

—Bill Cotter
World's Fair and Theme Park Historian

I worked in construction as a wire lather (reinforced concrete) in the summer of 1969 to help pay for graduate school at NYU. After completing a construction job in Manhattan, I went to the union hall to "shape" for another assignment. My name was called and I went to the window and the guy told me, "You're being assigned to Freedomland, kid."

"Freedomland?" I said, "It was torn down."

"Yeah, I know, but they still call it that. They're building a massive housing complex. Plenty of work for us, too."

So, I showed up at "Freedomland" that day and learned we were constructing Co-op City, or Cooperative City. I remember talking to the guys on the job site about the tall buildings being built on swampland in the northeast Bronx, and they all expressed concern that the buildings were not going to be safe. Well, the engineers and workers did such a good job that the buildings built on the former Freedomland site are still standing tall. Freedomland lives on!

—Joe Fahey
Born in the Bronx in 1940
Professor at Manhattan College

In the summer of '63 (1963, not 1863), my parents took me by bus 240 miles to the battlefield of Gettysburg. It was the centennial of the Civil War and, as a 10-year-old, I got hooked. Closer to home, just a few miles away, was Freedomland. My parents would take me to the Civil War section over and over again. At Gettysburg, I saw the battlefield. At Freedomland, I heard the roar of the cannon and through the smoke, the gleam of the bayonet. This is what it must have looked like between the Blue and the Gray.

I can truly say Gettysburg and Freedomland made me who I am today—a Civil War re-enactor and lecturer, a historical advisor to authors and filmmakers (such as *Gettysburg*, in which I also portrayed General A.P. Hill), and a past president of the Civil War Round Table of New York.

THANKS, FREEDOMLAND!

—Patrick Falci

I was a child during my very first visit to Freedomland in 1960. We spent the day working our way through the park, and it was twilight by the time we arrived at the Civil War ride. The gates were lit up by roaring torches, but they were already closing things down, as the horses were easily spooked in the darkness by the recorded gunfire. I saw the teams of horses being led away by torchlight.

All I got to do was visit the Civil War gift shop just outside the entrance. I had never seen so many Civil War things for sale all in one place. So we ended up missing the ride, but I couldn't wait to come back. And when we did, the Civil War ride became my all-time favorite thing to see at the park.

—William F. Finlayson
Past President, Civil War Round Table of New York

Freedomland was the foundation for my love of theme parks. Disneyland was a pipe dream growing up in the Bronx in the early 1960's. Who could afford plane tickets or have the time for a cross-country car trek? Solution: Freedomland, a 10-mile trip from my house.

Three things stand out in my mind: the Chicago Fire, the Civil War ride, and the Buccaneer ride. I was too little to pump the water on the Chicago Fire, but they allowed me to hold on to my dad while he pumped the water. I was thrilled by that.

I am a Disney World junkie inspired by the 64–65 World's Fair and even more so by Freedomland.

—Don Garofalo
Bronx Resident 1958–1978

So much of my life has been shaped by Freedomland. To me it will always be so dear to my heart. I've always loved trains and really enjoyed Casey Jones (a steaming and a rolling) on TV, the CNJ passenger trains which passed near my home, the miniature trains that ran on the City of Keansburg steamboat pier at Keansburg, New Jersey, and my dad's American Flyer train layout.

I wanted to go to Disneyland and after seeing the opening of Freedomland on TV, I really wanted to go. My sister, Virginia, and her boyfriend, Richie (my future brother-in-law), took me to Freedomland that very first summer. I was almost eight years old and the first thing we did was to ride on the horse-drawn trolleys, just like we were actually back in time. I especially enjoyed when our trolley veered to the side to pass an oncoming trolley. Then, seeing a real steam train up at the station was so fantastic and I could hardly wait to go for a ride on board.

Richie and one of the conductors brought me up to the locomotive (Monson No. 3) where the fireman showed me the fire in the boiler. I remember wishing that someday I might become a steam locomotive engineer. So many years later (1988), I would become one for the Walt Disney World Railroad.

The last ride that we went on during that first visit to Freedomland was aboard one of the harbor tug boats. Little Old New York was so cool and I can still recall the elves working at the Schaefer Brewery, Macy's shop, being truly amazed by the glass blower.

I fondly remember seeing both *The American* and *The Canadian* sternwheelers from the train and on my last train ride, during the last summer that Freedomland was open, seeing Louis Armstrong on the deck of one of the sternwheelers. He played his trumpet and waved a white handkerchief.

—Love, *John J. Gilson*

I remember seeing the Four Seasons at Freedomland. It was definitely on Saturday, May 23, 1964, and they did four shows, all of which I attended. They played their own instruments.

Lennon Sisters and train engineer. The Lennon Sisters (from left: Peggy, Janet and Kathy) meet one of the train engineers during the 1962 season. Courtesy the Lennon Sisters.

Bob Gaudio was on keyboards, Nick Massi played electric bass guitar, and Tommy DeVito played guitar. The drummer was session drummer Ronald Roach. He wasn't a member of the group. They definitely performed "Alone," their latest single, though it had been recorded a year or two earlier. It was on the Vee-Jay label and they had left Vee-Jay and switched to Philips. They only had two singles on Philips as of then, "Dawn (Go Away)" and "Ronnie." "Rag Doll," on Philips, was released four days later.

—Lew Goodman
Born and raised in the Bronx

I grew up within walking distance of Freedomland. I remember visiting the park four times—twice with my parents and sisters, once with cousins, and the last time with a group of friends from my grammar school at Holy Rosary in the Bronx. In addition to enjoying the rides and attractions, my fondest memory is of the glass blowers' shop. I would go to Little Old New York and be mesmerized as a bead of molten glass was blown and maneuvered to form a beautiful object. I think this influenced my appreciation and collection of fine crystal pieces.

—Barbara La Malfa
Bronx at heart

Being pretty young, I don't remember much during the building phase of Freedomland, but my parents told me that some of my family members were directly involved in its construction. My Uncle Benny was a crane operator, and he dug out the Great Lakes. My dad, being in the Teamsters Union, drove a dump truck on the weekends, delivering dirt. When it was completed, my parents took us to visit one weekend when our favorite TV personality from Channel 5 was going to be there. My sister, Liz, and I were very excited to meet "Uncle" Tom Gregory, the host of *Cartoon Playtime*, and we still have the snapshot of us with him to this day.

I clearly remember my dad holding me up to reach the pump so we could put out the Chicago Fire. I also recall my parents telling us that they saw Tony Bennett perform at the Moon

Bowl. Today, when I drive by Co-op City, I wonder if our kids would enjoy the park as much as we did.

—Nancy Laterza Manganiello
Former Pelham Bay Resident

Richard Morton loved the Bronx. He grew up on 145th Street near St. Ann's Avenue during the 1950s and continued to share his neighborhood memories with so many people. He was a frequent contributor to Bronx Facebook pages and helped many people reconnect with their childhoods or learn about the streets that their parents called home. Richard had fond memories of family outings to Freedomland, too. This photo of Richard at the park is shared in his memory.

Richard Morton. Courtesy the Morton Family.

I'm one of those people who can't remember what I had for dinner last night, but my memories of Freedomland remain fond and vivid some 55 years after visiting the park. The fog of time can't erase experiences like riding on a real, live mule...being "robbed" by masked bandits while on board a horse-drawn stage coach...furiously pumping water with other kids to help fight the raging Chicago Fire...and my personal favorite, seeing Robert E. Lee surrender to Ulysses S. Grant in front of Appomattox courthouse. Freedomland's creative team, many of whom earned their stripes at Disney, dreamed up a unique and entertaining amusement venue, the likes of which the world likely will never see again.

—Chuck Schmidt
—Journalist and author, *Disney's Dream Weavers, On the Disney Beat*, and others.

I can still remember my first trip to Freedomand. Sister Frances Paula made going on the Civil War ride a requirement and Mrs. Schreiber, our class monitor, instructed us that this was the first amusement that we had to experience in order to avoid hearing it from our beloved teacher. What a memory!

—John Tantillo
—Author, *People Buy Brands Not Companies*

CHAPTER TWENTY-ONE

Radio/Television Broadcasts from Freedomland

The thing I remember most about Freedomland were the parades and they would always drive me around in a Model T open roadster.

—Herb Oscar Anderson, WABC Radio

Many New York City and national radio shows were broadcast from Freedomland. Disc Jockeys and other radio-show hosts appeared regularly at the Braniff Space Rover or the Moon Bowl in Satellite City, at the Opera House and Saloon in the Old Southwest, or at the Hollywood Arena in San Francisco.

Disc Jockeys/Radio Personalities

- WABC. Herb Oscar Anderson ("The thing I remember most about Freedomland were the parades and they would always drive me around in a Model T open roadster."), Jack Carney (broadcast from Freedomland on June 6, 1961), Charlie Greer, Cousin Bruce Morrow, Farrell Smith, and Scott Muni. A June 23, 1962, issue of a trade magazine reported that "starting May 26, and continuing every Saturday night through the summer, Scott Muni, WABC, New York, is originating his 7–10 p.m. show from a 'Space Ship,' located just inside the 'Moon Bowl' at Freedomland, a local amusement center."

Muni also appeared at the Opera House and Saloon every Friday from 7:15 until 10pm during the 1961 season.

- WCBS. Oscar Brand, Stan Freeman & Bob Haymes, Allan Gray, Lee Jordan, Ed Joyce, Dick Noel, and Jack Sterling.

- WINS. Bob Lewis, Murray Kaufman (Murray the K), and Paul Sherman ("the crown prince of rock and roll").

- WMCA. "Dandy" Dan Daniel, Harry Harrison, Joe O'Brien, B. Mitchel Reed, Jack Spector, and Frank Stickle. During May 1963, tens of thousands of people cheered Freedomland's new season. Everyone enjoyed a parade of antique autos. B. Mitchel (born Burton Mitchel Goldberg in Brooklyn) was at the wheel of one car and he was joined by other "Good Guys and Gals" wearing WMCA's gold and black sweatshirts. Along for the ride were Dan, Joe, Phil, and Frank. At the time, WMCA was the only station broadcasting consistently two days a week from Freedomland (Saturday 7–11pm and Sunday 12–6:00pm).

- WMGM. Mike Lawrence, Jerry Marshall, and Norm Stevens, all during the 1960 season.

- WNBC. The same Jerry Marshall hosted his 7:10 to 10:30pm show Wednesdays and Thursdays at Freedomland's Moon Bowl when he was heard on WNBC. Jimmy Wallington was another station host who handled broadcasts from the park.

- WNEW. Phil McLean and Big Wilson. In a reply to a question from a trade publication, Malcolm John "Big" Wilson, Jr., said: "WNEW has been doing a half-hour remote pickup of top orchestras from Freedomland during my Saturday broadcast. The advantage is that we have brought back to radio the live sound of big bands. It is a pleasant change of pace which our listeners like. In a way, these pickups are similar to WNEW's monthly "Music Spectaculars," which feature the best musicians today in performances 'live on tape.'"

- WWRL. Hal Jackson.

"The Cool Ghoul"

John Zacherle (sometimes credited as John Zacherley) was a beloved figure on radio and television in both New York City and Philadelphia. He was a disc jockey and enjoyed a long career as a television horror movie host. Zacherle also hosted an animated cartoon show on WPIX-TV during 1963 and the teenage dance show *Disc-O-Teen* (sometimes written *Disco Teen*) for three years at WNJU-TV in Newark. Dick Clark of *American Bandstand* fame reportedly gave Zacherle his nickname, the Cool Ghoul.

Some Freedomland fans have indicated that Zacherle appeared at the park. These appearance(s), however, remain undated while the search continues for information and photographs.

MusicRadio77

As the 1961 season drew to a close, WABC hosted its 40th birthday celebration at the park. Everything at Freedomland was free for the 24,860 party guests on the night of October 6.

Freedomland's gates opened for WABC listeners at 6pm. Each fan was required to present a birthday card to save the $1.95 regular adult admission price. The fans danced at the Moon Bowl and listened to live broadcasts by WABC personalities. They also participated in a ruby hunt (ruby is the symbolic stone for 40 years). Each WABC guest was provided with the opportunity to find one of seven actual rubies (each valued at more than $250) that were mixed with 100,000 imitation stones placed in a huge treasure chest. A certified appraiser checked each stone as it was pulled from the chest.

Since WABC was 770 on the AM dial, 77 free chicken dinners were awarded to the holders of lucky numbers written on guest badges distributed at the beginning of the evening. The winners were hosted by WABC and the Brass Rail restaurant chain at the Plantation House. According to Freedomland officials, the party attracted the largest nighttime crowd in the park's first two seasons.

Moon Bowl Swing and Jazz

During the 1961 season, Freedomland announced that the music of live dance bands at the park would be broadcast on New York City radio station WNBC on Saturdays from 10:30 to 11pm. According to various newspaper accounts, the "first of the live remote broadcasts direct from the Moon Bowl dance floor in the amusement park's Satellite City will feature the music of Count Basie."

CBS Radio Network also aired the music nationwide on Sundays, beginning August 20, from 8:30 to 9pm Eastern Daylight Time. The featured orchestras included those of Jimmy Dorsey, Duke Ellington, Louis Armstrong, Benny Goodman, Woody Herman, and Lionel Hampton.

For the 1962 season, WNEW aired a weekly *Let's Dance* program hosted by Phil McLean. The show spotlighted Gene Krupa, Harry James, Stan Kenton, and Benny Goodman.

Clay Cole

Clay Cole was a disc jockey best known for his television dance program, *The Clay Cole Show*, that aired in New York City on WNTA-TV (originally a commercial independent and later PBS WNET) and WPIX-TV from 1959 to 1968. One of his shows, *Clay Cole at the Moon Bowl*, was broadcast from Freedomland on WPIX-TV during the 1963 season.

The first show aired on July 20 and it featured Joey Dee (of the Starliters) and Bobby Darin. The show opened with Jay and the Americans on a rooftop surrounded by flapping American flags and singing "Only in America." At that time, Jay Black (real name David Blatt) was the lead singer of the group.

Each Saturday night show featured big-band music for dancing under the stars on the Moon Bowl dance floor. Vaughn Meader as President John F. Kennedy from the comedy album *The First Family* also was a guest along with cast members from the album. Chuck McCann, popular for hosting TV kids shows, was one of those cast members, and also Clay's announcer sidekick.

During that same time, Clay Cole was the emcee of *Teen Age Fair*, a series of special programs that explored the world of young America. The shows aired from Freedomland on WOR-TV and represented teenage interests that included folk singing, surfing, karate, scuba diving, and the latest dance crazes.

Hosts Of TV Kids Shows

Just about every host of the popular children's television shows of the late 1950s and early 1960s in New York City appeared at Freedomland.

Ray Forrest

Ray Forrest hosted New York City's first and most unique kid's television variety series. *Children's Theater* was broadcast on Saturday mornings from 1949 to 1961 on WNBT-TV/WRCA-TV, which later changed its call letters to WNBC-TV. The program encouraged children in the studio audience, along with those watching at home, to see many places of interest, read good books, care for animals, and become involved in local activities. During its waning days, *Children's Theater* featured reruns of the color 1958 version of *Crusader Rabbit* cartoons, the first animated series produced specifically for television.

During 1960, Ray aired a series of pre-taped shows from Freedomland that provided his young viewers with a chance to not only see the park but to experience events from America's history. He taped his Freedomland shows for a period of five weeks. They became the most popular episodes of his show.

Sonny Fox

Sonny Fox is best remembered for hosting *Wonderama* on Sunday mornings from 1959 until 1967 on WNEW-TV. He also hosted four or five live shows each day for a week or two at the Hollywood Arena during the 1962 and 1963 seasons. Portions of the *Wonderama* shows at Freedomland were filmed and broadcast on select Sunday mornings. Magician and illusionist the Amazing Randi (James Randi) appeared with Sonny at some of these live shows.

"About 3,000 people filled the stands," said Sonny about the Freedomland shows. "Certainly not as intimate as in the studio and I felt I was a half-mile away from the kids, with whom I liked to interact."

For several years, Sonny Fox also hosted a Saturday morning show known as *Just for Fun*. The first year for the show was the same year he started hosting *Wonderama*. He left *Just for Fun* during the summer of 1965.

During the opening season of the park, a series format program reminiscent of another show (*Let's Take a Trip*) by Sonny was in the works with the management of Freedomland. A pilot show was scheduled for June 16, just before the park opened. The setting, according to newspaper articles, will allow Sonny "to point to various eras of American history for the benefit of the young at home and on location."

"I had my director from *Let's Take a Trip* help me," recalled Sonny. "We did one half hour with a short budget and included two kids from my other show. It was fun to get outside and be with the kids. It had potential, but we were not given the time to do what I wanted for the show."

Claude Kirchner

Claude Kirchner was a pioneer in children's television and served as the ringmaster of the popular *Terrytoon Circus* on WOR-TV from 1956 to 1962 and then *Merrytunes Circus* on the same station through September 1963. Earlier in his career, he hosted the nationally broadcast (ABC) show *Super Circus*. Among his sidekicks was Clownie. Claude and Clownie appeared frequently at Freedomland's Hollywood Arena.

"Many times, I accompanied Dad to his gig as ringmaster when Freedomland added a circus in 1961," recalled Lynn Lovalette. "Usually just the two of us, but sometimes my older brother or one of my friends would join us. We headed over via the Hutchinson River Parkway. Dad would say, 'Honeybunch, want to put the top down?' 'Yes!!' I'd reply and off we'd go in Dad's beloved white 1955 Olds convertible with red leather interior. Dad was not much for chit-chat, but anything he said to me was nothing short of adoration and I felt the same. Despite the silence, it just felt good to be around him. I was so proud of him.

"Once parked, we'd head over to the circus arena [Hollywood Arena] where Dad would change into his ringmaster suit and boots in a trailer. Sometimes he'd drive already dressed in his suit. I know it was hot for him in the summertime!

"I would hang out behind the scenes for a bit before heading out to scout the park. My favorite place was Casa Loca, that upside-down room where water ran backwards and balls rolled uphill. One could barely stand upright in there."

Early in his career, Claude was heard on radio in Milwaukee, Chicago, and other markets. He also was an announcer at the live performances of the swing bands that were broadcast on a Chicago station.

"One particular day, Dad told me how excited he was that the Glenn Miller Orchestra was playing at the park," remembered Lynn. "I think it was August 1961. Dad had announced for many of the big bands back in the 1940s in Chicago. He appeared outdoors at Grant Park and also at the Arganon Ballroom and the Trianon Ballroom where he'd broadcast live over the air. So, he was chomping at the bit to hear them at Freedomland and perhaps chew the fat with any remaining old-timers. It was a grand day for him!"

Chuck McCann

Besides his gig with Clay Cole, Chuck McCann hosted a yo-yo contest at Freedomland and was featured in several shows that WPIX-TV taped at the park that included Halloween specials.

The first Ben Cooper (Brooklyn manufacturer of costumes) Halloween show aired during 1961. Another show (*A Children's Halloween Party at Freedomland!*) that had been taped earlier was broadcast on Saturday, October 17, and again on Saturday, October 24, 1964. The program referenced an exciting 1965 season with new attractions, though Freedomland had filed for bankruptcy several weeks before the broadcast.

According to a description of the show, Chuck was situated near one of the park's sternwheelers and from that location he entertained a studio audience of children who wore Halloween costumes. He judged a costume contest and Laurel & Hardy films were part of the show. He also appeared with a creature or two from the Mine Caverns dark ride. A song from the show had the lyrics, "Oh what a party—a Halloween party—we'll laugh loud and hardy here—Don't kid yourself

(don't kid yourself)—it's not a dream (it's not a dream)—
IT'S HALLOWEEN!"

Other hosts of children's television shows who appeared at
the park included:

- Joe Bolton, known to kids as Officer Joe, hosted *The
  Three Stooges* and *The Little Rascals* shows on WPIX-TV.
  He appeared at the park with Moe, Larry, and Curly Joe,
  and his fellow television kid-show hosts.

- Bill Britten, who portrayed the New York City version
  of Bozo the Clown on WPIX-TV from 1959 to 1964.
  "Freedomland was a big park," he said, "and we always
  promoted it in our performances. It was a perfect place
  for kids. My feeling was these kids eventually would
  inherit our world and we needed to instill in them the
  proper values. Sometimes we succeeded and sometimes,
  I guess, we weren't successful. All of us tried our best to
  improve entertainment for kids and provide something
  that parents would love to have their kids watch. We just
  wanted everyone to have a good time."

- Uncle Tom Gregory, who was an announcer and later
  a children's show host on WABD-TV (later WNEW-TV
  and now WNYW-TV). From 1958 until 1965, he hosted
  the mid-afternoon show *Cartoon Playtime* that featured
  Looney Tunes and Merrie Melodies cartoons. Occasionally, he was a substitute host on *Wonderama*. During
  1965, he became the anchor of a late evening newscast,
  Faces and Places in the News, which was a predecessor
  to *The 10 O'Clock News*. It was on this newscast that he
  coined the phrase, "It's 10 P.M. Do you know where your
  children are?" that became popular with New Yorkers.

- Ray Heatherton was a singer, Broadway performer and
  a popular television personality known to kids as "The
  Merry Mailman." He appeared in Freedomland's Kiddie
  Show during 1962 along with Tom Gregory and Fred Scott.

- Captain Jack McCarthy, who hosted *Popeye* on WPIX-TV,
  appeared at Freedomland with the live Popeye show and
  the opening of a museum during the 1962 season.

- Uncle Fred Scott, an original cast member of *Captain Video and His Video Rangers,* was one of WABD-TV/WNEW-TVs most well-known and beloved cartoon show hosts. He hosted a variety of shows, including *Bugs Bunny, Felix the Cat, Diver Dan, The Deputy Dawg Show, Cartoon Circus,* and *Cartoon a Go-Go.* He succeeded Sonny Fox as the second and last host/performer of *Just for Fun* on Saturday mornings from Saturday, August 7, until Saturday, September 4, 1965.

- Joan Thayer, one of several women to portray the teacher on *Romper Room* in New York City, was Miss Joan when the program aired on WABD-TV, Channel 5. As the station became WNEW-TV, she continued to host the program for several more years. From Rockville Centre on Long Island, she appeared at Freedomland for the opening of either season two or season three.

- Some Baby Boomers recall that Sandy Becker and Fireman Todd Russell also appeared at the park. Their appearances, however, remain undocumented.

On June 16, 1961, a Friday night, WPIX-TV aired the children's special *The Visit to Freedomland.* The show was a pre-taped comedy/variety tour of the park that featured Officer Joe Bolton, Captain Jack McCarthy, Bill Britten as Bozo the Clown, and Chuck McCann, along with Paul Ashley's Laurel & Hardy puppets. Also appearing on the show were child actors Mary Ellen and Paul O'Keith (he would later portray Ross Lane on *The Patty Duke Show*). Comedy skits and songs were performed with musical accompaniment by Paul Lavalle, Freedomland's music director. The show aired one time and research has failed to locate a copy.

Elsewhere On The TV Dial

Besides the shows hosted for children and teens, adults also enjoyed a glimpse of Freedomland on the small screen. The most famous segment is the approximate 15-minute tour on *The Ed Sullivan Show* that appeared on the night of the park's debut (June 19, 1960). Ed taped the segment in advance, prominently featured the Chicago Fire, and even piloted a boat on the Northwest Fur Trapper attraction.

The television spotlight for Freedomland also included:

- The *Today* show with Dave Garroway featured a taped two-hour (7–9am) show from the park on Independence Day 1960. According to a newspaper critic, "it was a trifling production which lacked fluidity and interest."

- "The Memory of a Red Trolley Car" episode of *Naked City* featured the streets of Little Old New York in the opening four-minute scene.

- The show hosted by Joe Franklin, a New York entertainment icon and often considered the host of the first television entertainment talk show. He appeared at Freedomland on several occasions. The Freedomland Most Watchable Girl Beauty Pageant aired on Franklin's television show probably during 1962. The film exists in black and white and without audio.

- *What's My Line?* on which Ann Williams, as a guest, stumped the panel. She was the teenage elephant trainer at the Hollywood Arena.

CHAPTER TWENTY-TWO

Long-Forgotten Freedomland Stories

"You Are Being Watched" instead of "Please Do Not Touch"

—Freedomland Gardeners

Freedomland was a park of many stories. Some made news headlines. Many other tales were lost to time. Here are a few long-forgotten stories that are part of Freedomland's history.

1959

- From the beginning, park executives reportedly would gather frequently at Mario's Bar & Grill located on Fifth Avenue and 7th Street in nearby North Pelham.

1960

- Taxes for admissions were paid during early October after New York City filed a warrant for the delinquency. The city treasurer had announced that the park owed $148,200. A park spokesman indicated the issue was caused by an internal error.

- Freedomland appeared in the Macy's Thanksgiving Day Parade in 1960 and 1961, though photos and other information cannot be located to document those appearances. The park likely used one of its stage coaches, which also was used during neighborhood promotional appearances.

- One of the most successful promotions at the park during the opening season involved *Newsday*, the Long Island daily newspaper. About 22,000 people, including newsboys and their families, participated in the program.

1961

- Freeedomland displayed the Aeromobile 200, a wheelless automobile by Curtiss-Wright. It was an air-riding car that hovered over the ground on a stream of "fanned" air, much the same way a table tennis ball remained atop a stream of water.

- Broadway producer Alex Cohen reportedly turned down big money to direct Freedomland. He was behind more than 100 productions on both sides of the Atlantic, including the thriller *Angel Street*, comedies such as *Little Murders*, revues such as *At the Drop of a Hat* and *Beyond the Fringe*, dramas that included *84 Charing Cross Road* and *Anna Christie*, musicals such as *Dear World* and *A Day in Hollywood / A Night in the Ukraine*, and classics like *King Lear* and *Hamlet*. He also produced stage concerts for Marlene Dietrich, Maurice Chevalier, and Yves Montand, and was responsible for the international stardom of Marcel Marceau.

- A new attraction was five new-born burros appropriately named Bronx, Brooklyn, Queens, Manhattan, and Staten Island.

- Miss Freedomland ventured into the park's nearby neighborhood to choose Baby Freedomland as part of a promotion with a pharmacy located on Gun Hill Road.

- The Northwest Fur Trapper ride was invaded by neighborhood kids. At night, they scalped the braves and stole loin cloths. Each wig cost $15–$20.

- A July evening bomb scare occurred during a performance by Benny Goodman and his orchestra.

1962

- A Dorothy Kilgallen newspaper column reported that "it's supposed to be a deep dark secret, but when Freedomland opens for its third season in May it will have a circus and an aquatic show included for the price of admission."

- Gardeners have found that a sign that reads "You Are Being Watched" is more effective in stopping guests from picking flowers than the traditional "Please do not touch."

- Television's *Route 66* star George Maharis reportedly turned down a $7,500 offer for a one-night appearance.

- According to a park announcement, 14-year-old drummer genius Barry Miles played at Freedomland. Copies of his album, *Miles of Genius*, were given away as prizes to the under-20 crowd. As a preteen, he played with John Coltrane, Billie Holiday, and Lester Young.

- Dolls, paintings, and other items made in America's classrooms were displayed at the People-to-People Children's Center at the park to foster classroom exchanges with school children in other countries.

- *The Teenage Fair* was held for several seasons at Freedomland. Contestants would compete to obtain access to the Miss Teen U.S.A. competition. Other contests held at the park included "Most Watchable Girl" by the American Society of Girl Watchers and the "Miss High School of New York Pageant." Actor Troy Donahue hosted the "Most Watchable Girl" contest in 1962 and entertainer Jackie Gleason nominated Jan Crockett for the contest. Jan had appeared on Jackie's Saturday night variety television show and, at the time, she was a "weather girl" on New York's WABC-TV.

1963

- Evelyn Carrie liked cats—the big kind. She was an animal tamer from Tennessee, billed as "the only lady in the world who trains and performs with tigers and lions." She appeared at the Hollywood Arena.

1964

- As Freedomland was moving toward closure and bankruptcy, several business stories were floated in the press. The stories possibly could have been planted to give William Zeckendorf, Sr., more time, or credibility, as his Webb & Knapp company continued to falter, or the articles could have been trial balloons to camouflage the real story behind the closing of the park. Zeck, Sr., floated the idea that he ultimately would place a dome over Freedomland's 200 acres and convert the property into the world's largest shopping center. "It will be bigger than the Pentagon," reported one newspaper columnist.

- After Freedomland filed for bankruptcy, a Dorothy Kilgallen newspaper article reported that "a group of Hollywood producers is considering taking over Freedomland for a major New York studio site."

CHAPTER TWENTY-THREE

Freedomland in the News and in Books

Disneyland? It's Kids Stuff Compared To New Freedomland
—Headline from *The Hays Daily News*, June 1, 1960

Publicity

From strictly a publicity viewpoint, Freedomland was a public relations, advertising, and promotion executive's dream job. The park created endless photo opportunities and storylines. Though the media of the early 1960s was not as electronically robust as today, wire services, newspapers, newspaper syndicates, magazines, radio, and television eagerly covered the Freedomland story.

National, daily, and weekly newspapers heralded the opening of Freedomland and the publicity flow continued during the park's five-year run. News coverage was generated by Associated Press and United Press, syndicates such as the Newspaper Enterprise Association (NEA), and popular national columnists like Leonard Lyons, Dorothy Kilgallen, and Mel Heimer. Even Ed Sullivan looked for bits of information to include for his newspaper readers.

Magazines also loved the Freedomland story. Just in New York, color multi-page spreads were found in the magazines that accompanied the Sunday newspapers, including *The New York Daily News*, *The Journal American*, and *The Herald Tribune*. National magazines such as *Life*, *Look*, *Time*, *Newsweek*, and *Diners' Club* included single and multi-page articles and cover photos. The park was featured in *The Junior Fire Marshal* published for children by the Hartford Insurance Group and in audience-specific publications such as *Calling All Girls*.

Trade publications, specifically *Billboard* and *Amusement Business*, were packed with news from the park. Popular travel magazines such as *New York State Vacationlands* and promotional pamphlets for tourists featured Freedomland. On radio, interviews with park executives and celebrity entertainers were common, especially in the New York metro area. Freedomland appeared on many television programs locally and nationally.

Hot Off the Presses

Newspaper headlines heralded the opening of Freedomland.

"Freedomland Dedicated, It's Eastern Disneyland"
  —*Lincoln Evening Journal* (Lincoln Nebraska), June 19, 1960

"Newly-Opened 205-Acre Play Pen Boasts Rides, History For Tots"
  —*Lubbock Avalanche Journal* (Lubbock, Texas), July 13, 1960

The Canadian Sternwheeler. This Freedomland publicity photograph was distributed to media across the country. Stories and photos also appeared in foreign publications.

"Freedomland U.S.A.—\$65 Million Wonderland Newest N.Y. Attraction"
> —*Berkshire Eagle* (Pittsfield, Massachusetts), July 6, 1960

"New York's Freedomland Stresses History And Nostalgia"
> —*Courier-Journal* (Louisville, Kentucky), July 24, 1960

"Disneyland? It's Kids Stuff Compared To New Freedomland"
> —*Hays Daily News* (Hays, Kansas), June 1, 1960

"'Freedomland Park Draws Huge Crowds On Opening Day"
> —*Odessa American* (Odessa, Texas), June 20, 1960

"New Freedomland Amusement Park Traces American Heritage"
> —*The Post* (San Mateo, California), May 25, 1960

"U.S. Stages Old Times Pageant: Super Disneyland In The Making"
> —*Sydney Morning Herald* (Sydney, New South Wales, Australia), February 27, 1960

Advertising

Considerable newspaper advertising was developed by the park while many other ads were promoted by sponsors and others that wanted to connect with the excitement that was Freedomland U.S.A.

- Supermarket newspaper advertisements were found as far as 100 miles from the Bronx. The Grand Union supermarkets throughout the region participated in park promotions that were published frequently in newspapers.

- A Pennsylvania fashion show at Hazelton High School was promoted with an advertisement in the *Plain Speaker*. Anyone who attended the show was eligible to enter a contest to win a family of four weekend at Freedomland.

- Van Heusen shirts publicized the "My Dad's The Greatest" contest with an advertisement in the June 2, 1961, edition of New Jersey's *Asbury Park Press*. Seven great dads, one at each of seven local Bamberger stores, "will win complete dress, sports, lounge and beach wardrobes plus a day trip for the family to Freedomland, U.S.A." Football dad Frank Gifford was the judge.

- The Howland's Department Store in Bridgeport, Connecticut, featured a newspaper ad in *The Bridgeport Post* for Keds sneakers: "Kids! Get your Freedomland coupon worth $1.13 with every purchase of U.S. Keds. Buy them at Howland's right now and enjoy a day at Freedomland...America's greatest fun value!"

Many hotels in Manhattan advertised great deals for rooms, discounts, and close proximity to tourist attractions. The Hotel Commodore on 42nd Street and Lexington Avenue indicated that the location was a "direct subway line to Freedomland, U.S.A." This hotel was owned by the company that owned Freedomland. The still luxurious Hotel Concourse Plaza at 161st Street and the Grand Concourse near Yankee Stadium also advertised in out-of-town newspapers. One ad indicated "NEAR FREEDOMLAND" even though it was a distance of almost eight miles.

Freedomland advertising bills were posted on the plywood walls that surrounded Manhattan construction sites and ads were featured on subway platforms and city billboards. Out-of-town tour companies advertised day trips to New York and specifically to Freedomland. These included Keystone Tours and Leon Miller Tours (agent for Greyhound) of Pennsylvania. A newspaper advertisement for Leon Miller Tours read:

Sept. 16–17 2-Day Tour To

FREEDOMLAND and N.Y. City

The world's largest Amusement Park.

164 rides, attractions, etc.

See the great Chicago Fire, Little Old New York, the largest buffalo herd and 2 baby buffalo, a great Civil War battle, the old Santa Fe Railroad with its real steam locomotive, the San Francisco earthquake, the old Western Opera house with real western acts and music, see the Great Lakes Stern-Wheeler Steamboat and 164 other rides, attractions, etc.

$29.50 includes admission and all rides

(Children under 12, ½ fare)

Read About Freedomland

One of author Richard Price's novels (*Freedomland*) incorporated an abandoned theme park—Freedomtown—that is based on his memories of living in the Bronx and visiting the park. The book became a film.

Activist, film historian, and author Vito Russo included the park in his book, *The Celluloid Closet*. His concerns about LGBT portrayals in media led to the formation of the Gay and Lesbian Alliance Against Defamation (GLAAD). He visited Freedomland on a day trip with his younger brother and a handful of neighborhood friends during its opening season. They traveled on the IRT subway line from 125th Street and Lexington Avenue, but Russo failed to notify any parents. A group of frantic adults were waiting when the kids returned to the Harlem neighborhood.

References to Freedomland can be found in a variety of other fiction and non-fiction books such as Paul Anka's *My Way*, Genna Sapia-Ruffin's *Delivered from Temptation*, and Nicole Mary Kelby's *The Pink Suit*.

CHAPTER TWENTY-FOUR

Freedomland Faux Pas

Freedomland had become a center of "commonplace and vulgar mass unrestrained teen-age entertainment."

—Lawsuit by Benjamin Moore & Co.

A common thread among theme and amusement parks is the accidents, mistakes, and other mishaps that occur along the way. Freedomland had its share—a fire before the park opened, malfunctions on opening day, tax liens, injured stage coach riders, lawsuits, and a robbery.

Fire Destroys Buildings (1960)

On the night of March 23, a three-alarm fire at the construction site destroyed six small and unfinished structures. A half-mile-long relay of hose lines, according to newspaper reports, helped move water to the flames from a hydrant at Baychester Avenue and Bartow Avenue. At the time, the cause of the fire was undetermined. No estimate of damage was revealed and no injuries were reported in the press. Some of the charred remains were salvaged for props for the Chicago Fire attraction.

Fort Laramie? (1960)

The fort in the Great Plains was known as Fort Cavalry. However, in several early media stories, including the pictorial feature in the June 21, 1960, issue of *Look*, the fort is referenced as Fort Laramie. It is not known if the name actually was changed before the park opened, or if this was a public relations error.

No Milton Berle Appearance (1960)

George Wachsteter was an illustrator and caricaturist who worked for newspapers, magazines, and broadcast networks. His caricature drawing for the opening of Freedomland once was mislabeled to indicate that comedian Milton Berle appeared in an opening night show at the park.

Tax and Payment Liens Filed (1960)

Due to the financial problems at the Webb & Knapp company, tax liens for work at the park were filed by several vendors. These included:

- October 4. Controlled Weather Corporation of 1157 Third Avenue in New York City filed a lien for $122,763 for labor, air conditioning, and heating. Webb & Knapp was not satisfied with the completion of the contract. Capitol Steel Corporation of 1150 Avenue of the Americas in New York City filed a lien for $15,358 for steel to construct the Freedomland Inn. A separate lien of $2,501 was filed for steel for a restaurant in the same facility. A Webb & Knapp spokesman said these contracts would be paid.

- November 10. Turner Construction Company filed a mechanic's lien for $3.6 million, the remainder due on a general contract for a large part of the construction of the park. The work was performed jointly with the Aberthaw Construction Company. Payment of $10 million had been made on the contract.

Stagecoach Accident (1960)

A few days following opening day, a serious accident involved a stage coach. A wire-service news story reported that the coach overturned on June 25 and injured ten riders, including three children. The coach had eleven riders, six adults, and five children. According to the driver, the four horses apparently were startled by the train whistle. The left rear wheel of the coach became stuck in soft ground on the shoulder of the paved trail and tipped the coach. One girl from Cleveland and a woman from New York City, who suffered a spine injury, were hospitalized.

One of the riders recalled that the horses spooked and bolted as the coach rolled down the last hill and that people rushed to the scene to lift the coach off the seriously injured people.

Robbery at Gunpoint (1960)

Most Bronx residents during the 1960s heard the story about the inside robbery. Back then and over the years, the story was embellished with altered facts.

One claim was that the robbers, after grabbing the money from the payroll office, took off in a motor boat across the park's Great Lakes. If they did that, they never would have left the park since the waterway was made specifically for Freedomland and did not include an outlet to permit an escape by a boat.

The facts:

- Three men stole a 16-foot outboard motorboat on August 25, chugged up the Hutchinson River to Mill Creek, and beached the boat near the park.

- Two nights later they pulled stocking masks over their faces, armed themselves with two foreign-made shotguns and a pistol. They forced Edward Chelli, a Freedomland laborer, to help them enter the cash-control building. Inside the building they found Clifford Birschner, the head cashier, and two other employees, Anthony Robertson and Edward Semeonin, counting the night's receipts. They herded the four employees into a vault, took $28,836, and returned to the boat.

- The boat was abandoned upriver near a car that one of the robbers had parked in the vicinity.

- Police checked about 2,000 present and past employees and learned that a 25-year-old former convict had worked at the park as a carpenter. The two accomplices, one also 25 and the other 36, were arrested with the former employee.

- All the thieves had previous convictions. All were charged with assault, robbery, and violation of the weapons law.

- Detectives found $14,653 of the money in their Bronx homes (1950 Edison Avenue, 432 Zerega Avenue, and 344 Swinton Avenue). A plastic bag hidden under stones at the bottom of a tropical fish tank in the home of the former employee contained $3,000. The soggy bills were stuck against the walls of a Bronx police station to dry, and that picture appeared in newspapers across the country.

- Two of the robbers received five to eight years in prison and one received seven to nine years in jail.

Bronx Historian Thomas X. Casey provided a postscript to this crime story. His aunt, Betty Castelli, was a Freedomland employee. As an office clerk, she was able to obtain a few free passes and she and her husband attended night events with Tom's parents.

"It would be later in the 1960 season that I would get a chance to go," explained Tom, "but it was the events of August 27, 1960, that made me beg to visit. The newspaper headlines the next day told the story of how three real-life pirates robbed the receipts of the day. The newspapers also referenced them as buccaneers, just like the ride at Freedomland, because they escaped via an outboard motorboat they stole from City Island. As a nine-year-old, I envisioned it all. They dressed as bandits and rode up on horses from Orchard Beach and entered the bank in Little Old New York. After the robbery, they changed clothes to become pirates and jumped into a speedboat to a spot where a beautiful gun moll kept the car running while the men changed into suits. I had to get to the scene of the crime.

"My Aunt Betty had her vision of the story. She was brought down to Foley Square and grilled by Eliot Ness and the Untouchables. They were not asking her about Al Capone. In her fantasy, it was the mob, or, more specifically, the Mafia. My aunt got all dressed up for the grilling, but it turned out to be only a few questions by the NYPD. My aunt did mention to us all that if the robbers had gotten the payroll, which was at a different location than the receipts, it would have been over $80,000 versus $28,000. When I got to Freedomland in early September 1960, all evidence of the crime was gone, but I still had the actors performing a stage coach robbery to enjoy."

Danny the Dragon Mishap (1960)

The popular attraction with children was involved in a minor accident toward the end of the first season. Two young brothers from the Bronx were injured, one with a broken nose and the other with a bump on the forehead, when the last car tipped in the six-mile-per-hour Danny the Dragon ride. According to park photographer John Wagerer, a Freedomland security officer thought the injuries were much worse and actually called for a Catholic priest.

Danny the Dragon. A ride on Danny's tail is a memory still recalled today by many Baby Boomers who were young children during the early 1960s.

The Sidewalk Moved (1962)

Freedomland's Moving Sidewalk in Satellite City was the scene of a minor accident in July. A woman from Pottstown, Pennsylvania, stepped on the conveyance, slipped, fell, and broke her right arm and wrist. The accident was front page news in her hometown newspaper.

Benjamin Moore Lawsuit (1962)

Benjamin Moore & Company, a paint and varnish manufacturer that was an original sponsor of the park for the Science of Color exhibit in Satellite City, sued Freedomland for breach of contract. The complaint indicated that the company had leased exhibit space with the understanding that Freedomland would be "an historical and educational family recreation and entertainment center...to be maintained with dignity and propriety." The company alleged in the suit that management changed the character of the park to appeal to teen-age jazz enthusiasts.

In a ruling dated September 18, 1962, Supreme Court Justice Saul S. Streit dismissed the $150,000 suit that charged the park had become a center of "commonplace and vulgar mass unrestrained teen-age entertainment." In the ruling, the judge stated:

> There is no obligation in the lease by which the landlord obligated itself to maintain a "Freedomland" so as to appeal to any special class or to prohibit any special class of people from visiting "Freedomland."

Singers Not Compensated (1963)

Pop singers Jack Jones, Kathy Keegan, and Tina Robin all performed at Freedomland and all filed a grievance of nonpayment. As of October 1963, they applied to the American Guild of Variety Artists to receive money from the bond deposited with the union. The issue appeared in Dorothy Kilgallen's syndicated newspaper column.

Tornado Ride Mix-Up (1963)

A frequent story that surfaces involves Tornado and Earthquake, both manufactured by Arrow Development, and the rumored switch of passenger cars for these dark rides.

The Tornado ride closed after the 1962 season. It was shipped to Kennywood in West Mifflin, Pennsylvania, where it appeared from approximately 1964 to 1966. Then, it was packed and shipped to Storytown USA in Lake George, New York. The Earthquake ride lasted through the last season of Freedomland (1964), though that part of the park was walled off during the final year. The ride was purchased by Cedar Point.

The inaccurate story is, due to a shipping mix-up, the Tornado ride cars slated for Kennywood were shipped to Cedar Point with the Earthquake ride while the Earthquake ride cars went to Kennywood with the Tornado ride. The car designs, reportedly, were so similar that both parks decided not to correct the shipping error.

The actual timeline, though, does not follow the narrative. Tornado blew out of Freedomland at the end of the 1962 season and soon was operating in Kennywood. Earthquake did not leave the Freedomland property until after the 1964 season and it opened at Cedar Point during the 1965 season. When referencing the dates of operation for these rides at Freedomland, Kennywood, and Cedar Point, the story about the interchangeable vehicles is not credible. However, anything is possible!

Check Problems (1964)

During the park's waning days, some employees were issued bad paychecks totaling between $2,000 and $3,000. According to Freedomland officials, "a mixup in deposits caused some checks to be returned for insufficient funds." The total payroll was $60,000.

Misidentified Photographs

Over the years, pictures and information have been published with incorrect references to Freedomland. Among the errors:

- A photo of the 1964–1965 New York World's Fair skyway sometimes is misidentified as the Freedomland Tucson Mining Company Ore Buckets ride soaring above the park.

- Several Freedomland photos appear in the August 1, 1960, *Life* magazine cover article about America's new amusement parks. One photo of a young boy receiving a haircut in an old-time barber shop is misidentified as occurring at Freedomland. The scene actually was Cowboy Town near Dallas, Texas. Another photo of two young boys holding a gun on a prisoner behind bars has been misidentified as the jail at Freedomland. This photo also was taken Cowboy Town.

CHAPTER TWENTY-FIVE

1964: Freedomland's Final Season

I...was paid $100 a week, a handsome sum for a teen in those days.

—Terry Buchalter

After the 1962 season, Freedomland sold Tornado. During 1963, Freedomland began to market the availability of other attractions to the entertainment industry. On the block were Earthquake, the bull boats from the Northwest Fur Trapper attraction, four stagecoaches, and a sternwheeler.

Changes at Freedomland

A park's success often is determined by its ability to adapt and successfully infuse necessary changes and upgrades. Billed as a history theme park when it opened, Freedomland was altered during subsequent years while it maintained history-themed attractions. To help boost attendance, management added the Moon Bowl for the second season to attract older teenagers and younger adults to the new outdoor dance floor. The Hollywood Arena was added for shows. During its final two years, non-historic thrill rides and skill games arrived at the park.

New York area newspaper articles, on several occasions, indicated that Freedomland management was interested in year-round operation of the park. Ideas floated by William Zeckendorf, Sr., included a small ski slope, a Christmas celebration, a bowling alley, and an indoor trotting track. Freedomland, though, failed to embrace the concept to generate additional income.

If management wanted Freedomland to survive and prosper, it would have explored new streams of revenue that also may have included:

- A stage/movie theater, or dinner theater, for Little Old New York.

- New York and Chicago decorated for Christmas with carolers, events, and shopping.

- A Santa Fe Rail Road version of a Santa Claus train riding around the quiet park.

- Satellite City as a venue for a Halloween Fright Fest or a science-fiction festival with connections to television shows of the time such as *The Twilight Zone*, *The Outer Limits*, and even *The Jetsons*.

- Winter conversion of the Moon Bowl dance floor into an ice rink or a showcase for ice sculptures.

Some members of management, including possibly the Zeckendorfs, silently may have preferred to count the days until the park closed and the land could be prepared for a new project. Rather than seek innovative opportunities to generate more long-term revenue, Freedomland management continuously slashed payroll. The plan reduced the entertainment value by eliminating cowboy shootouts, bank robberies, and other features that complemented the park's historic attractions.

Concessionaires grumbled that they were paying more per square foot in rent than they could recover as profit. One food vendor complained that management never could settle on a plan that would attract people to the park and that the public became confused by changing attractions and admission prices.

During 1964, areas of the park resembled an abandoned movie set or ghost town. The park sold surplus copies of its opening season park guide and the San Francisco page in the 1962 guide now contained a large sticker: "WE'RE FIXIN' IT FOR YOU! CLOSED IN ORDER TO BUILD...a BIGGER and BETTER FREEDOMLAND."

Much of the history backdrop now was overshadowed by thrill rides and games of chance. Many of the latest amusements were located in the New Orleans and Satellite City areas.

Games for Fun

During the last season, Terry Buchalter worked for the Games for Fun concessionaire.

"It was my first job after graduating from Taft High School prior to starting at City College," said Terry, who lived at 2829 Sedgwick Avenue in the Kingsbridge section of the Bronx. "Underage at 17, and not able to work the games of chance, my job was to stock the game booths (called 'flashing the pit') and maintain the inventory of rag dolls ($.35 each), plush toys (poodles $2.50 each), and plastic back scratchers that came packed in huge quantities from Faye Schwartz' Fable Toys in Brooklyn. The largest stuffed animals, touted by the carnival barkers working the games as $120 poodles, only cost that per dozen. When my co-worker, Johnny Glickman (son of the New York sports broadcaster), quit mid-summer, I rose to his position handling the prize inventory and was paid $100 a week, a handsome sum for a teen in those days."

Games for Fun, according to Terry, operated several attractions at Freedomland and at the 1964–1965 New York World's Fair. The owner of the company was Irvin Feld, the music industry manager who, in 1967, bought Ringling Brothers Circus. The company's game offerings included coin toss pits, pinball gallery, water gun races, balloon darts, and a softball toss into fruit baskets (balls always would bounce out unless a person aimed for just inside the rim).

"One day, Irvin came to visit Freedomland with his daughter, Karen Irma Feld," recalled Terry. "She was allowed to pick any stuffed toy from the stock and I presented her with the plush toy poodle that she wanted. Many years later, she and her brother were in the news over a $110 million lawsuit over Irvin's estate."

The games of chance at Freedomland were supervised by Allen Bloom. At the age of 11, Allen swept floors for pharmacy and record shop owners Irvin and Israel Feld. As the Felds branched into entertainment, Allen stayed with the company and managed road tours for Buddy Holly, Richie Valens, the Drifters, the Coasters, Frankie Lyman, Paul Anka, Bill Haley and His Comets, and J.P. Richardson (the Big Bopper). He also managed the first U.S. tours of the Beatles and the Rolling Stones. As the company became involved with the circus, Allen helped launch the careers of many circus stars.

"My recollection of Allen was as a cigar smoking, self-described high-school dropout who got to his position working the southern carnival route," added Terry. "Years after my Freedomland days, while attending the circus with my children, I was surprised to see his name listed as a Ringling Brothers executive in the circus program."

Most of the employees at Freedomland during 1964 were college students who were interested only in summer employment.

"My brother, Barry, had worked there the prior year while he was student at Hunter College [later Lehman College] in the Bronx," continued Terry. "The more colorful employees, though, were the true carnival workers.

"Jack was the company mechanic who kept all the pinball machines in operations. These were the classic electro-mechanical ones with flippers that responded to body language, barely resembling the electronic games that replaced them. The Curly Washburn character played by Jack Palance in *City Slickers* could have been his stunt double. Jack was always one of the first to arrive each morning. After pouring a sludge-filled cup of day-old coffee out of the urn that was always plugged in overnight, he would pull a grease-laden screwdriver out of his back pocket and stir in enough sugar to induce diabetes in an elephant. It was Jack who drove me to get a tetanus shot after I was stung by a bee I disturbed in the shaggy fur of a stuffed monkey I was hanging up in the pinball parlor. Sadly, one morning that summer, Jack failed to appear, and we later found out that he had died in his sleep.

"Artie was a dyed-in-the-wool carnival professional who also worked as an auctioneer," according to Terry. "He was proud to be known as Froggy the Gremlin for his distinctive throaty style of speech reminiscent of the television puppet on the Andy Devine shown known as *Andy's Gang*. He would entertain us with his impression of the barker who worked the Coney Island Wax Museum. I can still hear his gravelly voice urging patrons to 'see Carol Chessman in the gas chamber and

Lina Medina, the eight-year-old mother from Peru, all on the inside, big as life.' It was Artie who would encourage the staff to car pool out to Coney Island after closing hours to ride the dodgem cars and eat at Nathan's."

Terry said that a particularly amusing college student worked the coin toss booth. "On busy weekends, when the largest crowds gathered, he would use his oratory skills to work the crowd into a frenzy of participation which we were schooled to call a 'tip.' Dimes would rain down onto the table, as patrons, whom we referred to in true carnival slang as 'marks,' would vainly attempt to have their coin land on one of the painted circles. No prize unless the circle's color showed all around. During a particularly good 'tip,' he would happily exhort the 'marks' to 'throw your money away.' When he spotted a guy in a pair of particularly unflattering shorts, he would broadcast, 'I'll buy you the bottom half of that pair of pants if you win.'"

Terry's memory extended to one of the park attractions that had been closed for the 1964 season. The Blast-off Bunker in Satellite City originally was a reproduction of a Cape Canaveral control room in which visitors witnessed a simulated rocket launch from start to finish.

"This attraction, which no longer was part of Freedomland's offerings, became the stockroom where I worked among the stuffed toys during that summer. Ironically, from 1976 to 1996, I was to find myself under another space-themed dome in that same general vicinity. As a New York City science teacher, I was the director of the planetarium in the Co-op City school complex. I often quipped that I had greater tenure than any other employee in the school since I could trace my roots back to Freedomland. During that time, while speaking with a contractor working in the school about my Freedomland summer, he said he had a gift for me that he had been saving for many years. The following day, he presented me with a copy of the park's souvineer guide book. I often thumb through this memento of that first summer after high school and regret that the World's Largest Entertainment Center is only a memory."

Freedomland's Fate

The character actors who remained at the park learned about Freedomland's fate only a few weeks into the 1964 season. Along with other employees, they were told about the financial difficulties and that everyone would feel the effects as Freedomland remained open until the end of the season. Managing Director Art Moss said the park would open during 1965 with many changes and innovations as it consolidated to just Little Old New York, Old Chicago, and Satellite City. Employees were advised that a housing development would rise on adjoining land and that another option was the relocation of Freedomland to Florida.

While the Zeckendorf landowners battled insurmountable financial issues, the thrill rides and games of chance were added to the park by Hyman Green as he and a pension fund of the International Teamsters Union gained control of the property and operations. To continue to draw crowds and earn every possible buck that last season, management regularly promoted park activities and the opportunity to "win a brand-new Ford Mustang" in connection with WINS Radio.

Then, on Sunday, September 13, 1964, Freedomland ended its run at 11pm.

CHAPTER TWENTY-SIX

The Zeckendorfs and Webb & Knapp

Freedomland...was a device to hold the land...

—William Zeckendorf, Sr., New York
Times News Service, 1970

The land clearing and construction for Marco Engineering's Magic Mountain started during 1957. The partially completed park operated for only several seasons. Pleasure Island was more successful, lasting 10 years (1959–1969). Freedomland operated for five seasons (1960–1964) and Six Flags Over Texas continues to prosper since it opened during 1961.

The first three parks faced a variety of financial, construction, and other issues that hampered long-term success. Magic Mountain and Pleasure Island incurred huge development and management costs that could not be sustained by either park. Management (and mismanagement) decisions led to bankruptcies. Freedomland's destiny was similar, but with an interesting caveat. The park, unknown to the public, became a placeholder for the land's future residential and commercial development.

While conceived and built by C.V. Wood and his company, Freedomland's fate was in the hands of others, including the Webb & Knapp landowners (William Zeckendorf, Sr., and William Zeckendorf, Jr.), investors, city planners, and politicians. While the elder Zeckendorf stated in public that he liked Freedomland and hoped it would succeed, he admitted years later that the park was a temporary occupant until variances could be obtained to construct large apartment buildings on his marshland. The development that became known as Co-op City had been conceived during the late 1950s.

Contrary to public and private opinions at the time, including that of the New York media along with amusement park executives, Freedomland U.S.A. was not an entertainment flop. Freedomland was visited by about 1.5 million people during its first year and grossed about $4.5 million. Home attendance for the New York Yankees was 1.6 million that year. Before Disneyland opened, Knott's Berry Farm received approximately the same amount of guests each season. Freedomland's attendance was a considerable achievement for the time, especially for a northeast venue with a short season. Attendance was adequate through 1963, too, though at least one theme park owner at the time believed that the actual numbers may have been downplayed by management.

The Marshland

The land Freedomland occupied was owned by the Zeckendorfs' Webb & Knapp company. The parcel was obtained about nine years before Freedomland opened to receive its first guests.

During 1951, the senior Zeckendorf reached an agreement to move the Ohrbach's department store located on 14th Street in Manhattan to an existing building on 34th Street. This deal eventually included another party and another parcel of land.

A broker who represented James Butler visited Zeck, Sr. The broker told him that his client's family was looking for a land deal. The family owned Yonkers Raceway just north of New York City. Many years earlier, the Butlers had purchased property in the Baychester section of the Bronx. The family wanted to place a race track on the site, but it never built the attraction. The Butlers owned approximately 400 acres and the family wanted to swap that land for property that would generate income.

Zeck, Sr., offered his property on 34th Street. It was generating $150,000 annually after charges were paid on a $5.4 million mortgage. The Butlers agreed to the deal upon learning that the Ohrbach's store would become a major tenant. Zeck, Sr., traded one acre in New York City with a high mortgage for four hundred acres located in New York City without any mortgage. He always had eyed the Bronx property for its potential for development.

With the success of Disneyland, real estate developers, investors, other business executives, and politicians across the country wanted to open similar parks. The theme park fever eventually arrived in New York, and the Zeckendorfs had the connections and owned the perfect location.

Zeckendorf's Business Philosophy

The elder Zeckendorf's desire to have Freedomland located on his Bronx property dovetailed with his overall real estate and business philosophy. He believed that any appraisal of land should ignore its current use, whether it was vacant or contained structures. Demolition followed by development, he often stated, can have a magical effect on the land's resale price.

Leading up to Freedomland, Webb & Knapp managed projects in various stages of development in Denver, Montreal, Washington, New York, Chicago, St. Louis, Boston, Hartford, Cincinnati, Cleveland, and at least a half-dozen other cities. Selling and purchasing properties and buildings, taking second and third mortgages, selling mortgages, and scraping together money to pay off mortgages or notes that had been recalled was as common an occurrence at Webb & Knapp as developing a piece of land. According to the real estate baron, Webb & Knapp sometimes was twirling the baton and at other times beating the drums. It always was leading the parade.

When Freedomland arrived, Zeck, Sr., and Woody already were business associates. He was invested in Woody's Magic Mountain, Pleasure Island, and the upcoming Six Flags Over Texas parks. Macy's commitment to open a replica of its original New York City store at Woody's Freedomland possibly was attributed to Zeck, Sr., who earlier had persuaded the company to open a store at his Roosevelt Field shopping center on Long Island.

Webb & Knapp's Financial Problems

Before the groundbreaking for Freedomland, Webb and Knapp experienced a financial twinge. The company and its subsidiaries had lost $6-plus million during 1958 in contrast to a $3 million profit during 1957. The loss was the company's first decline since the firm began to operate in the real estate arena. Zeck, Sr., attributed the problem to large operating expenditures and the high interest of borrowed money.

Zeck, Sr., had conducted a one-man business since he obtained control of the company that was a corporate entity with public shareholders. Webb & Knapp bookkeeping, reportedly, was a mystery to virtually all outsiders and, some commented, that it also was a mystery to the head man. The problems would magnify during the years of Freedomland's operation.

The elder Zeckendorf was the king of the largest real estate empire ever assembled up to that time. Webb & Knapp was the leading redeveloper of urban land in the country and maintained interests in other countries. Father and son committed $500 million to construction.

But, Webb & Knapp had spread itself thin over too many projects. All needed cash. The company also owned 120 Broadway near the tip of Manhattan, the largest building in the downtown area. It eventually became a curse for the Zeckendorfs. Webb & Knapp purchased it for $10 million in cash plus $8.5 million in company debentures. The only unsecured debentures issued by Webb & Knapp contributed to the destruction of the company.

As Freedomland opened on the Zeckendorf land, other construction projects were in various stages of development. Many had peaked or were near completion. Too many were unprofitable investments. To ease the financial burden, properties were sold, including New York City's Chrysler Building, and new investment partners were brought into projects. Webb & Knapp borrowed millions of dollars to repair current problems and to generate future income.

Zeck, Sr., searched for new deals with the hope that just one would correct the course of his teetering ship. One such project involved his friends at Yonkers Raceway. Reportedly, Zeck, Sr., attempted to negotiate a Freedomland-Raceway merger that was rejected by the Raceway's board of directors. However, during October 1961, a 33 percent interest in the multi-million dollar track was sold to International Recreation Corporation of which the Zeckendorfs were invested and served in management. In an Associated Press report, the purchasing corporation was identified as the operator of Freedomland. The transaction reportedly involved $17.5 million for shares of stock.

The deal did not improve the bottom line. During 1962, the company faced increasingly difficult circumstances. While the elder Zeckendorf admitted that he did not clearly hear the alarm bells, he did acknowledge that his hotels drained cash, Freedomland suffered losses, and the Roosevelt Field shopping center was not making money.

"The only project and property which we already had a few qualms about in 1960 was Freedomland Amusement Park, situated on the three (sic) hundred acres of Baychester swamp-land we had acquired in a swap for Orhbach's store," Zeck, Sr., wrote years later to place his failure on the park rather than on his business management. "We got into Freedomland the way the United States got into Vietnam, back-sideways, without really intending to, and only to clean up the mess somebody else had left behind."

With this statement and the following reflections, Zeck, Sr., re-wrote his personal history. He had been "all in" on Freedomland from the first day, yet he blamed others for its failure. The Zeckendorfs already were well-versed about the opportunities and risks of theme park investment through their association with Woody's Magic Mountain, Pleasure Island, and Six Flags Over Texas. A photograph of Zeck, Sr., at Freedomland has been difficult to locate (he was at the park often, according to some sources), but he was captured in at least one photo, circa 1959, at Pleasure Island.

"The idea of Freedomland, as fallout from the explosive success of Walt Disney's fabulous Disneyland, was wafted eastward by one C.V. Wood," wrote Zeck, Sr. "Wood is a promoter's promoter, a terrific, enthusiastic idea man who could sell snow to Eskimos. Wood had worked with Disney on Disneyland. He was at some point eased out by Disney, but not before convincing himself and a number of other people that Disneyland's success was really a matter of Wood's rather than Disney's ideas and management. Wood put together a masterful presentation of his Freedomland idea. The idea was to create a star-spangled amusement park, an America-in-miniature, to which hordes of easterners would flock.

"It was a great idea, beautifully presented. Sober outfits such as Paine, Webber, Jackson & Curtis lined up to help underwrite the show. Rather early in the game the project proved to be over-promoted, over-expensive, and under-financed. Too late for us to do much about it, it turned out to be misconceived, grievously mislocated, and utterly mismanaged, but Webb & Knapp, at the outset, was perfectly safe. We were merely the landlords. We didn't have a penny in the project. All the publicity and traffic Freedomland generated was bound to increase the value of our real estate. How could we lose? We leased them the land."

The comment that Webb & Knapp's role solely was that of a landlord (charging the park $15–16 million for rent, a sum that would have crippled similar projects of the time) was a fabrication. The Zeckendorfs .were involved personally, financially, and managerially with the companies that managed the park on their land.

During the first season, builders and suppliers threatened park operations for nonpayment of services. Convinced that Freedomland was a good investment that would provide financial dividends, the Zeckendorfs poured more money into the park. But, a few months after the park opened, a national media report indicated that the park already faced critical financial issues:

> Freedomland...has been no fun for its promoters. Last week they were scratching to round up fresh capital to pay the park's bills and keep it operating. The woes of Freedomland began even before the first spade of earth for the 205-acre playground was turned. A plan

to sell stock to finance the venture flopped; William Zeckendorf's Webb & Knapp, which owned the land and leased it to Freedomland promoter, the International Recreation Corp., had to buy 40 % of the stock for $7,000,000. This financing proved too little—partly because builders overshot the estimated $17.5 million construction cost by $4,500,000.

Year after year, the park siphoned away Webb & Knapp funds and credit. The one silver lining for the Zeckendorfs was that Freedomland attracted attention to the land. Zeck, Sr., later admitted that the park "was a device to hold the land" until Co-op City was approved for construction.

In mortgaging assets to obtain more capital to start more projects, the Zeckendorfs always moved around huge amounts of debt. The problems for Webb & Knapp developed before Freedomland. Short-term debt doubled between 1956 and 1959 while interest on loans and other expenses quadrupled. By mid-1961, the company owned $100 million in debt. Money flowed out faster than the Zeckendorfs could bring it in as an asset. Hundreds of employees were dismissed and payments were months in arrears for top executives. The Zeckendorfs became trapped in the cycle of spiraling costs and mounting taxes.

The senior Zeckendorf's days were battered by constant demands for payment on overdue mortgages, sinking funds, bank notes, and other obligations. To meet these payments, he went on a furious campaign to sell assets while creditors hit him with lease evictions, default judgments, and liens. His hotel business was failing, and according to news accounts, the older properties in New York were losing the competition against the new facilities constructed in anticipation of demand associated with the New York World's Fair. Webb & Knapp poured more than $10 million into the hotels and lost $4.5 million.

To protect his investment, Zeck, Sr., who had stayed out of most International Recreation Corporation management decisions, stepped in and took charge of the park. Webb & Knapp fired or demoted Freedomland's managers and cut operating costs from $40,000 to $25,000 a day. Adult admission rose from $1 to $1.50. By August 1961, Webb & Knapp owned both 40 percent of the stock and the $4 million of unpaid construction bills. The stock that had been issued at $17.50 plummeted to a low of $6.25. To meet the payments, Zeck, Sr., prepared a plan for new financing to save Freedomland and the Freedomland Inn, the unbuilt hotel that would become compromised with a failed entertainment venue.

With a typical Zeckendorf complicated financing plan, Webb & Knapp purchased $11.5 million in convertible debentures from International Recreation Corporation, using $3 million to pay construction bills. The remaining $8.5 million purchased the leases of Webb & Knapp's Astor, Manhattan, and Commodore hotels in New York City. With the purchase of the debentures, Webb & Knapp positioned itself to obtain further control over Freedomland and own an $18.5 million stake in it. The park now was managed by the Zeckendorfs. By taking over the hotels, Freedomland was placed in a position to have a year-round income with hotel profits offsetting park losses.

By 1963, the Zeckendorfs acknowledged that Freedomland was in serious financial trouble. Webb and Knapp, which also was in a precarious financial position, began an all-out liquidation. One large July deal (25 properties worth $75 million) involved 100 attorneys working constantly for two days. Later that month, the elder Zeckendorf staged a giant public auction of another group of 25 properties from which he hoped to receive $8.5 million.

Through all this turmoil, Zeck, Sr., put a positive spin on his work. "Why, we're responsible for $3 billion worth of construction in North America," he said in a published interview, "and we're still here to tell the story. I think that's incredible."

Zeck, Jr., by his estimates, said that the company lost $12–15 million with Freedomland. "Our getting involved in Freedomland hurt the financial position of Webb & Knapp more than anything we've ever done," he said in a published report. Meanwhile, Webb & Knapp and National Development Corporation continued to collaborate to develop the remaining unimproved property in the Baychester section of the Bronx for residential, commercial, or industrial development.

To help the Zeckendorfs pay mounting debts, property liquidation eventually included a portion of the Freedomland site. On June 30, 1964, the property south of the current Bartow

Avenue now occupied by the outdoor shopping center was purchased from the Zeckendorfs for a $25 million first mortgage loan to National Development Corporation. The buyer was the pension fund of the International Teamsters Union. The fund had connections with Hyman Green, who already owned an interest in National Development Corporation. The pension plan operator was the Central States, Southeast, and Southwest Areas Pension Fund. The security for the loan included 149 acres of land leased as the site of Freedomland and additional acres (various reports indicate both 200 and 258 acres) adjacent to this tract. A second mortgage of $4.3 million was floated against the property.

The seven-year pension fund loan maintained an interest rate of 6.5 percent annually. Proceeds were used to refinance previous short-term loans that were outstanding against the property. The loan also enabled National Development Corporation, according to the official announcement, to proceed with the planning for the major improvement it expects to erect on the Bronx property. Before the sale to the pension fund, Zeck, Sr., had stated that he might consolidate the park to 30 acres and build a residential complex around it. He also floated the idea of an indoor shopping mall.

The transfer of 80 percent Webb & Knapp interest in its consolidated subsidiary, the National Development Corporation, to Hyman and his associates, who owned the other 20 percent of the corporation, was accompanied by another transfer. Webb & Knapp surrendered its entire controlling interest of close to 60 percent stock in the International Recreation Corporation and its wholly owned subsidiary, Freedomland, Inc., to National Development Corporation. The company and Hyman now possessed complete oversight of the theme park.

The loan was secured by real estate owned by National Development Corporation at Dunedin Beach, Florida, where Webb & Knapp was associated with the Honeymoon Isle project that involved Hyman and his brother, Irving Green. This project, which also included a $4 million loan from the pension fund, allowed Webb & Knapp's marine division to dredge St. Joseph's Sound and fill residential sites and a public beach at Dunedin Beach. The developer of that property,

Woodrow V. Register, stated, according to Florida newspaper reports, that the New York business transfer would not affect the Florida project nor the plan to bring Freedomland to the beach. Woodrow said that "we are taking a long look and will watch Freedomland this summer. If it looks good, we hope to bring it here. But we don't plan to bring a white elephant. It would be a nice industry for this area."

Under terms of the transaction, according to published reports, Webb & Knapp maintained an option to reacquire the 80 percent interest in National Development Corporation in December. Meanwhile, Hyman, as the new president of National Development Corporation and with ties to the Teamsters Union, also succeeded Zeck, Jr., as president of the International Recreation Corporation and Freedomland, Inc.

Optimism for Freedomland

Hyman supported Freedomland after he surveyed the park and other amusement parks in the New York area, telling newspapers:

> We have every reason to be highly optimistic about the future of Freedomland. Originally designed solely as a theme park, it has become necessary to broaden Freedomland's base to include more thrill rides and fun features to attract repeat business. Certain themes will be maintained, but our aim now is to make it not only the largest and finest amusement park in the country, but a profitable enterprise as well.

CHAPTER TWENTY-SEVEN

Bankruptcy and the Building of Co-op City

Freedomland was as good as or better than Disneyland.

—Anonymous blog comment

Public statements by Freedomland officials during May 1964 revealed their optimism that the New York World's Fair would help increase business at the park and other entertainment venues in the greater New York City area. Management at Freedomland, Palisades Amusement Park, Coney Island, Rockaway Playland, and Rye Playland agreed that the fair would boost tourism to New York and that many more people would patronize the parks.

"We've been advertising all over the count[r]y for five years," said a Freedomland official in a newspaper report, "and it should pay off now," adding that visitors had said that they had found very little at the fair for children and, as a result, arranged to visit Freedomland.

Shortly after this statement, *Amusement Business*, a trade publication, reported:

> The park is nearly sliced in half. ... Originally projected as a Disney-type theme park, Freedomland now abounds in standard riding devices and a host of concession games.

On September 15, 1964, Freedomland, Inc., filed a petition for bankruptcy with the United States District Court for the Southern District of New York. The International Recreation Corporation attributed Freedomland's troubles to competition from the New York World's Fair. Liabilities were listed at

$27,041,000 and assets at $9,741,000. Filed under Chapter XI of the bankruptcy laws, Freedomland's petition sought permission to continue in business under court supervision and with court protection against lawsuits of individual creditors as it attempted to pay bills. According to the petition, the controlling interest in Freedomland was owned by Hyman Green, the president of the National Development Corporation.

The creditors listed in the bankruptcy petition included International Recreation Corporation for $11,625,700, National Development Corporation for $2,059,000, the interests of William Zeckendorf, Sr., and William Zeckendorf, Jr., for $1,194,964, and the Internal Revenue Service for $311,446. According to the filing, Freedomland income from admissions to the park was about $3 million during 1962–1963. Income from 1964 attendance was $734,000. The amusement park, the petition stated, wanted to reduce its land size from 85 to 30 acres, as previously stated by William Zeckendorf, Sr., and might finally show a profit while construction of a planned housing project would begin on the remaining land.

Freedomland never opened for the 1965 season. The court arrangement failed and on August 30, 1965, Freedomland was adjudicated a bankrupt. Attractions and supplies were sold to other entertainment venues as the property was prepared for housing and commercial development.

Teamsters Pension Saved

During August 1965, the pension fund of the International Brotherhood of Teamsters saved its $25 million investment that had been tied to the collapse of the Zeckendorf empire. At about this same time, one of the fund trustees, James R. Hoffa, and a number of borrowers from the fund were convicted of defrauding the fund.

The rescue operation, tied to the decision to develop the land, was administered by the fund, retired businessman and philanthropist Abraham E. Kazan, and the assistance of the State of New York, New York City, and more than 80 lawyers. The fund received its money when the Freedomland site and an adjoining 200 acres were sold to a new nonprofit corporation known as Community Services Inc., which issued an initial check of $13,465,891.54. The nonprofit gave the fund a mortgage for the property now occupied by the outdoor shopping center to cover the remainder of the finances and it also assumed responsibility for the loan.

Co-op City Rises

Six months after Freedomland filed for bankruptcy, the housing project of about 15,000 middle-income cooperative housing units for approximately 40,000+ people was announced to the public by New York City Mayor Robert Wagner and New York State Governor Nelson Rockefeller. Money for the $300 million project was raised through the sale of public bonds by Morgan Guaranty Trust and guaranteed by the State of New York through the legislature agreement to commit taxpayers to back the project.

Co-op City was built by the United Housing Federation. UHF had been established about 15 years earlier by the same Abraham E. Kazan who headed Community Services Inc. The Amalgamated Clothing Workers of America also was involved in the project. Jacob S. Potofsky was president of ACWA, a combination of housing cooperatives, labor unions, and civic organizations, and he was on the UHF board. The housing project received aid from an approximately $260 million multiple-decade mortgage loan from the New York Housing Finance Agency and, also for a handful of decades, a 50 percent city tax abatement on the value of the property. The primary mission of UHF was housing production and not urban renewal. UHF organized and built cooperative communities throughout the city under New York State's Limited-Profit Housing Companies Law of 1955 known as "Mitchell-Lama" for its two sponsors, Senator MacNeil Mitchell and Assemblyman Alfred Lama.

UHF used financing from savings banks, insurance companies, union pension funds, and other conventional sources along with direct mortgage loans from the state. UHF emphasis was on high-rise, large-scale projects to meet a mass need for low-priced housing. UHF formed the Riverbay Corporation to own and operate Co-op City.

Most of Co-op City's housing was placed on Freedomland's parking lot and its Little Old New York and Satellite City-themed areas. The final section of housing was built east of the Hutchinson River Parkway, but this land never was occupied by Freedomland.

A May 1969 document that reviewed the creation of Co-op City was sent to members of the Institute of Current World Affairs, a nonprofit that continues to operate today. Updated details about the activity on the Baychester land included several interesting observations:

- The National Development Corporation agreed to sell 300 acres for just $1.50 per square foot [$15,561,342], reserving for itself two smaller, strategically located plots, one for commercial development, the other for an industrial park. It was a shrewd deal...the value of the reserved acreage would rise with every thin dime of UHF investment in Co-op City. Eventually, UHF spent another dollar per foot for sand fill, five million yards of it, fine, white, and eight to ten feet deep all over the site.

- The National Development Company has yet to play its hand, so no one knows officially what will happen to those adjacent plots of land, but engineering models have been seen.

Architectural critics brutally assessed the housing complex. The project also was criticized socially for luring the middle class out of other Bronx neighborhoods and heightening the awareness of the deeper problem of white middle-class flight from the city. But, the problems for Co-op City ran deeper than its above-ground appearance, related social issues, and various financial concerns. The buildings were supported by more than 50,000 pilings designed to reach bedrock, and the underground utility distribution network, stairs, ramps and building entrances were vulnerable to movement and settlement caused by water moving through the soil. Cracks appeared in walls and damage occurred to sidewalks, entrances, and terraces.

An April 2004 article in a publication for New York City homeowners reported that a town hall meeting had been organized for Co-op City residents to discuss pertinent issues. One resident, a professional property manager, had resigned from Riverbay Corporation's 16-member board in "utter frustration and disgust." She said that the huge cooperative was built on land originally purchased by private developers to be the home of Freedomland.

"They bought the site," the woman was quoted in the article, "knowing Freedomland would fail, knowing that then they would then own the land to build Co-op City and they could sell it to the state of New York. Co-op City was built on a lie. There's been greed, corruption, money under the table."

The Shopping Center Property

For more than a decade, the land south of Bartow Avenue, where the outdoor shopping center now is located, had remained undeveloped ground. This area had contained most of the park's attractions: Old Chicago, the Old Southwest, the Great Plains, San Francisco, and New Orleans.

The property's conversion into the shopping center began during the early 1980s. A few of Freedomland's western buildings had remained on the site until that time, creating a ghost-town image on the southern horizon. The building with the designation as the last survivor was one of the two structures that had housed the Tucson Mining Company ore bucket sky ride. Located in Old Chicago, this building was known as the turnaround house, since, initially, the skyway returned guests to the ride embarkation point located in the Old Southwest.

Several people who visited Co-op City during that time recall this last stand of Freedomland. The building decayed as it became surrounded by the marsh and reeds that reclaimed the property. A few people hoped to venture to the building, but they were warned that water from Eastchester Bay again flowed in and out of the property and that the ground was muddy, unstable, and filled with rats.

Another small portion of the original Freedomland terrain, though outside the park boundary, remained undeveloped until 2012. At the time of the park, this land at the south end of today's outdoor shopping center in the corner part of the property bounded by the New England Thruway, the Hutchinson River Parkway, and secondary roads had been designated for the Freedomland Inn. The hotel foundation had been covered by landfill. An indoor mall and its garage now occupy the property.

Historic Site Destroyed

The opening chapter of this book noted the historic nature of the land within the vicinity of Freedomland. An historic site also was located on park property.

Pinckney's Humack was a rock island about 400 feet from modern Baychester Avenue, originally within the marshes of what became known as the Hutchinson River. Historians documented that Indians, specifically Siwoney, used it possibly as a fishing location. Discarded oyster shells and wood ashes were located on the property along with some pottery. The name Pinckney's Humack (also referred to as the Prickly Pear) was provided by European settlers to the hummock, or island, on Philip Pinckney's grant of meadowland. The property was part of the Thomas Pell grant acquired from the local Indians during 1654.

During the time of Freedomland, this location remained preserved, though not interpreted, between the park and a car lot. The location eventually was destroyed with the April 1998 construction of several retail box stores within the Bay Plaza Shopping Center.

Theories About Freedomland's Demise

Many people who never saw Freedomland have claimed, falsely, that it was doomed to fail as a theme park. Though it was different than any other entertainment park ever created, and this includes Disneyland, Freedomland would have been successful for many years, possibly decades, if the key people involved in its debut were interested in its long-term success. During its five seasons, Freedomland's overseers moved the park closer to the day that they could alter it, downsize it, move it, or declare bankruptcy—and present the plans for Co-op City.

Many reasons and excuses for Freedomland's demise have been documented over the years, and this includes the debate about the role of the New York World's Fair. Any of these reasons, separately or collectively, may have contributed to problems at the Bronx theme park.

Among the many theories:

- The park was poorly capitalized. While stock was sold to the public, not enough shares were sold to raise the necessary money, causing more money to be borrowed from financial institutions or invested by Webb & Knapp.

- The concept was doomed by a poor business plan. The cost of building and operating the park was underestimated while the potential number of guests each season was overestimated.

- America's entertainment tastes were changing. The local "family parks" popular during the 1950s were becoming passé.

- Though Disneyland was a success, many other parks across the country continued to struggle financially or close the gates.

- Time was ripe for families, with access to new cars and new roads, to travel around and see the country rather than vacation close to home.

- Freedomland never opened year-round (only about 120 days each season) to generate additional revenue. The months without income drained the budget. Some contracts, especially union contracts, were negotiated on a calendar year, reportedly driving payrolls to new heights within the amusement industry. Maintenance, security, and fire staffing was required year round.

- New York is a city with a summer season that operates from Memorial Day to Labor Day. High school and college workers were not available at other times.

- The land was more valuable for development than with the entertainment center that occupied it. The world's largest cooperative housing project became necessary for city construction jobs, to maintain within city limits the residents fleeing the blight of the South Bronx, and to reap financial and political rewards.

- Harsh winters required mandatory and expensive spring touch-ups throughout the park.

- Little money was available for major new attractions (other than the non-history celebrity entertainers) after the park made its debut.

- The 1964 summer riots in Harlem were floated as an excuse by park management for the reason of decreased tourism to New York City.

The World's Fair Excuse

The success (though it lost millions of dollars) of the 1964–1965 New York World's Fair, which attracted tens of millions of people to Flushing Meadows Park in Queens, often is cited for the eventual failure of Freedomland. This reason was stated by Freedomland management in the bankruptcy filing. However, a number of Freedomland fans long have maintained that the World's Fair did not contribute to the park's demise. The anticipated and eventual popularity of the fair only provided the owners with a convenient public excuse as Freedomland's attractions were systematically curtailed, bankruptcy was filed, and plans were presented to develop the property.

Competition from a world's fair, which was a known entity before Freedomland was announced on May 25, 1959, initially did not concern park management. Since most people attended the fair only a handful of times during its two years, the attraction did not significantly diminish attendance at the other New York venues that included Freedomland.

Over the years, the World's Fair excuse for Freedomland's bankruptcy has become an urban legend.

Woody's Insights About Freedomland

Soon after the park closed, C.V. Wood contributed his insight about Freedomland. Woody said that his creation never was a completed park. The project, he stated, exceeded its budget and Freedomland never recovered from the extra millions of initial debt incurred by opening day. He added that Freedomland just did not have the final appearance that was the difference between a good and excellent park.

Woody had been surprised by the amount of additional "payments" that Marco Engineering provided to the unions. He knew about the high union rates, but he did not expect the extra costs such as unwarranted overtime. City officials made blatant demands for favors. Permits for certain attractions were delayed but quickly obtained with "special" application fees.

Woody reportedly stated that he knew the park would not last as the Zeckendorfs had other ideas for the land rather than wait for a profit to be made on Freedomland. Some people have indicated that Woody also cited competition from the World's Fair, but this sentiment requires further documentation.

Many of the issues faced by Freedomland were revealed to Walt Disney during his involvement with the New York World's Fair. Though Walt had contemplated a northeast option for a new park, the various labor, construction, and weather issues in the region, along with his personal experiences at the fair, convinced him to build in Florida.

Real Estate Wins

"Show business is a funny thing," Zeck, Sr., said about Freedomland in a media interview. "You're either a flop or a success. We were a flop. I guess from now on we should stick to the real estate business."

Actually, the bottom line for the Zeckendorfs and others was that the property occupied by Freedomland proved more profitable for development than it might realize as the world's largest entertainment center. Plans for development of the marshland actually began before the park was built. New York City's political and business leaders were aware that new homes (in the form of 30 apartment buildings from 24 to 33 stories on the site) eventually would be needed for the many residents who would flee the urban blight that had started to infect the southern portion of the Bronx.

The blueprint allowed Freedomland to operate on a portion of the property for five years. Multi-story buildings were constructed to house the attractions. By remaining intact on marshland for five years without incurring damage or settling issues, the Freedomland structures, it now is believed, allowed developers to receive the proper property variances that eliminated a 15 to 20-year monitoring period before high-rise buildings could occupy the site.

Charles J. Ursadt, an attorney who worked at Webb & Knapp and later helped create the New York State Urban Development Corporation (now the Empire State Development Corporation), addressed New York City land value and development in his book published in 2005. This excerpt is revealing as the dates coincide with the operation of Freedomland:

> On January 26, 1960, the Port Authority announced plans for a single fifty- to seventy-story office tower on the East Side, south of the Brooklyn Bridge, near several housing projects that were already in the works. The authority included an adjoining hotel in its plans. But New Jersey withheld its necessary cooperation, holding out for a better commute for its residents, who arrived in Downtown Manhattan by rail on the Lower West Side via the aging "Hudson Tubes." To satisfy everyone, the Port Authority moved its project westward and added a new terminal for the commuter lines, which it would also take over. The development also became more ambitious. It would rise as twin towers, 110 stories each, at the edge of the Hudson River. ... It was an auspicious time for such a project. New York City's mayor Robert Wagner would be up for reelection in 1962, and he was all too aware that the city had lost about two hundred thousand jobs since 1950 as service industries replaced factories. The World Trade Center construction project

would create jobs—many of them—as did several large state-sponsored housing projects in various stages of planning or development at the time, such as Rochdale Village in Queens and Co-op City in the Bronx.

—*Battery Park City: The Early Years*

Additional Insights

Charles R. Wood, the business executive and creator of Storytown USA and Gaslight Village in New York's Lake George region, purchased a number of attractions and other items from Freedomland after the bankruptcy ruling. Non-attraction items included office furniture and, according to a statement made by Charley, he found copies of park records.

Charley never accepted the public reasons, specifically the competition from the World's Fair, for Freedomland's bankruptcy. He stated that the park's closure probably had more to do with the difficulties caused by the other Zeckendorf investments and the involvement of politicians, Hyman Green, and other interests.

A few years ago, an anonymous comment to a blog post endorsed the heart-felt memories of the many people who worked at the park or visited it countless times:

> Freedomland was as good as or better than Disneyland. … Freedomland was not a cheapened Disneyland at all, and as far as the attendance it was very good for the first 4 seasons, and waned in 1964 but still adequate. Freedomland's closing was for one reason and that was to get alot of money quickly for a housing project. Which was part of a building plan in 1959 when Freedomland was announced. Sure, it was tough financially the first year and other years, but it was also that way for Walt and Roy when Disneyland opened. … Had it not been for a show on ABC, Disneyland could have become Co-op City Anaheim style.

CHAPTER TWENTY-EIGHT

Freedomland's Connections to Other Parks

This structure was first built at Freedomland, in the Bronx, N.Y.

—Postcard from Clark's Trading Post

Fans of theme and amusement parks are aware of the frequent comings and goings of attractions. Some attractions are retired due to maintenance expenses. Others fall out of favor with succeeding generations of guests. Some attractions forfeit real estate footprints for the latest thrill coasters.

Throughout its five seasons, Freedomland also added and subtracted attractions. When the park closed, remaining attractions were destroyed or moved to other venues.

Cedar Point

Two Arrow Development dark rides—Earthquake and Buccaneers—were sold to Cedar Point in Sandusky, Ohio. Buccaneers was renamed the Pirate Ride. These attractions enjoyed a popular following with a new audience. Each attraction lasted about another two decades until the park morphed into a coaster park. Earthquake operated from 1965 until 1984 and the Pirate Ride operated from 1966 to 1996.

Clark's Trading Post

A number of structures and other items from Freedomland still can be seen at Clark's Trading Post in Lincoln, New Hampshire. The Clark family has a long tradition—more than 80 years—of family entertainment and they have incorporated Freedomland into the park.

The main entrance to the park is Freedomland's reconfigured Chicago train station. The original octagon-shaped station was reconstructed as a rectangle to accommodate more people. Many of the original building features, including the cupola, clock, and ornamentation, remain for the station and the platform. A Clark's postcard from years ago featured the station:

> This structure was first built at Freedomland, in the Bronx, N.Y. Later dismantled and brought 360 miles to Lincoln, N.H., it was rebuilt a bit larger and more ornate— typical of the most beautiful stations of the 1890s.

Freedomland's Santa Fe railroad station, a prop building and hideout for the bandits who robbed the train, also was relocated to the park. Most recently, it served as the park's Segway Safari rental stand and souvenir shop. The building interior was unfinished when Clark's purchased it, confirming its prop building status at Freedomland.

For about 40 years, park guests who enjoyed Clark's popular bear shows sat in the same plastic bucket seats from Freedomland's Space Rover. These seats were replaced a few years ago, but the fencing around the bear ring still includes metal clamps purchased from the Freedomland clearance sale.

The Tuttle Rustic House is Clark's version of a crooked house. It was created from the same blueprints and incorporates many of the same optical illusions as Freedomland's Casa Loca. The fencing surrounding the Tuttle family cemetery plot originally decorated Freedomland's New Orleans landscape.

The old-fashioned light posts, along with park benches and trash cans, also are from Freedomland. Clark's 1884 fire station was constructed from bricks originally used in Freedomland buildings.

The figure of a man dressed as an aviator, or astronaut, and that appeared at the inside top of Freedomland's Braniff Space

Rover, also made its way to Clark's Trading Post. But, its fate is unknown to the Clark family. Additional items have remained in the park's back lot all these years—surplus light posts, extra Space Rover seats, metal roofing from the entrance booths, and decorative wood trim from the Brass Rail Steakhouse.

The Freedomland buildings were inexpensive. Insurance may not have been necessary to obtain ownership and to remove the structures.

Dave Clark recalls that it cost his family about $250 for the Chicago train station building. It was dismantled and loaded onto a tractor trailer. Dave and his brother, Eddie, were just out of high school at the time. Their father, Edward, brought them to the Freedomland site to accumulate materials. About every two weeks, Edward would drive from New Hampshire to the Bronx, and when he arrived the trailer was loaded. It took five hours to haul the materials to Clark's Trading Post.

The Clark brothers were not at Freedomland when all the good items were auctioned or purchased. They had to wait until Clark's closed for the season. They arrived in the Bronx during October 1965 and stayed on-site through the winter. The brothers were not provided with much money during their time in the Bronx, so they could not stay at a local motel. They occasionally ate dinner on nearby Gun Hill Road, but mostly they ate cold beans and stew inside one of the Freedomland buildings. They slept in buildings without utilities during that winter.

Forest Park Highlands and Knoebels

Forest Park Highlands of St. Louis, Missouri, was the city's largest and best-known amusement park. During its early years, the park maintained a theater and one of the largest public swimming pools in the country. The end occurred in a flash when fire destroyed most of the park on July 19, 1963.

Aero Jet was among the surviving park attractions. Installed during June 1956, the ride consisted of about a dozen two-person cars that spun in a circle. Riders could adjust the height. It arrived from Germany, where it had been used for a number of years. Following the fire, the ride was sold to Freedomland, but no documentation exists of the sale. After Freedomland closed, the ride was sold to Knoebles in Elysberg, Pennsylvania, where it continues to operate today.

Kennywood Amusement Park

When C.V. Wood's attention was focused on Six Flags Over Texas and other projects, his favorite ride was removed from Freedomland. After the 1962 season, Tornado was sold to Kennywood Amusement Park in West Mifflin, Pennsylvania, where it operated for several seasons. The attraction received a new façade that re-created a large barn.

Tornado then was sold to Storytown USA (now Great Escape) in the Lake George, New York, region, where it operated from 1967 until 2002. Space was limited at Storytown and the park installed only about three-quarters of the original ride.

Storytown USA/Gaslight Village

Storytown USA, a fairy tale-themed amusement park owned by businessman Charles Wood, opened during 1954. Charley purchased a number of Freedomland attractions for the park. He also opened his Gaslight Village park nearby. That attraction closed a number of years ago and it may have included Freedomland's Casa Loca.

Charley purchased Freedomland's green Danny the Dragon train for Storytown. A handful of years ago, it was located in park storage. The destination of the second Danny from Freedomland remains a mystery. Charley also purchased Freedomland's King Rex Carrousel (for a reported $100,000), the Crystal Maze mirror house, the Mule-Go-Round, and pieces of interior scenery from the Mine Cavern dark ride for the park's train tunnel. Certain other items, including the moose, giant cowboy boots, and a sawmill worker spinning on a log, were obtained from the Northwest Fur Trapper ride and still may be seen at the park.

The Crystal Maze building was used for a food concession and then an administration building. The train and tunnel were removed a few years ago. The Mule-Go-Round is believed to have been sold to the now defunct Pirates World in Florida.

Rose Ann Hirsch, in *Kiddie Parks of the Adirondacks*, wrote:

> In 1964, the short-lived Bronx, New York, amusement park Freedomland, U.S.A. closed permanently. Charley Wood purchased several rides from the park auction, including the Sky Ride, an antique Dentzel carousel, and Danny the Dragon. Danny's bright colored serpentine body served as seats for passengers. A track was embedded in an asphalt trail that went up a hill through a coppice of trees and over the train tunnel.

An often repeated inaccurate story, as in the aforementioned book, is that Freedomland's Tucson Mining Company sky ride operated at Storytown. The Storytown sky ride actually arrived from New Jersey's Palisades Amusement Park. The Freedomland attraction, according to a 1965 newspaper article, was sold to Tower View Amusement Park across from Niagara Falls, New York. If the sky ride actually arrived at Tower View, Charley subsequently could have purchased it, or parts of it, but he never installed the attraction at his park. Research about Tower View Park has not documented any definitive record for the purchase of one sky ride from Freedomland or the sale of one sky ride to Charley.

On December 16, 1989, individual pieces from the Freedomland/Storytown/ Great Escape carrousel were auctioned by Guernsey's auction house in New York City. The total price for 69 figures (at Freedomland, the ride included 72 figures) was $1,321,227, with a 10 percent buyer's premium of $132,122, making the individual purchases total $1,453,350. Besides horses, the figures included rabbits, cats, bears, ostriches, deer, giraffes, mules, pigs, and one each of a tiger and lion. Some of the items were stripped of paint. Others were refinished and some were auctioned with a protective fiberglass coating.

The coating likely was applied at Freedomland. According to Bill Finkenstein, owner of WRF Designs, a carrousel restorer and appraiser in Plainville, Connecticut, the fiberglass is similar to glaze on a doughnut. The fiberglass resin reacts with fiberglass tape and actually damages the carrousel figures.

"Condensation builds up between the fiberglass and the wood, and this affects the detail of the piece," said Bill. "The detail is found in the first couple of inches of the figure."

The use of fiberglass to protect a piece from chips, dents, and the weather was not unique to the King Rex Carrousel, added Bill, who has been involved in this industry for about 40 years. He knew Charley and he prepared the figures for the auction. He stripped the fiberglass from some of the animals and discovered serious deterioration in some pieces that required significant restoration.

During August 1990, Guernsey's held an auction in Saratoga Spring, New York, that included figures from a variety of other carrousels and also featured panels, chariots, and a rounding board from the former Freedomland attraction. As of November 1990, several of the pieces were among the world-record auction prices for carrousel items. These included a standing Dentzel horse with flag ($64,900), a Dentzel tiger ($63,800), and a Dentzel lion ($57,200). A chariot was priced at $5,500.

"Years later," said Bill, "Charley felt bad about auctioning the carrousel and selling it in pieces. A carrousel is a beautiful attraction, but it also is history."

A few years ago, a spokeswoman for Great Escape indicated that Chance Rides, an amusement rides manufacturer, created "castings of the [original figures]" and the assumption was made that fiberglass castings of the Freedomland Dentzel figures were incorporated into the park's new Grand Carousel. Recent research, however, has determined that the castings were not of the carrousel's original Dentzel animals. The animals on the most recent Great Escape attraction were fiberglass castings of old figures from other carrousels.

The figures, frame, panels, mechanism, and the rest on the Grand Carousel are from Chance Rides stock materials. For the fiberglass reproductions of old carrousel figures, Chance craftsmen employed cast molds of hand-carved animals to produce new versions that preserved details of the original pieces. Most figures were molds of antique horses produced by Wendell "Bud" Hurlbut (a designer, builder, entrepreneur, and theme park creator) along with Dentzel and Philadelphia Toboggan Company figures.

After the auctions, several pieces of the Freedomland attraction found a home at the New England Carousel Museum in Bristol, Connecticut. One is a carved wood inside upper panel. Featured in the main gallery, the panel is about two feet in height and depicts an Indian warrior charging on horseback. A mirror from the ride also can be found in the museum's lobby. It is set in a wood frame with the addition of three light bulbs. Pictures from Freedomland indicate that the original mirror panels did not include lights. The panel and mirror were restored by WRF Designs.

As for Gaslight Village, pictures have been located of that park's crooked house. It might have been the Freedomland Casa Loca with a much different outer shell, but an accurate story has remained elusive to this day.

The Gaslight Village attraction was known as Mystery House. The assumption is that Charley may have purchased the entire Casa Loca cabin and moved it. One person who remembers the house at Gaslight Village indicated that the decor was not as complete as the version in the Bronx. The attraction was removed during 1987 or 1988, and several people claim that it was moved to the nearby Magic Forest park. Information remains incomplete to determine, undisputedly, if Casa Loca was relocated or if it was destroyed at Freedomland.

New York World's Fair

Freedomland sponsors Schaefer Beer and Borden left the Bronx after the 1963 season for Queens and the New York World's Fair. Both sponsors posted signs at the respective Freedomland exhibits to indicate a return at the end of the fair. The Last Supper wax exhibit, added during 1963, also relocated to the fair.

Freedomland was promoted at the fair through discount coupon books. Each coupon provided $1 savings on admission during the 1964 season. Freedomland also was promoted on three-inch by three-and-one-half-inch pieces of paper collected by visitors at the fair's Qantas airways exhibit. Each paper included a promotional message on the front bottom (one for 1964 Freedomland) along with information about a tourist attraction anywhere in the world. A separate paper featured Freedomland in a tourist attraction message.

The fair appeared in media contests across the country, and the grand prizes were trips to New York City to visit the fair. Contest winners also were offered opportunities to enjoy other New York attractions, including a day trip to Freedomland.

Freedomland's cowboys appeared at the fair in an unknown number of performances during the 1964 season. Marshal Ben Rossi, his horse Navajo, cowboys that included "the famed Freedomland gunfighters," stunt men, and Indians appeared in a western show that included champion roping and precision bullwhip cracking at the Transportation & Travel Pavilion.

Pirates World

Located in Dania, Florida, Pirates World existed from 1967 until 1975. It is possible that it received Freedomland's Mule-Go-Round from Storytown USA and stories have been told that it also received Casa Loca from Gaslight Village. But, the dates of the crooked house removal from Gaslight Village do not correspond with the dates for Pirates World. If Casa Loca moved to Pirates World, the transfer likely would have occurred soon after Freedomland closed, confirming that the Gaslight Village Mystery House was a different structure.

Pirates World did secure the Pirate Gun Gallery from Tower View Amusement Park that originally had been located in the New Orleans section of Freedomland. Its destination after Pirates World closed remains a mystery.

Quassy Amusement Park

A New York Harbor tugboat, *Totsie* was shipped to Quassy Amusement Park, one of the few remaining trolley parks in the nation. It is located in Middlebury, Connecticut. Owner George Frantzis was four years old when *Totsie* arrived at the family-owned park.

"The boat had a flat bottom," recalled George. "It was a great boat and we've never been able to find another like it. It had charm."

The boat took park guests on a pleasant spin on the lake. Artwork of the boat appeared on Quassy memorabilia from that time.

The boat was not easy to maintain. The base consisted of about eight inches of concrete and it mostly was made from plywood, making it a maintenance nightmare. It sunk on the lake a couple of times and Quassy had to fiberglass the hull each year.

"We decommissioned her in 1998," added George. "She was dismantled and placed into five dumpsters."

The location of *Pert*, the other Freedomland tugboat, has yet to surface.

Six Flags Great Adventure

The sky ride at this park in Jackson, New Jersey, has connections to Freedomland. While the cables and cars are not from the Bronx park, most of the towers once held up the Tucson Mining Company ore bucket ride. The towers have been in place since this park opened during 1974.

Six Flags Over Georgia

This park originally was owned by Texas business executive Angus G. Wynne, Jr. It opened during 1967 and many of its original attractions mimicked those seen at Freedomland. Several Freedomland creators were involved in the project.

Among the attractions was another version of the tilt house. Known originally as Casa Loco, the attraction was renamed Casa Magnetica and it contained many of the same effects.

Six Flags Over Texas

This park in Arlington, Texas, also was owned by Angus. As Freedomland opened, C.V. Wood and his Marco Engineering team were creating the park.

"The secret," according to Woody's comments at the time in a Texas newspaper, "is to tell a big story—one that everyone at all ages can enjoy 'escaping' into. ... It's like working on full-scale three- dimensional jigsaw puzzles with the real thrill coming as the pieces fit together and the scene comes alive."

Similarities between Freedomland and this park included themed areas, street designs, and attractions such as a sky ride, freeway, river adventure, plantation house chicken restaurant, crooked house, and burro rides.

Space City USA

A 1960s park concept for Huntsville, Alabama, Space City USA never opened its gates. Glen Robinson of Skylim of Alabama was involved in its planning, design, engineering, and initial construction. During the development phase, Glen touted his expertise with Freedomland and several other Marco Engineering parks. Nothing more is known about his connection to Freedomland.

Tower View Amusement Park

Located on the Canadian side of Niagara Falls, Tower View Amusement Park was situated across from today's Konica Tower (originally Seagram Tower). The park opened during May 1962 and closed during 1967 to prepare the property for commercial development.

Among its amusement park attractions was Whirlpool. A nostalgic park website questions if this ride was created by Arrow Development while indicating that the attraction was based on the Disneyland Tea Cups ride. The ride absolutely was created by Arrow and specifically as Freedomland's Spin-a-Top attraction for the New Orleans-themed section. The cabs, decorative towers, and the centerpiece with the Mardi Gras features all appeared at Freedomland. The Pirate Gun Gallery from Freedomland also was moved to this park and later relocated to Pirates World in Florida.

Another attraction—a Swiss sky ride—was to be installed on a slope near the park, but research indicates that the concept was dropped when the steel cables and possibly the towers, reportedly from Freedomland's Tucson Mining Company sky ride, could not clear customs. The cables could have been sold to Storytown USA, but this has not been confirmed with documentation. The towers have been at Six Flags Great Adventure in New Jersey since 1974.

CHAPTER TWENTY-NINE

Freedomland Commemorated

FREEDOMLAND USA
THEME PARK
On this Co-Op City site in 1960–1964
was the entrance to Freedomland USA
"The World's Largest Outdoor Entertainment Center"
A true theme park shaped in the map of the United States,
with rides, attractions and performers depicting the history
of our country in an education and entertaining manner.
—Freedomland plaque, Co-op City, The Bronx

In a flash, Freedomland was gone. The attractions were auctioned or sold, and the ground was prepared for the Co-op City housing project. Freedomland was wiped off the map—its own and the coordinates of the Bronx landscape.

Almost 50 years from the park's last day, on August 17, 2013, a plaque was unveiled on the site of Freedomland. The day's ceremonies welcomed several hundred Freedomland fans. John Bulakowski, Bob Mangels, and this book's author coordinated the various events and the dedication. Among the special guests were original park employees Frank Adamo (maintenance) and Ben Rossi (entertainer), Lynn Lovalette (the daughter of television ringmaster Claude Kirchner), Bronx historians, and local politicians. An audio greeting was received from television celebrity Chuck McCann and displays of Freedomland memorabilia captivated the audience. Discussions, questions, and stories about the park and its attractions filled the day.

New York Congressman Eliot Engel reminisced about his connection as a teenage employee during the 1963 and 1964 seasons. He said he made the best milkshakes. Soon after Co-op City opened, the Engel family lived in one of the buildings. New York State Senator Ruth Hassell-Thompson recalled the fun of Freedomland and indicated that she still possessed the sketch of her created by a park artist. Additional special guests included Michelle Sajous, the director of community relations for Co-op City's Riverbay Corporation, and Bernard Cylich, chairman of the historical committee of Riverbay's board of directors.

The plaque was placed close to the location where the large flagpoles with the Freedomland name greeted guests as they entered the property by car or bus. It is situated on the north side of the present Bartow Avenue, occupying a location in the shadow of residential buildings that stand on the Little Old New York section of the park.

CHAPTER THIRTY

Postscript

It remained an amusement park zoning district.

—Michael Davis

During November 2017, several electronic signs were erected at the corner of Baychester and Bartow avenues at the entrance to Co-op City. A triangular sign that rose about 70 feet featured one of the Freedomland bumper stickers. A smaller sign at street level displayed the Freedomland car/luggage decal. Many people started to wonder if a comeback was planned for Freedomland.

The signs were the idea of Michael Davis. He is the founding partner of the Plymouth Group, a real estate investment company that invests in transitional and value-add properties throughout the five boroughs and in selected markets nationwide. Michael purchased the property about four years earlier from the operator of the Exxon station on the site. He demolished the station to build several stores. The signs on the site are third-party advertising signs and Michael incorporated the Freedomland messaging during the testing phase.

"The zoning for the property is unusual," said Michael. "It has the same zoning as a section of Coney Island. It remained as an amusement park zoning district, and this is the reason we were able to erect these signs that are not permitted in almost every other area of the city."

While Freedomland did not appear on the signs beyond the tests, Michael has expressed interest in commemorating the park on the site. While too young to have experienced Freedomland, his grandparents took his father and uncles to the park. He always has been fascinated with the concept of Freedomland and, with this property, he has been provided with an opportunity to tell its story.

A concept plan, according to Michael, is to create a mural dedicated to Freedomland on the back wall of the stores. The wall is about 140 feet wide and 20 feet high. Michael welcomed input from the Freedomland community to provide ideas, photos, and guidance for this potential visual tribute to Freedomland.

Freedomland U.S.A. Fun Facts

C.V. Wood founded the Mind Science Foundation, a charitable, scientific, and educational institution to coordinate, support, and extend the study of the human mind. He also was a member of the Board of Governors of the American Stock Exchange.

Freedomland's natural wonders were "transplanted" to the park. Regional plants were allowed to flourish in natural habitats that included scale-sized forests, a rebuilt Rocky Mountains, a miniature Great Lakes, and the panorama of the western plains. Foliage included squash growing on the vine, desert plants in the west, magnolias and oleanders in New Orleans. Buffalo grass, rare water lilies, palm trees, birds of paradise, New Zealand flax, orchids, banana plants, and corn stalks were located throughout the park.

During the 1961 season, a sign at the main entrance read "Babes in Arms Admitted Free." So, a young man literally carried his girlfriend up to the gate and demanded that she be admitted at no cost. She was, but within minutes management removed the sign.

During the 1960 season, women's feet were "air-conditioned" by a scented spray offered at a park shoeshine salon. The service was provided without charge by Esquire Shoe Care Products. The spray was promoted to "instantaneously revivify, relax and refresh" tired feet. Women guests also could have their shoes shined at no cost—and tipping was not permitted. This promotion identifies just one of the many differences between the parks of the 1950s and 1960s and the parks of today. Photographs from Freedomland showcase guests who were dressed much differently than those who wear t-shirts, shorts, and sneakers at today's parks. Men wore collared shirts and slacks. Women wore stylish dresses, hats, and heels. Children rarely wore jeans or sneakers.

Freedomland was organized to serve more than 50,000 hamburgers, hot dogs, sandwiches, soda, milk, and coffee each hour at specially designed snack stands throughout the park. Restaurants and other eating places were able to accommodate 30,000 people an hour.

At any given time, the local bank branch could become a staged crime scene. According to *The Freedomland Enterprise*, "Members of the city's gangland brazenly entered the bank to force funds from frightened tellers. Fortunately for the savings of law-abiding citizens, the local constabulary was not asleep. The criminals were apprehended as they were making their get-away, and fell under a rain of night sticks."

From the nearby community of City Island, residents could hear the sounds of Freedomland, especially the train whistle. Boys would ride their bicycles and hide them in the bushes by the bridge, and then walk around to the entrance of the park.

Since no one has worked for Freedomland for more than 50 years, the term "Friendly Freedomlander" was adopted by the Freedomland Facebook page (Freedomland U.S.A.: The World's Largest Entertainment Center) when it was unveiled in 2011. Anyone associated with the page and with other Freedomland social media now is considered a "Friendly Freedomlander." Anyone reading this book also is a "Friendly Freedomlander."

Freedomland scouts scoured the country for herds of buffalo, wild mustangs, mountain burros, trained mules, and the pinto ponies that visitors enjoyed at the park. Anyone who thought the animals on the Freedomland mule trail moved a bit slow, proof may have been located in an October 20, 1960, classified ad published in a Hudson Valley newspaper by the Lazy-L Ranch of Highland, New York: "LAZY-L RANCH, will have all their leased horses and rodeo stock at the ranch this weekend including saddle horses, work horses and 6 pairs of mules from Freedomland..."

The May 13, 1961 *Asbury Park Press* syndicated column by Dorothy Kilgallen included this brief mention: "Shepard's Journey name of new rocket ride being built at Freedomland." The ride may have referenced popular NASA astronaut Alan Shepard, but additional details are not known about this attraction.

Three actors at Freedomland banded together to promote themselves as the new version of the Three Mesquiteers. The original "The Three Mesquiteers" was an umbrella title for a Republic Pictures series of 51 Western B-movies released between 1936 and 1943. Eight films starred John Wayne. The series was based on novels by William Colt MacDonald. During 1960, Freedomland's John Conant, Don Crabtree, and Buddy Farnan filmed a reel to promote themselves as the Three Mesquiteers. John portrayed Tucson Smith, Don was Stony Brooke, and Buddy was Lullaby Joslin. We reckon the idea never amounted to a hill of beans.

The pool table used in Casa Loca reportedly was purchased by the park for an unknown sum and found in the Bowery section of New York City.

Phyllis Stein was at the heart of the 1970s American early punk scene. Her roots traveled back to Freedomland, where, at about 12 years of age, she first was introduced to live music. The show featured the Ronettes.

About 20 couples decided to set their wedding dates while soaring high over Freedomland in the Tucson Mining Company ore buckets. One couple could not afford a honeymoon to California so they spent 14 hours at the park. They cruised on the Great Lakes, drove an antique car through the vineyards, helped extinguish the Chicago Fire, and danced in the Moon Bowl to the music of the Tommy Dorsey Orchestra. When park management learned about the "honeymoon trip," Freedomland provided the couple with dinner at the Brass Rail Steak House.

Chuck McCann was close friends with comedic actor Stan Laurel. The actor never visited Freedomland, but he knew about the park. In a letter on stationary from the Oceana Apartment Hotel (849 Ocean Avenue, Santa Monica, California) to a mutual friend who was an audio engineer, Stan wrote: "Am happy to know the news about Chuck [McCann] & everything is OK with his L&H [Laurel & Hardy] program—I can fully understand not hearing from him, he's certainly had his hands full these last few weeks—Freedomland, W.P.I.X. show & taping the Sunday morning show plus all that travel back & forth. I imagine (hand on the hip) 'HE'S ALL FAGGED OUT'! I guess by now, he's all rested up & back to normal again but he's foolish to take on so much work, its (sic) a terrible strain on the nerves & system in general & lack of sleep etc. then's (sic) the wear & tear OF GOING TO THE BANK & that laughing routine is murder especially when you can't control yourself!!"

Reporting on the day the gates first opened at Freedomland, an industry publication concluded its article about the huge grand opening success with: "The future will prove whether Freedomland has staying power; for 1960 it most likely will meet it projected goals. The outdoor amusement industry will be visiting and analyzing and—from comments during the initial weekend—borrowing.

Shortly before the 1966 film *The Russians Are Coming, The Russians Are Coming*, Soviet Premier Nikiti Khrushchev wanted to visit Disneyland when he was in California. He became angry when security issues prevented him from meeting Mickey Mouse. His New York movements were limited when he attended sessions at the United Nations, so he never visited Freedomland. He decided to take matters into his own hands. The Russian leader indicated that his country would build its own version of Disneyland and Freedomland, boasting that the park would be three times larger than Freedomland on 650 acres outside of Moscow. A mock Lunik space vehicle and a model of an atomic ship were to be among the education features for children. Attractions would involve astronomy and marine life. Did the park open? Nyet.

Acknowledgments

I wish to thank the many people who have shared memories, photographs, stories, leads, and questions for the Freedomland social media pages and this book. Without you, the many separate puzzle pieces that convey the Freedomland story would be lost to time. I wish to express special thanks to:

- John Bulakowski, a Queens boy with vivid teenage memories, who has provided research support about all topics related to Freedomland and who has become a highly valued Freedomland friend.

- Bill Cotter, a world's fair and theme park historian, who has shared memories, research, and photography of Freedomland and other parks and fairs that enjoyed common bonds during the 1960s.

- Bill Finkenstein and the family-owned WRC Designs (Plainville, Connecticut) for expressing decades of love for America's carrousels and for his contributions to the post-Freedomland storyline of the King Rex Carrousel.

- Dexter Francis, an Arrow Development historian, for sharing the history of this company's involvement with the Disney parks, Freedomland, and many other parks.

- Cate Mahoney of the New England Carousel Museum for valuable information about the history of carrousels and, specifically, Freedomland's King Rex Carrousel.

- Ricky Riccardi and Sarah Rose of the Louis Armstrong House Museum and Archives (Queens, New York) for their assistance in documenting Satchmo's performances at Freedomland.

- Chuck Schmidt, a journalist and author, whose books about Disney parks have been published by Theme Park Press and whose *Goofy About Disney* blog has weaved the connections among Freedomland, the Disney parks, and the 1964–1965 New York World's Fair.

- Daniel Robinson and Anne B. Stauffer of the National Carousel Association for valuable assistance about the history of the Freedomland King Rex Carrousel.

- The Bronx historians: Thomas X. Casey, the late John McNamara, Jorge Santiago, and the late Bill Twomey. Thomas has shared many stories and theories about Freedomland at presentations throughout the borough and several appear in these pages. John, who wrote about the Bronx and presented tours throughout the borough, befriended me during the 1970s as I was expanding my interest in Bronx history specifically and American history in general. Jorge has been honored by the New York City Parks Department for his research about the land within Pelham Bay Park and the uncovering of artifacts that date back to the early English settlers and Native Americans. Bill continued the tradition of research, writing, and providing tours of the Bronx, and he was present, despite failing health, at the unveiling of the Freedomland commemorative plaque. Thank you also to the East Bronx History Forum that meets regularly to maintain and share all the history of the borough.

Some of the information in this book about *The Canadian* sternwheeler that found a second home at Johnsonville Village is from the Greetings From Johnsonville Village website (johnsonville.omeka.net) and to the research of Luke Boyd.

Finally, thanks to the many other historians, researchers, Freedomland employees, park guests, and their children and grandchildren whose experiences were incorporated into this book.

About the Author

Michael R. Virgintino is a marketing communications executive who began his career in the newsrooms of New York City area radio stations. He has directed corporate, nonprofit, and product-branding initiatives that rely on public relations, public affairs, corporate social responsibility, community relations, and related strategies. He also is an historian who writes about the American Revolution, the Civil War, and other topics, and he has, over the years, offered his communications capabilities to support the preservation of American history and historical sites across the country. He grew up in the shadow of Freedomland and created the popular Freedomland Facebook memory page several years ago.

ABOUT THEME PARK PRESS

Theme Park Press publishes books primarily about the Disney company, its history, culture, films, animation, and theme parks, as well as theme parks in general.

Our authors include noted historians, animators, Imagineers, and experts in the theme park industry.

We also publish many books by first-time authors, with topics ranging from fiction to theme park guides.

And we're always looking for new talent. If you'd like to write for us, or if you're interested in the many other titles in our catalog, please visit:

www.ThemeParkPress.com

• •

Theme Park Press Newsletter

Subscribe to our free email newsletter and enjoy:

- Free book downloads and giveaways
- Access to excerpts from our many books
- Announcements of forthcoming releases
- Exclusive additional content and chapters
- And more good stuff available nowhere else

To subscribe, visit www.ThemeParkPress.com, or send email to newsletter@themeparkpress.com.

Read more about these books
and our many other titles at:

www.ThemeParkPress.com